"The ultimate self-help book for people who want to optimize their lives in these turbulent times."
—*Dean R. Spitzer, Ph.D.*
Author of <u>SuperMotivation</u>

"It has been said 'where there is a will, there's a way.' Tom Ruddell's book *The MECCA Factor* gives you both! Tom not only *discusses* success principles, he *demonstrates* them. *The MECCA Factor* is a guide, a goal and a gift — all rolled into one great way of life.
— *Bill Quain, Ph.D.*
Author of <u>Reclaiming the American Dream</u>

"Normalcy in our lives is laced with unscheduled events. To have a fulfilling life and provide for a good means of income, you must master uncharted as well as charted waters. Tom Ruddell has voyaged those waters and lays out a course of self-direction without dependence on government or corporate bailouts."
— *Gov. Bob Martinez, former*
Governor of Florida & U.S. Drug Czar

"With delightful wit and pure wisdom, Tom Ruddell extends a powerful invitation for us to fully experience professional and personal growth. He has provided a remarkable road map for the journey from where we are to where we want to be."
— *Carol Maier*
Human Resource Development Consultant

"Some great insight and direction from someone who 'walks his talk.'"
— *Linda Bailey*
Employee Relations Consultant

"It's all here. If you are willing to really work for your success, *The MECCA Factor* is the workbook to use."
— *Stephen A. Stumpf, Ph.D.*
Dean, College of Business

"What a thought-provoking system for self-impr 'Self-help book' would be a gross understatement. Thi plete success manual, ammunition included!"
— *Jeff Ruffo*
Entrepreneur

"Read *The MECCA Factor* — then, Refocus... Reread!!!
— *Laura M. Fortson*
YMCA National Training Staff

"Any book that can touch the hearts and minds of my students is a miracle. *The MECCA Factor* is such a book. Every parent should give their children a copy of Tom Ruddell's book — an excellent map to the roadway of life.

— Michael K. Mitchell, Ph.D.
Teacher of life skills and science,
Alaska state reform school

"Stop being a victim of corporate re-engineering! *The MECCA Factor* will give you the skills to re-engineer your own life beyond survival toward success and happiness."

— Suzanne Gibson Wise
Executive Director, Family Service Centers

"This book offers its readers a myriad of ways to empower themselves and others in their professional and personal lives. The emphasis is that by empowering others to be successful, we become more successful in our own lives."

— Linda R. Farfante
Mental Health Professional

"Tom Ruddell has written an important book that can be useful to anyone seeking a more successful life. This is a compelling book which is literally full of helpful and useful suggestions as each of us finds a niche in the world of the 21st Century. I consider it a 'must-read'."

— Greg Gardner, Ph.D.
College Communication Department Chair

"If you want to zero in on exactly what it takes to be successful, Tom Ruddell's *The MECCA Factor* is the blueprint to follow. Read the book and feel better about not only surviving, but winning!

— Patricia A. Straughn
American Institute of Banking education director

"A fascinating literary, self-help trip delivered with humor and inspiration. A product of Tom Ruddell's broad experience. A 'must' on any serious reading list."

— Chester G. Elias Jr.
President, The Advantage Group

THE MECCA FACTOR

5 IMPERATIVES FOR A SUCCESSFUL LIFE

SECOND EDITION

TOM RUDDELL

Capstar Corporation
Tampa, Florida

1997

Printed in the United States of America

Library of Congress Catalog Card Number: 96-096446

ISBN 0-9649284-1-8

Meccanize!® is a registered trademark of Capstar Corporation

Cover & internal graphics designed by Bryant Graphics, Inc.

Contents

The **MECCA** Factor

To Nancy

Acknowledgements

Thanks run deep for this book. Knowing where to start is easy. Were it not for Nancy, my partner in life for more than 34 years and my partner in business for the past half dozen, there would be no book. Her love, her faith in me and her decade-long gentle whisperings to "write the book... write the book..." did more to help it happen than a wheelbarrow full of little Round Tuits.

Among those who edited, or reviewed, the manuscript and/or contributed valuable ideas are:

- Susan Dellinger, Ph.D., superb encourager and internationally known author, speaker and workshop leader.
- Greg H. Gardner, Ph.D., professor and chair of the Department of Communication at Rollins College.
- James E. Gilbert, Ph.D., retired president of East Stroudsburg University.
- The Rev. Charles L. Greenwood, Captain, USN (Ret.), and Pastor Emeritus of Palma Ceia Presbyterian Church, Tampa.
- Dan Hessler of Compact Publishing Company, who was an early contributor of ideas to the *Meccanize!*® process.
- Cindy Kocher and Linda Farfante, two highly knowledgeable professionals from the field of mental health.
- Anne Maers, book marketing consultant extraordinaire.
- Carol Maier, an outstanding corporate training and development executive who now is a master trainer for two of Capstar Corporation's programs.
- Jo-Anne Pitera, Psy.D., human resources development director and psychologist, who added much perspective to this book.
- Jeff Ruffo and Dr. Dan Mullett, two great mentors, friends, business associates and role models.
- Plano Valdes, Ed.D., a gifted management development expert and long-time mentor and friend.

A dozen or more others were most helpful in producing this book, too. It was Linda Bryant's superb cover design and inside graphics that give the second edition its special look. And thanks as well to Daniel I. Dees for his thorough review and proof reading of the manuscript.

The personal values represented here were instilled many years ago by two wonderful parents, Loretta and Bob Mitchell, whose love and support, like the battery-powered pink rabbit, faithfully keeps going and going.

Life's richest blessing, however, is to see strong values and success principles grow in the generations to follow. So it is with our son Geoffrey, and our daughter Jennifer who, with her husband Rickey Crowe, added a fourth generation to our family, a beautiful little bundle of joy and boundless energy named Cassandra.

I owe a lot to scores of people and character-building experiences over the years. To name but a few:

• Valley Forge Military Academy, where self-discipline, motivation and a strong sense of duty and honor were instilled.

• Joseph B. McFadden, professor emeritus of journalism at Lehigh University, who inspired what became three-plus fulfilling decades in the communication field.

• Jack K. Busby, retired chairman and chief executive officer of Pennsylvania Power & Light Company, who set standards of integrity and concern for people that are lost on much of Corporate America today.

• The International Association of Business Communicators and its outstanding leaders, including Jake Wittmer, Norm and Rae Leaper, Roy Foltz, Lou Williams and Lynda Stewart.

But greatest thanks go to where the greatest thanks for *everything* in life should go — To God Almighty.

Tom Ruddell

P a r t   1

Your Context

What's Going On & What to Do About It

- Welcome to a Whole New World
- A Short Course in History
- "Continuous White Water"
- An Ongoing Search for Stability

To live your life to the fullest, begin by understanding the world around you. Then be willing to help change it for the better.

Chapter 1

Welcome to a Whole New World

- Stunned Awakenings
- A Ritual Called "CROP"
- And Then What Happens?
- So Where Are You Headed?
- Where Do You Get Your Strength?

Seven-plus years into the turbulent 1990s, look back to the moment the decade began — the moment when four couples at a quiet New Year's Eve party toasted "a prosperous new decade."

It's easy to see why the four couples had become good friends. They met through their church, shared many values and epitomized an increasingly rare union known as the Traditional Nuclear Family.

In total, they had more than a century of happy marriages — no divorces — and 10 grown children, all of whom turned out well.

Besides church, the four women were "old-fashioned" housewives, mothers and community volunteers.

The four men were successful in four different career pursuits. Loyal to their businesses, they shared a strong work ethic, enjoyed what they did and looked forward to continued success.

Clearly, here were four couples who lived responsible, productive lives — people who, by doing the right things over many years, could look forward to living out their golden years with considerable financial security.

For an hour or so before uncorking the champagne, the couples had chatted about the uneasiness and uncertainty as the 1980s drew to a close. The strong economy of the mid-1980s had faltered. Businesses of many kinds were wracked by takeovers, management upheavals, abrupt change. The 1987 stock market crash had sent shock waves through the economy, although stocks had rebounded.

As the four couples waited for the televised descent of the

lighted ball atop the Allied Chemical Building in New York, they traded upbeat expressions of confidence that the 1990s would bring a return to the career advancement, economic stability and financial prosperity they had enjoyed for so many years.

And when the big lighted ball reached the bottom of the mast and the band struck up the timeless strains of "Auld Lang Syne," their hugs, kisses and toasts reflected joyful optimism that the decade leading to a New Millennium would be *great* years for everyone.

There would be career success. There would be continued opportunities to serve the community. There would be more time to spend with families already expanding with grandchildren. And, after some final professional hurrahs for the four men, there would be financially secure retirements blessed with plenty of travel, golf, fishing, boat trips, long visits with children and grandchildren — all the joys of prosperous and active retirement.

With glasses raised at one past midnight on Jan. 1, 1990, that was the dream. The reality?

Stunned Awakenings

Within 14 months of that New Year's Eve party, all four men would be out of work.

Ten weeks after celebrating the advent of the 1990s, one of the four, a well-regarded corporate executive, was called out of a meeting and summarily fired by a new CEO.

A few months later, another of the men, who was a broker in the collapsing commercial real estate business, was forced to dissolve his partnership, close his office and retreat to an office at home with sales prospects near zero.

Not long after that, another of the men, a 30-year veteran retailer, was terminated after a takeover by a rival company.

Finally, the fourth man, who ran the profitable half of a two-division company, was told by his CEO that he would have to work without a salary because the other division was losing money. When he objected, he was fired.

An entire circle of good friends. All had stood together at the advent of the 1990s and, like millions of others, expressed hope for tomorrow and had faith in the future. And, like millions of others, each saw an abrupt end to a successful career. Each saw the dream of a financially secure retirement upended by a flood of change that seemed to obliterate the old paradigm:

> Work hard for many years, be loyal to your employer and you will be rewarded with job security, success and a secure retirement to live your "golden years" in comfort.

That paradigm, of course, didn't die with the noise-making and glass-clinking in the opening minutes of the 1990s. Events of the 1980s had installed a whole new language of change — leveraged buyouts, greenmail, downsizing, flat organizations, junk bonds, white knights, poison pills and the like.

Other, equally daunting aspects of the paradigm had changed as well. Where most married women once were housewives, by the mid-1990s some 80 percent now held down one or more jobs. And then the news media began introducing "the four-job family" — he has two jobs and she has two jobs.

Where most families once were traditional units in which the same two parents raised children of their own, some 70 percent of American families had become "non-traditional" with one parent remaining, two people raising children of various parentage, same-sex couples demanding marital and parental status, etc.

For many, if not most people, traditional or not, fulfillment of dreams is not what happened in the 1990s. The decade brought accelerated change, broken dreams, shattered faith in (and loyalty to) employers and a greater proclivity for despair.

A Ritual Called "CROP"

No one is fired anymore. He or she is "deselected for retention" or, to use the more popular term, "outplaced."

To a great degree, the mechanics of outplacement have taken on the characteristics of a science and the process of outplacement has become something of an art.

Books and manuals have been written on how to do it. Seminar leaders proclaim good and bad techniques. In the 1980s and early 1990s, hundreds of consulting firms had turned it into a growth industry, with specialists earning six-figure incomes alongside bankruptcy lawyers and auctioneers.

To the acronym lover, the new ritual of professionally handled outplacement could be called a "CROP" — Corporate Rite of Passage.

Outplacement can take many forms, depending on whether the CROPer is disposing of a single individual or droves of people, and whether the CROPee is an entry-level clerk or a company officer.

In the "humane" iterations of large-scale CROPs, groups are brought together, given the bad news and turned over to outplacement professionals who whisk them off to structured programs that start, typically, with a half hour or so in a classroom learning how to prop up self-esteem and end with well-formulated campaigns to find new jobs.

Of course, not every organization brings in the professional CROPmeisters or even attempts to be humane about it. The horror stories abound:

- Grim news is withheld from employees who one day are shocked to show up for work and find the place boarded up and surrounded by armed guards.
- Rumors and anxiety are allowed to build for months in an information vacuum until the axe finally falls, almost as blessed relief.
- A nine-year veteran corporate accountant with a good work record looks up from his desk to find himself flanked by security people with cardboard boxes. They tell him he had just been "let go." After supervising the packing of personal effects, they confiscate his ID card and company keys and march the hapless soul out the door, all to make sure he doesn't steal anything on the way out.
- A veteran marketing vice president loses her job in a bank takeover and, after 21 years of loyal service, is given two weeks' severance pay and a two-hour class on how to write a resume.
- A vice president of a large company returns from a business trip and plays back his phone mail messages. The second or third message is the voice of his boss informing him that he has been terminated and should clean out his desk.
- A manager at a power plant, heading home after a long day, is flagged down by the guard at the gate, who tells him to step out of the car. He is handed a piece of paper informing him that he has been terminated and is to surrender his ID card, plant keys and key to the company car he was driving. He is motioned toward an awaiting taxi and given a number to call in the morning.

The most-fortunate among the outplaced, of course, are those treated to a properly executed, full-blown CROP presided over personally by one often referred to as "The *Firing* Manager."

In the best of circumstances, the ritual comes as no surprise. Quite often, though, the CROP*ee* is in total shock, either because the CROP*er* has been thoroughly secretive about what is to come or because the CROP*ee* has been unable or unwilling to see storm clouds gathering.

In any case, the CROP itself, especially in the process-conscious bastions of Corporate America, is to be swift and relatively painless. It's like a doctor giving an injection. It hurts less when the needle is inserted quickly rather than pushed in slowly.

The CROP*ee* is brought before the CROP*er* who, in the presence of a witness, usually from the Human Resources Department, imparts the bad news as swiftly and directly as a bullet fired through the head.

According to the how-to "manuals," the CROP*ee* is to be given a short, simple and direct reason for why the execution is taking place. The CROP*ee's* listening ability, however, often plummets to a point somewhere below zilch — especially if he or she loved the company, liked the work and had no strong inklings of impending demise. The "why" question rarely seems fully answered.

This is followed by an instant outpouring of professional support while the CROP*er*, like Pontius Pilate washing his hands of Christ's impending crucifixion, withdraws to find a basin and towel.

On cue — in effect, at the sound of the "gunshot" — there appears a professional outplacement counselor. The counselor's job? Catch the Corporate Corpse before it messes up the Corporate Carpet and cart it off to a structured process of professional re-incarnation.

And Then What Happens?

Millions of people have lost jobs, have had their pay cut, their workload increased and have had any number of other unpleasant things happen to them in the workplace. They either put such circumstances into perspective and deal with them, or they don't.

> Life is 10 percent what happens to you
> and 90 percent how you react to it.
>
> Charles Swindoll

Some of the happiest people in America today are people who lose their jobs; if, that is, they are able to muster the wisdom, fortitude and courage to figure out what's going on around them and then go forth and *do* something about it.

I was completely devastated and asked the counselor to help me break the news to my spouse. I gave most of my life to that lousy company and this is what I get in return! There's no way I'll ever be able to get a job like that or earn anywhere near as much money. My life is ruined! I need a drink.

Freedom! Sure I was shocked. Yes, I'm disappointed. But I feel sorry for the poor people who have to keep working there! I know my spouse and I can work through this and will come out of it even stronger than before. We will look at every option. We'll do whatever it takes—and win !

It's been said the only difference between the words *Bitter* and *Better* is "*I*".

Subtle differences separate other pairings as well. "*I-M*" is all that separates *Victim* and *Victor*. You can go straight to "*H*" to the "*N*"*th* degree on the ever-so-small difference between *Whiner* and *Winner*.

And, of course, you can soar to as great an Altitude as you want in life if what suits you to a *"T"* is a winner's *Attitude* that helps you get *Better* and *Better* and become a *Victor* over every one of life's challenges — a true *Winner!*

To handle the waning 1990s and plunge into the New Millennium with a winning spirit is to recognize the fundamental differences between the worlds of yesterday, today and tomorrow.

There are underlying constants and underlying variables in these worlds. Yesterday, the constant was stability and the variable was change. Today, it's the opposite. The constant is change and the variable is stability. As for tomorrow, you can count on even *faster* change and on *relative* stability based largely on your ability to become resilient and to develop stronger personal values.

So Where Are You Headed?

Life is a journey. It always has been, always will be. The big question is: "To where?"

Back when stability was the constant and change was the variable, it became ever-so-tempting to chart a course for "Utopia." As you'll be reminded soon, even the U.S. Government was strongly committed to building a "Great Society" in which people were to be guaranteed stability and shielded from the sting of change.

The fatal flaw in any attempt to build a Utopian society, whether in a nation, a family or a workplace, can be put in the bluntest of terms: *The problem with Utopia is there ain't no such place!*

Pull your dictionary off the shelf and check it out:

> An imaginary and indefinitely remote place...An impractical scheme for social improvement...Utopian: Having impossibly ideal conditions, especially of social organization...Proposing or advocating impracticably ideal social and political schemes.

Have you been charting a course for Utopia in your job or business? In your family life? In your spiritual life? In your attitude toward life in general?

If so, be encouraged — especially if you're among the millions who may feel they've been trying to climb a faulty success ladder that's leaning against the wrong building.

If that is the case for you, the underlying problem all along simply may have been trying to chart a course through life toward a destination that doesn't exist — a course that will almost *guarantee* more faulty ladders and more wrong buildings.

"Life is a journey." That metaphor is too powerful to abandon just because the destination may be unclear or, like Utopia, impossible to reach.

This book explores another destination for life's journey. It is a destination that you — or anyone — can reach if you choose to. It is a destination of *attitude* rather than physical location. It is not the sort of destination in which your journey ends, but one in which your journey can continue in a spirit of joy, achievement and self-fulfillment.

It embraces all three parts of this book.

In this part, *Your Context,* it offers hope and encouragement as you discover both the obstacles and opportunities that abound in these times. In Part 2, *Your Conquest,* it helps you develop a game plan to overcome obstacles and seize opportunities. Finally, in Part 3, it becomes *Your Curriculum* through which you can gather the wisdom and courage to carry out your game plan — and win!

Where Do You Get Your Strength?

Are you a "self-made" person who draws most of your strength from within yourself? Do you draw it from the people around you? From a higher power?

Two observations:

• The vast majority of the greatest, most successful men and women in recorded history drew most of their strength from a power they saw as greater than humankind, and

• It has been the world's great religions that have provided the preponderance of guidance and strength to the billions who have populated the earth since the beginning of time.

Consider the Ten Commandments, brought forth by Moses and recorded in The Old Testament. Consider The New Testament and the Gospel of Jesus Christ.

Hindus are guided by The Upanishads, Buddhists by The Dhammapada, Jews by the Talmud, Muslims by The Koran.

People of faith draw strength from a power greater than themselves, guided by spiritual prophets and leaders as diverse as Elijah, St. Paul, Muhammad, Joseph Smith, Guru Nanak, Martin Luther, Confucius, and Mary Baker Eddy.

It is from one of the world's biggest religions that the name of this book and the new destination were derived. The derivation does not embrace the teachings of that particular religion, but captures a meaning that can be uplifting to people of *all* faiths, as well as those who are struggling to find a spiritual basis for their lives.

Over the centuries, Mecca, the city in Saudi Arabia that is the birthplace of the Prophet Muhammad and site of the temple, spawned a bountiful harvest of *second meanings* well-suited as a destination for life's journey. Search through a library shelf of dictionaries and you'll turn up second meanings for Mecca such as these:

> Reaching a longed-for state of happiness...Fulfilling important life goals...A center of activity sought as a goal by people sharing a common interest...An ultimately desirable place to be...Any place that a person longs to visit or reach...

In keeping with the beautiful and ancient metaphor that life is a journey, there is *another* way in which Mecca has special meaning.

For millions of the Muslim faithful, Mecca is the destination of a journey — a pilgrimage known as the Hadj. For most, it is a journey made but once in a lifetime.

Of course, the Hadj seeks Mecca as the most spiritually fulfilling place to visit. But you can seek "Mecca" as the most fulfilling *attitudinal* place from which to press on with your journey through life.

A third way that Mecca lends special meaning is its importance as a focal point:

> Turn, therefore, thy face towards the holy temple of Mecca; and wherever ye be, turn your faces towards that place.
> *The Koran*
> Chapter 2

Concentrate on where you want to *be* in life. You're more likely to get there if you keep your eyes focused on the right direction — on *that place.*

In this book and in associated seminars and materials, quotation marks are used out of respect when referring to "Mecca" as a destination. Later, you'll discover a third meaning, expressed in capitals: MECCA, the acronym for 5 Imperatives for a Successful Life. Those five imperatives can be *The MECCA Factor* for your successful journey through life.

The self-evaluation and planning process, presented in Part 2 of this book, is known as *Meccanize!*® which is a registered trademark owned by Capstar Corporation.

Chapter 2

A Short Course In History

- 7 Decades From Which to Learn
  The 1920s: A Time to Party & Cast Off Inhibitions
  The 1930s: A Time to Struggle & Help Each Other
  The 1940s: A Time to Fight & Revel in Victory
  The 1950s: A Time to Fulfill the American Dream
  The 1960s: A Time to Rebel & Challenge Our Values
  The 1970s: A Time to Anguish Over What's Happening
  The 1980s: A Time to Change Direction & Focus
- The 1990s: Time to Renew the American Spirit

We've always been a nation of dreamers. Our nation was founded on dreams, especially dreams of freedom. From the beginning of our republic, we've sustained ourselves on dreams of triumph over tyranny, whether the tyranny of a foreign power or the tyranny of want. For more than two centuries, we've nurtured dreams of greatness in our young. For many, to be rich *is* The American Dream. To be rich is to be *free*.

Now, as the 1990s come to a close, we pause to ask: "What has *happened* to the American dream?"

According to some very disconcerting studies, America has brought forth a generation of young people — the so-called Generation X — who are becoming the first Americans in history to be worse-off financially than their parents, even considering the half dozen or so economic depressions that have plagued us over the past 21 decades.

Not only will the emerging generation be worse off financially but, according to other studies, they will be the first *less educated* than their parents. What impact will *that* have on the American dream?

We need not go all the way back to the American Revolution to understand the 1990s and what's ahead in the New Millennium.

The 1920s is a good place to start for two reasons: (1) it represents the formative years of the senior-most people among us, albeit most of them long since retired, and (2) it represents a period in which Americans made their greatest-ever shift in personal values.

It also was the first decade for which it is fairly easy to ascribe a theme, just as we can ascribe themes to the other decades that separate then from now. These themes and characteristic flavors offer us insights into the current decade, especially the lessons learned and the legacies left by each of those 10-year blocks of time.

The 1920s: A Time to Party & Cast Off Inhibitions

We call it "The Roaring 20s" for, in the aftermath of World War I — The War to End All Wars — it was a time to party and prosper and experiment with new lifestyles.

There were flappers and bootleggers and "revenooers"; there was Fatty Arbuckle and the Keystone Kops; bathtub gin, the Charleston and vast opportunities to buy stocks on the margin.

At least three profound influences took root in the 1920s — influences that affect our lives to this day and have become the legacy left to us by the 1920s:

• *Electronic media.* Instant transmission and receipt of information began as millions tuned in to their crystal sets and primitive radios.

• *Women's rights.* With the newly won right to vote, women began exerting major influence on the political and economic scenes.

• *Organized crime.* Prohibition shifted demand for alcoholic beverages from legal sources of supply to illegal ones, thus elevating organized crime to the level of big business.

When the 1920s ended, the party ended as well.

The 1930s: A Time to Struggle & Help Each Other

A shroud bearing a single word hangs over the Decade of the 30s: Depression.

America didn't realize it was in a depression until more than a year after the October 1929 stock market crash. It was the pin-stripes-and-cigar people who were doing swan dives out of office windows, not Joe Lunchbox. Unlike today, stocks, bonds, commodities and such were games largely played by the well-to-do few.

Newspapers heralding the start of the decade were filled with optimism. The pundits predicted a big upswing by the end of 1930 with a return to prosperity. The Federal Reserve System would turn back the tide of decline. The party would resume. It didn't.

Many years later, someone observed what the pundits of 1930 were soon to learn: "Forecasting would be easy if you didn't have to mess around with the future."

There are characteristics of the 1930s that should influence our thinking as we make our personal journeys toward the New Millennium. Unlike the 1990s, with millions of families having *disintegrated* over economic issues, families in the 1930s *got stronger* as people shared in the economic hard times and looked after each other.

The darker the days, the bigger the dreams. Many people focused on positive, uplifting entertainment that, unlike today's bombardment of violence and hedonism, lifted the spirits and underscored a personal payback from positive values. Millions got a boost from screen portrayals of glittering wealth, lilting musical extravaganzas and a steady stream of slapstick comedies.

Here is the legacy left to us by the 1930s:

• *The welfare state.* For the first time, the federal government played a massive, nationwide role in the economic well-being of individual Americans. The federal income tax which, from its enactment in 1913 had helped balance the federal budget, became an instrument of wealth redistribution. Social Security was imposed, luring many toward "absolution" from the responsibility to provide for themselves and for their parents in the "golden years." Consequently, with personal savings pitifully low, millions of Americans now face retirement in the 1990s as virtual wards of government.

• *Large federal debt.* Federal surpluses in the 1920s were making a dent in the debt left over from World War I. It was in the 1930s, however, that the federal government set a pattern of racking up annual deficits that ultimately turned the world's largest creditor nation into the world's largest debtor nation, our position by the 1990s.

While the economy already was recovering by the end of the 1930s, it took what today would be an unthinkable event to bring a return to prosperity: a world war — a *second* world war.

The 1940s: A Time to Fight & Revel in Victory

In the 1920s, we learned how to have fun and to be influenced by mass media. In the 1930s, we learned how to make do with little but still have hope — even big dreams.

And the 1940s? We learned to sacrifice — our lives, if necessary — for a cause clearly and demonstrably greater than ourselves. Above all, we learned that, with a clear objective, faith in our leaders and an ironclad national will, Americans can accomplish *anything*.

Much of where we are today is a legacy of the 1940s:

• *World leadership.* With the devastation of Great Britain and the collapse of the British Empire, America became the most powerful nation on earth, assuming all the obligations and burdens of the role.

• *A world view.* Millions of Americans, accustomed to life within a few miles of where they had been born, experienced other parts of the world and came home with a much different view of life.

- *Industrial power.* We cranked up our old manufacturing facilities, added new ones, and ran them flat out to help our bombed-out allies blast three other industrial powers back into the last century. Then, without modernizing much of our own enormous means of production, we helped allies and ex-enemies alike build modern production facilities that became more efficient than our own.

- *The Bomb.* Nuclear weapons greatly raised the stakes in relationships among nations, setting the stage for limited wars with objectives not as clear-cut to us as the crusade against the Axis.

When World War II finally ended and the troops started coming home, however, we felt *entitled* to the good life. That spawned the greatest legacy of the 1940s: A population explosion called The Baby Boom.

"What's the first thing you're going to do when you get home?" many a returning serviceman was asked. The standard reply: "Make love to my wife." The followup question brought out the best in barracks humor. "The second thing? Put my duffel bag down!"

Millions of new Americans came into the world in the late 1940s. They were born to parents who had experienced the want of the Great Depression and the pain of war.

Most parents were determined to shower upon their children all the things they never had, a penchant with effects far greater than a boom in the toy industry. It was a time-bomb of basic values that set off an explosion unheard and unfelt until the baby-boomers hit their teen years in the 1960s.

The 1950s: A Time to Fulfill the American Dream

In many respects, the 1950s represented the last decade in which we clung to traditional American values. We had started to shed some of those values in the 1920s, but the adversity of the 1930s and the 1940s caused most of us to refocus on strong family units, the work ethic and faith in God.

In the 1950s, we still were largely a society of nuclear families — one father/breadwinner, one wife/mother/ household manager, 2.5 kids, one dog, one cat, one *suburban* house with picket fence and, as a result, *two* cars (one a station wagon for mom to use as a family transportation system and one for dad's commute to work).

The 1950s also were the last decade of relative stability in America. We liked Ike, and many applauded at least the initial efforts to root out "godless communists" from every nook, cranny, government bureau and classroom.

Besides the Baby Boomers, here are some of the legacies of the 1950s which still influence us today:

- *Television.* It was invented in the 1920s, kept on the shelf in the 1930s because no one could afford it, introduced in the 1940s to wealthy tinkerers who liked to watch test patterns and, in the 1950s, began having enormous impact on nearly every household in America.
- *The automobile.* The 1950s made two-car households the norm, launched the Interstate Highway System and sounded the death knell for profitable public transit in American cities. Getting places became a *private* matter in the 1950s. And who cared about polluting the air with gas guzzling, chrome-plated road locomotives?
- *Suburban sprawl.* Ex-Seabee construction expert William Levitt showed us how to carve cloned communities — Levittowns — out of cornfields. And thanks to the automobile, we became commuters, seeking the good life farther and farther from where we worked and shopped. As higher-income people moved out of urban areas and a phenomenon called shopping centers began making trips downtown unnecessary, the 1950s began the urban decay that now haunts us.
- *A sense of "gap."* Complacent from being king of the world's mountain, we got a shocking wakeup call named Sputnik in the 1950s. For the first time, we saw a "gap" between ourselves and the Soviet bloc in science, technology and education. Suddenly, we saw ourselves losing our status as the nation that produced the best of everything.
- *The middle class.* Until the 1950s, America's middle class was relatively small. We had an enormous blue-collar and agricultural population and a small percentage of people who were wealthy. In between was a middle class largely perceived as doctors, storeowners and factory managers.

In the 1950s, we began expanding the middle class to such a degree that "low class" and "high class" virtually disappeared and, in their places, came two new terms: "lower middle class" and "upper middle class."

Government solutions to America's problems were the main focus of the 1930s and 1940s. We shifted back toward the private sector in the 1950s but, by the end of the decade, many were discontented and crying out for change.

By 1960, enough over-indulged Baby Boomers ("spoiled brats," some might say) had gotten old enough to cause major migraine headaches for their parents, not to mention local police departments and draft boards.

The 1960s: A Time to Rebel & Challenge Our Values

It started with the Beatniks in the late 1950s. Unsmiling, often unwashed and costumed in black, they lamented life, wrote bad poetry, and smoked substances of dubious legal status.

Hair was a dominant value of youth in rebellion, both in the

1950s and 1960s. But while the former decade featured meticulously crafted "duck cuts," the latter decade managed to sidestep shampoo, combs, Vitalis, pomade and barbershops.

Male Beatniks grew beards and preferred lengths of clothes-line to belts. Female Beatniks favored long, black hair uninterrupted by curls or even kinks and used irons and ironing boards to iron hair, never clothes.

The Beatniks of the late 50s were a relatively small segment of our youth, but the Hippies of the 60s became the pacesetters for a widespread counterculture. The peace symbol became the dominant rune — on jewelry and jackets, tattooed on various parts of the anatomy and spray painted on walls.

Transportation of choice was the clapped-out Volkswagen micro-bus, the dirtier, more dented and festooned with slogans and peace symbols, the better.

By the time of Woodstock, nonconformity had even developed its own set of prevailing standards.

> The only thing a nonconformist hates more than a conformist is another nonconformist who fails to observe the prevailing standards of nonconformity.
>
> Bill Vaughn,
> *The Kansas City Star*

But the scary side of the 1960s was the unprecedented, nation-wide call for the destruction of American institutions.

Radical groups of self-centered young people, urged on by some leftist professors and pro-communist agitators, called for the over-throw of the federal government. Fear of anarchy spread as ROTC buildings were set afire and riots and violent demonstrations were organized and sparked by groups whose behaviors were out of synch with their names.

There was a non-violent coordinating organization that con-doned violence, a powerful student group espousing a democratic society whose members shouted down people disagreeing with their radical agenda, and various outfits whose "peace" nomenclature accepted violence and even murder "for the sake of peace."

Dr. John A. Howard of the Rockford Institute put pen to paper and tongue to cheek, and came up with this witty yet all-too-true assessment of the 1960s. He called it "Never Mind Over Matter":

> God is dead! The culture's shot.
> The youth, it seems, have gone to pot.
> The norms have vanished from the scene.

America will soon be "green."
Hooray for sex! Indulge the ego!
(Just so it's mine, not yours, amigo.)
Whate'er is fun, go have a bunch.
Milt Friedman's wrong, here's your free lunch.
So live it up! Postpone all care!
Your dirty jeans are debonair.
If wisdom is what you would find,
Consult your feelings, not your mind.

Tragically, the 1960s was also the decade of political assassinations. John F. Kennedy, Martin Luther King, Robert F. Kennedy and other leaders fell to assassins' bullets, enshrining memories beyond actual accomplishments and advancing their ideas beyond the boundaries of contemporary public acceptance.

Assassins are like the federal government. Each, it seems, accomplishes the opposite of what is intended.

Among the legacies of the 1960s:

• *Rebellious youth.* America has always been blessed with teenagers, and teenagers have always flapped their wings in a quest for independence. But the 1960s gave us the first crop of teenagers who had been showered with material things, given relative amnesty from discipline and introduced to what later became known as the Boob Tube. TV also helped raise to levels of entitlement the expectations of those who didn't share in prosperity and equal opportunity.

• *The anti-nuclear movement.* It was during the 1960s that nuclear weapons and peaceful use of the atom became lumped together, costing America its position as world leader in energy production and skewing our national energy mix toward costlier, more environmentally unfriendly fuels. Japan, which had a far-greater reason to fear nuclear technology than the United States, soon would surpass us in the percentage of electricity production coming from nuclear fuels.

• *Drugs.* While it's true that opium and bootleg liquor caused public concern during the 1920s, and other decades were marked by bouts with public drunkeness and use of "dope," it was during the 1960s that marijuana and hallucinogenic drugs simultaneously became instruments of degeneration and badges of social acceptance within a large segment of our youthful population. The "drug culture" was firmly established and would continue virtually unabated.

• *Degradation of the national will.* Vietnam was the first major war in American history that depended almost entirely upon professional soldiers for leadership and draftees to do most of the fighting and dying. In every other major war, it was the citizen soldier who rallied to the cause, provided a strong measure of leadership and fought hard to win and get back home. America's first "television war" left us torn. On the one hand were moral questions and escalating costs, both in lives and in dollars. On the other was the patriotic desire to serve honorably and to remain unbeaten in foreign wars. We lacked the will to do what it would take to win. We also lacked the will to maintain our technological and manufacturing-edge. More and more foreign-made cars came ashore and production of many consumer goods began shifting offshore.

  • *The War on Poverty.* The welfare state was established in the 1930s, but it was the War on Poverty, declared in the 1960s, that clearly shifted responsibility from people caring for one another to the federal government and new layers of bureaucracy. As with other massive government efforts to affect social change, the War on Poverty would accomplish the *opposite* of its goals, relegating to poverty millions of Americans who, otherwise, may have found reasons to lift themselves *out* of poverty.

Each decade since the 1920s ended with a loosely defined mandate for change. When the 1960s ended, we were anxious to get the Vietnam War behind us and focus on enabling more segments of our population to enjoy the American Dream.

The 1970s: A Time to Anguish Over What's Happening

We began to shift focus from violence to more traditional means of redress, thanks to changes in government but also to the tragedy at Kent State University in Ohio where campus rioting led to the deaths of four students. While there were many campus demonstrations and protests to follow, including outrage over Kent State, the tragedy brought an abrupt end to violent behavior on campus.

After destroying millions of dollars worth of property, throwing bags of human excrement at National Guard troops brought in to restore order and engaging in all manner of other animalistic behaviors on campuses from coast to coast, Kent State was the rudest of awakenings for a generation of self-centered youth in rebellion. The violent temper tantrums virtually ceased.

For the riot leaders, who whipped up anger, then disappeared into the crowds when the arrests started being made; for the thousands lured into destructive behavior; and to the many who didn't participate but thought the rampage was somehow justified, it was as though a giant message had finally gotten through:

> Attention all young people burning down buildings, injuring police officers with rocks and bottles and engaging in all other forms of violent behavior: It has now been demonstrated very clearly that you can get hurt doing this.

The 1970s also was the decade in which some of the radicals of the 1960s, who warned their peers never to trust anyone over 30, started — guess what? — turning 30.

We hoped that after 1971, when we lowered the voting age from 21 to 18, our youth would trade in placards and Molotov cocktails for political parties and ballots. It didn't work out that way, especially after we were treated to the spectacle of the first U.S. president in history to resign from office in disgrace.

Participation in national elections grew in the 40s, 50s and 60s. With 18-20-year-olds added to the electorate, the 1970s saw participation *drop* by more than 10 percent.

The legacy of the 1970s includes:

• *Loss of faith in political institutions.* Watergate, the Pentagon Papers, the resignation under fire of first the vice president and then the president, questions about regulatory effectiveness following the Three Mile Island nuclear accident and a host of other events and factors, including the perceived weakness of the Carter White House, all helped us toward the view that big government would neither solve our problems nor help us fulfill the American Dream. We became ready for *less* government and *more* individual initiative.

• *The end of resource self-sufficiency.* Not since our dependence upon the British for tea in the 1700s had we allowed ourselves to become so dependent on foreign powers for important resources as we did for oil. Nationwide shortages in 1973 and 1979 provided successive wakeup calls. With nuclear power development hamstrung, with environmental and economic limitations put on domestic oil production and with our love affair with gas-guzzling land yachts continuing, we managed in the 1970s to go beyond the point of easy return on the substance that fueled American prosperity in the years that followed World War I — gasoline.

• *The end of anti-militarism.* With the Vietnam War finally over, along with the draft, the 1970s set the stage for a strong peacetime, professional military. Young people found it easier to support a stronger military force, perhaps even to use it, now that it had become unlikely they'd have to put themselves at risk by actually participating. The quality of America's fighting forces began to increase as the military services became more respected and as young people began turning to the military for fulfilling careers.

• *The bitter taste of inflation.* Interest rates soared well into the double digits as the decade came on an end, with mortgage interest topping 20 percent. We learned some painful economic lessons, most notably the need to bring costs of production under control and become more competitive in the world economy.

The 1970s set the stage for a massive change in direction, both politically and economically.

The 1980s: A Time to Change Direction & Focus

To some, the 1980s was "The Decade of Greed and Excess." To others, it was "The Golden Age of American Capitalism." A single coined-word became the lightning rod of the 1980s: *Reaganomics.*

It's easy to blame Reaganomics and the conservatives for the economic mess of the 1990s. After all, Ronald Reagan was president through much of the debt buildup and we tend to blame our president when bad things happen — especially when hit in our pocketbooks.

What *was* the cause? Let's call it "SoFoNo-nomics."

SoFoNo stands for the dark side of the American Dream — belief in the Free Lunch. We *say* we don't believe in the Free Lunch, but our voting habits show otherwise.

More than voting across the board for people who represent steadfast and consistent economic values and agendas, we split our tickets and also voted the SoFoNo ticket — Something For Nothing.

To the White House, we sent whoever promised the lowest taxes and biggest cuts in spending. To Congress, we sent those who promised the most benefits.

If nothing else, Reaganomics demonstrated that lower taxes tend to increase economic growth and, as a result, overall receipts to the federal treasury.

As demonstrated, the *constant* is the percentage of Gross Domestic Product (GDP) that flows to the U.S. Treasury — no matter what percentage of people's incomes is "confiscated" by the Internal Revenue Service. The *variable* is the growth rate of the GDP. Over time, the higher the tax rate the lower the growth of the GDP. Conversely, the lower the tax rate the higher the growth of the GDP.

So how did the economics of the 1980s contribute to the financial mess of the 1990s? George Bush, who once called Reagan's fiscal philosophy "voodoo economics," supported Reaganomics for 10 years. Then, not "reading his own lips," he bowed to pressure to hike taxes in 1990 and was left holding the bag on election day in 1992.

During the campaign, President Bush described the problem perfectly, but to millions of deaf ears:

> Our problem is not that we tax too little
> but that we spend too much.

Years earlier, Reagan's fellow movie actor, the profligate swashbucker Errol Flynn, put it less eloquently but in more colorful and personal terms:

> My problem is that my net income is exceeded
> by my gross habits.

Since the 1960s, entitlements had been the second constant in the federal equation, along with lower taxes. Despite rhetoric to the contrary, we strayed further from the idea that each of *us* — not the federal government — should take responsibility for our own lives.

But tax cuts, along with the gross spending habits of Congress, weren't the only objects of economic focus during the 1980s. Where greed was concerned, many fingers pointed at Corporate America.

CEO's entered the decade with salaries averaging 25 times those of their lowest-level workers. At the end of the decade, they were averaging *91 times* as much as "Joe Lunchbox."

The news media, never known to pay their reporters all that well, were filled with stories of multi-million-dollar pay-and-perk packages. And when the average American's "real income" began to decline, many became outraged by stories of companies raising executive bonuses while laying off workers.

The 1980s spawned additions to our language that became synonyms for corporate greed: "greenmail," "golden parachutes," "hostile takeovers," "junk bonds" and "leveraged buyouts" (LBOs).

Where greed is concerned, the instantly infamous memo from a savings & loan executive to his bond salesmen said it all:

> Remember that the weak, meek and ignorant are
> always good targets.

The legacy of the 1980s is much more than that of America becoming the world's leading debtor nation.

Among the negatives there are positives, including these:

• *Communism collapsed.* As the decade closed, the Soviet Union collapsed along with most other communist regimes, bringing the long and burdensome Cold War to an end. Despite our faults, the U.S. became the No. 1 role model for a greatly expanded free world.

• *The world became a safer place.* As more and more fingers were taken off nuclear triggers, the atomic scientists turned back their ominous Doomsday Clock for the first time since 1945. The biggest dangers shifted from what a nuclear holocaust would bring upon us to dangers we *bring upon ourselves,* such as AIDs and violent crime.

• *We became more competitive.* The quality of U.S. goods became the highest, on a world scale, since the 1940s. And while painful, many of the cutbacks, consolidations and restructurings made us all the stronger to compete in world markets.

• *We became more generous.* The image of greed wasn't the whole picture in the 1980s. We became more generous than ever. The more we had, the more we were willing to give to charity. Annual giving to charities by individuals, corporations and foundations grew 55 percent faster in the 1980s than in the previous 25 years.

What 7 Decades Should Have Taught Us

Having just made a quick review of seven decades of U.S. history that span today's youngest to most elderly people, there is one question that should nag all of us: "Have we *learned* anything to help us into the New Millennium?"

What do you think, considering:

Decade	*What We Should Have Learned From It*
1920s	Huge problems can result when government intervenes too much through tough controls on human behavior, and not enough through common-sense safeguards on the U.S. economy.
1930s	The faster road to economic recovery is the road along which people are rewarded for being productive in a robust and innovative private sector, not the road littered with governmental obstacles in which people are punished for being rich.
1940s	When Americans will unite behind a common cause, we can do more with less far faster than any other nation in the world.
1950s	The worst thing we can do to our children is give them everything we didn't have, such as nice homes, TV sets, toys and cars, while denying them what they need most, such as loving discipline, moral and spiritual values, and the kind of education that will help them be productive, self-fulfilled and successful.
1960s	If we're ever to engage in a foreign war, make sure the cause is right, our motives are open and honest and, that we can muster the national will to win it quickly with minimal loss of human life.
1970s	We can't become all we can be as a nation if we elect to the highest offices in the land people who have strong leadership and weak moral values or strong moral values and weak leadership.

1980s   We can't have it both ways. If we are to dig
ourselves out of a moral and economic morass,
we must take responsibility for our own
actions and take charge of our own destinies.
We also must work together to achieve common
goals that reward productivity, innovation,
positive values and moral behavior.

The 1990s: A Time to Renew the American Spirit

One of the most popular television shows of the 1980s was "Lifestyles of the Rich and Famous." Millions of Americans tuned in, not to become enraged by the lifestyles but to raise their dreams of one day becoming rich and enjoying similarly opulent comforts and toys.

As we entered the 1990s, however, millions watched those dreams fade and many downsized their own dreams to fit the lifestyles of the poor and struggling.

Tons of trinkets from the 1980s ended up in a small but gruesomely symbolic phenomenon of the 1990s — the "Yuppie Pawn-shop." Unlike the dingy pawnshops that served the down and out for a century or more, these purveyors of pre-owned upscale playthings deal in Rolexes and cellular phones more than guns and bowling trophies.

What is to become of us as we head toward the New Millen-nium? Economic collapse? A renaissance leading to America's most-golden age?

Buffeted by a nightly typhoon of negative television news and awakening each day to the phobic prose of people who buy ink by the barrel, many Americans have been responding to the 1990s in one of three ways: (1) scared to death, (2) not understanding the situation or (3) in denial.

If you are among those who are scared to death, your fears may be underscored by the next chapter and eased somewhat by the chapter after that.

Meantime, it has become easier to "not understand the situa-tion." News consumption is on the decline, while TV viewership and other forms of entertainment remain high. Sickened by a nightly half hour of local killings, drug busts and rapes, followed by another half hour of economic gloom on the home-front and tribal warfare overseas, it's far less stressful to flip among mindless sit-coms and, to use the new vernacular, "lay on the sofa and just rot."

The sum of 1, 2 and 3 are people who are frightened, un-informed and unrealistic. The winners in the 1990s and beyond will be those who overcome the daunting woes by becoming courageous, well-informed and pragmatic.

Take stock for a moment. That light at the end of the tunnel —

do you want to believe it's daylight while knowing deep down it's the headlight of an onrushing locomotive? If you accept it as a locomotive, do you also accept that, to survive, it will be necessary (1) to act rationally while pressed against the wall and (2) find a less perilous route on which to continue your journey through life?

What *is* ahead? Lay all the forecasts end to end and they'd circle the globe, leading to no conclusion.

It used to be that the best way to create a small fire was to rub two Boy Scouts together. These days, you can get a raging conflagration by rubbing two economists together, especially when flanked by liberal and conservative pundits on a cable-access political shoot-out.

To be effective in planning the rest of your life's journey, make some key assumptions about what the close of 1990s and the dawn of the New Millennium will be like.

There are at least 10 major trends to consider when planning all aspects of life's journey, including education, careers, family relationships and, most important, the size, shape and nature of your vision for the future.

The extent to which you understand these 10 trends, overcome their challenges and seize their opportunities, is the extent to which you can help renew the American Spirit.

Let's begin with the first five.

Chapter 3

"Continuous White Water"

- 5 Worrisome Trends & What to Do About Them:
  1. *Intense Competition Everywhere*
  2. *Instability of Large Institutions*
  3. *Reinvention of the Workplace*
  4. *Awash in Professionals*
  5. *Crime & Violence as Daily Threats*
- For Every Action, A Reaction

Life is like white-water rafting on a fast-running river.

If you've been white-water rafting, you know that, properly conducted, it's fun, exciting and reasonably safe.

Ideally, professionals brief you on what to do and how to work as a team. Coaching and practice help you make it through each set of rapids to calmer waters ahead — but always with some risks.

Life *always* has been like white-water rafting. No matter how privileged or well-prepared, you won't be blessed with a life *totally* free of turbulence and risks.

In the decades that preceded the 1990s, life offered plenty of white water and there were times, such as the depression in the 1930s and World War II in the 1940s, when millions were sluiced through circumstances and events over which they had little or no control.

But most people who lived through those times were able to draw strength from, and take comfort in, families that stayed together, neighborhoods where it was safe to walk the streets at night, workplaces where employees who were loyal and who worked hard could expect job security, and faith in a living and loving God.

When tragedy struck, more often than not it had nothing to do with individual choices. Such tragedies as polio epidemics and the midwestern dust bowl of the 1930s were "acts of God." Other tragedies were matters of chance, such as a low draft number or being aboard a troop ship that was torpedoed in the icy North Atlantic.

Yes, you are still faced with acts of God, be they floods, earthquakes and the like, although modern technology has greatly improved your prospects for survival. And there still are matters of chance, such as being on an airplane caught in windshear, although your odds of arriving safely on modern aircraft are vastly better than in the so-called "good old days" of travel by horse or in a 1939 Ford roadster without seat belts or air bags. Acts of God and matters of chance will always be with us.

What makes *these* times so perilous, however, are not acts of God or matters of chance, but bad or questionable personal choices.

It's *personal choices,* not acts of God, that have one in five Americans carrying a sexually transmitted disease. The AIDs epidemic is *not* the same as the polio epidemic. Until the development of vaccines, there was little people could do to keep from being struck down by polio, other than avoiding people known to have the disease.

There is plenty that individuals can do to avoid the scourge of AIDs and other sexually transmitted diseases. Each of us can choose to behave morally or immorally. If everyone had chosen to behave morally in the past, there would be no AIDs, no syphilis, gonorrhea, herpes, etc. And if everyone would choose to behave morally in the future, those diseases eventually would fade from the scene.

It's personal choices, not bad company, that attract people to illicit sex, drugs and crime. And there are personal choices on how to deal with those problems.

Should children be taught that sex out of wedlock is morally wrong or that it's "okay" so long as they practice "safe" sex?

While some people demand that schools or the government do something about drugs, teenage pregnancies and the like, others think *parents* should take more responsibility for their children.

Perhaps — just perhaps — fathers should spend more than the current average of *seven minutes a week* in meaningful conversation with their children.

Perhaps — just perhaps — mothers should forego career fulfillment or a bigger household income and *be there* for their children, at least in their early and formative years.

Perhaps — just perhaps — *both* parents should work harder on their relationship with each other so their children could grow up as part of a loving family unit instead of being cast upon the continuous white water of step-parents, step-grandparents, half-siblings, mommy or daddy's live-in "friend," custody battles, court visitation rights, and life among a dysfunctional gaggle of steps, halfs and exes.

It's *personal choices,* quite often, and not "business circumstances beyond our control" that prompt employers to lay off employees while fattening executive bonuses and stockholder profits.

It's *personal choices,* not "entitlement to better circumstances," that prompt employees to steal from employers, whether in cash, office supplies or by withholding their less-than-the-best efforts.

And, yes, it has been *personal choices* and not an evil conspiracy by politicians that racked up a national debt that is soaring past the combined debt of all other nations on earth.

While more than 80 percent of Cambodians *risk their lives* to exercise their right to vote, less than half the eligible Americans even bother to exercise the simple personal choice of going to the polls.

So now is a time of continuous white water and, perhaps, a time of greater willingness by people to accept more responsibility for their rafts being on the wildest of rivers.

What's ahead? There are plenty of trends to be concerned about, but here are five that portend *more* white water. You may find threats in these trends. But you may also find hidden among them some incredible opportunities.

In light of these trends, it will be the *personal choices* you make that will determine your future success and happiness.

1. Intense Competition Everywhere

Competition has become so intense in America and elsewhere that law-of-the-jungle analogies abound.

The gazelle, to cite one such analogy, wakes up in the morning knowing that failure to run faster than the fastest lion will result in being eaten alive; the lion knows that failure to run faster than the slowest gazelle will result in starvation.

In business, competition means more than U.S. companies competing with foreign companies. It also means competing effectively with each other to produce the best products at the lowest prices.

Economies of scale gained in domestic markets help make U.S. goods and services more competitive in foreign markets. Research and development costs covered through the sale of goods on the domestic scene provide opportunities for U.S. companies to penetrate foreign markets where R&D frequently is paid for by the government.

And global competition includes the willingness of individual employees, often working in teams, to produce new ideas, new methods, and new products to "beat the competition."

Looking back over the last four decades, there are two main reasons U.S. companies didn't kept pace with foreign companies: (1) prices were too high and (2) quality was too low.

U.S. laborers, egged on by powerful unions, became far-and-away the highest paid workers in the world. U.S. industry decided to make do with existing technology in order to cover high labor costs and optimize the next quarter's profits. Is it any wonder, then, that many U.S. companies couldn't compete well in the world market?

Example: Day after day, in a large shipyard in Massachusetts some years ago, three men installed electrical wiring in a merchant ship under construction.

While the other two watched, the member of the carpenters union installed a wooden backing to a steel bulkhead. Then he sat down and dozed while a member of the pipefitters union attached a conduit. Then the second man sat down and dozed as the third, a member of the electrical workers union, fed wire through the pipe.

Meanwhile, in Taiwan, a worker making a quarter of what the lowest-paid of the Massachusetts threesome was getting, performed all three jobs. Surprise! The U.S. shipyard closed. The shipyard in Taiwan did a brisk business and hired more workers.

> It does the worker no good to have an employer who can't make it in the marketplace.
>
> Jeffrey H. Joseph
> U.S. Chamber of Commerce

Does this mean America can't compete in the world market for things that float and go to sea? Not at all.

While big U.S. shipyards were struggling for survival, smaller U.S. boat-builders were turning out — at competitive prices — the world's finest motoryachts.

Thousands of new jobs were created in the 1970s and 1980s and everything was going pretty well in the export market until, in the midst of a recession, Congress decided to "punish the rich" by slapping a 10 percent luxury tax on yachts. The rich never were punished, for they simply stopped buying yachts.

Sales went down, unit costs went up, and once again, government drove a nail into the coffin of U.S. competitiveness. Yards closed, thousands of Americans lost their jobs, and yacht-builders overseas took the lead in one of the few markets in which America had been leading the world.

When the luxury tax was finally repealed, some jobs were restored but many others were lost forever. The industry was left scrambling to regain its competitive edge.

When companies cut costs, when the U.S. dollar stays favorably priced against foreign currencies, and when the U.S. government finds ways to level the playing field of international commerce, American products become more competitive in world markets, sales increase and more jobs are created.

And what about quality?

In the 1950s and 1960s, U.S. automobiles became a world-wide joke. Detroit factored "planned obsolescence" into the auto-ownership equation and saw breakdowns as a key to parts sales. Size and flashy geegaws were supposed to hide poor design and shoddy workmanship.

The Germans, who were turning out high-quality cars of superb design, referred to the typical American automobile as a *"Strassenkreuzer"* — literally, a "boulevard battleship."

It took the pressure of global competition to make a difference. When nearly one out of four cars sold in America was an import, the wakeup call was heard, and it was time to reinvent the American automobile and the way it was made.

There has been enormous progress:

• Quality improved to the point where some American cars were ranked among the world's best.

• The Germans went wild over Ford's new Probe GT, waiting lists in Japan and Europe for Harley-Davidson motorcycles grew to six months or more, and foreign car sales in the U.S. weakened.

• The quality of Japanese cars made in America by American workers became superior, in some cases, to the same cars made in Japan by Japanese workers.

• A leading maker of British luxury cars turned to its new American owner to improve quality and design.

• Owner satisfaction surveys began showing more justification to "buy American" and keep more U.S. jobs from disappearing.

But America will have to do a lot more than buy its own products to regain a favorable balance of international trade.

> With trade barriers falling, no company's national turf is protected from overseas competition. When the Japanese — or Germans, French, Koreans, Taiwanese, and so forth — are free to compete in the same markets, just one superior performer can raise the competitive threshhold for companies around the world... Good performers drive out the inferior, because the lowest price, the highest quality, the best service available from any one of them soon becomes the standard for all competitors.
>
> Michael Hammer & James Champy
> *Reengineering the Corporation*

Long-term U.S. success in the global marketplace will depend on some fundamental questions:

• *Are you willing to work harder than the competition?* Perhaps no nationality works harder than the Japanese. And Americans in the 1990s are working harder at their jobs, on average, than at any time since 1945. But younger Japanese are challenging the system in which their parents have been working themselves to death.

Personal choice: How hard are you willing to work?

• *Politically, are you willing to help get rid of government disincentives to work hard?* Public policy for decades has focused on what amounts to penalties on people who work hard and want to be more productive in their work lives and personal lives.

> In America, we tax work, investment, employment, savings and productivity while we subsidize non-work, consumption and debt. It's time we start to reverse this trend.

> Jack Kemp

Personal choice: What people and platforms will you vote for in the next election?

• *If you are in business, are you willing to invest in the latest and best technology and equipment?* When coupled with a willingness to work hard and the incentives to work harder, having the best technology and equipment is certain to raise overall productivity beyond that of our international competitors.

The results of working harder, and of restructuring, consolidating and modernizing, kept productivity in U.S. businesses rising steadily for many years and kept it ahead — quantitatively, at least — of nearly every other country in the world. But what of the future?

> In the private sector, the biggest obstacle to higher investment is the tax code. The U.S. taxes savings and capital at a higher rate than any other industrial nation, even hitting corporate profits twice — first as company income, second as dividends.

> *Wall Street Journal*

Personal choice: If you are a decision-maker, what will you decide to invest in — and lobby for?

• *Will you help muster political strength to ease the crushing burdens of government regulation?* People may be willing to work harder, especially with incentives. Business may be willing to invest in the best technology and equipment. But we won't be fully competitive until the shackles of government regulations are loosened.

Examples: Workers compensation, at least in some states, is enough to make an employer think twice before putting people on the payroll to help grow and become more competitive. Try to find out during an interview whether a prospective employee might be prone to defraud the company through a liberal state workers compensation system, or in other ways, and you can be sued.

Ask a prospect what his or her intentions are regarding having a family, which could affect future job performance and payroll costs, and the wrath of government and a legion of advocacy groups may come crashing down on your company.

Hire too many people, and you cross thresholds beyond which you face the costs of wheelchair ramps, devices for the hearing impaired, months of family leave for men *and* women, etc.

> An essential strategy for this small business is never to hire anyone under any circumstances for any reason. By keeping our company limited to family members as partners and, when necessary, by using vendor services and our informal network of people willing to work with us in mutually beneficial ways, we can make a good return on investment while avoiding all the paperwork, regulatory red tape and legal risks of having people on a payroll.

> President of a Small Firm

What used to be called "fringe benefits" have grown into onerous burdens for employers. What used to be a shocking occasional incident of fraud by "one rotten apple in the barrel" has turned into a day-to-day occurrence as workplace theft continues to rise.

What used to be one clerk with a primitive office machine to handle a factory payroll has turned into a department of people with sophisticated computers hard-pressed to keep up with constant changes in federal, state and local regulations and requirements.

The implications of government over-regulation in the international marketplace are crystal clear. Consider the burdens of a single federal agency, the Food & Drug Administration (FDA):

> The average research cost of every new drug, two thirds of which goes to meeting FDA requirements, is $230 million (not a typographical error). One pharmaceutical company calculated that it spent more on forms and paperwork than it did on all research for cancer and other diseases. American citizens might be better served if these funds were diverted to research in Japan and Germany, where more research would get accomplished and eventually trickle back to help cure disease in America.

> Philip K. Howard
> *The Death of Common Sense*

A reduction in red tape would be an important step in getting more people back to work, too. But no matter how much government intrudes or doesn't intrude in the workplace, the ability of American business to compete effectively and, as a result, create good jobs in which people are paid well and treated fairly, will depend on the single question — a major personal choice — that is vital:

• *Are you willing to increase enormously the investment in education, both collectively and individually?* Unless you are, there's no way that the U.S. will be able to triumph in global markets.

When insurance companies fly applications and other paperwork to a foreign country for processing, the reason has as much to do with finding enough literate, intelligent people to do the work as it does with finding people who are willing to work harder for less money.

The fact is that America is facing a *shortage* of skilled labor. That's good news for people willing to make educational investments in themselves, especially in areas involving technology.

How can we have millions of people out of work and face a labor shortage at the same time?

Part of it relates to *over-supply* of middle-managers and people with educations limited to history, theater arts, ethnic studies and the like. But much more is related to an *under-supply* of people who can read, comprehend and communicate well, who have first-rate technical skills and who possess a strong work ethic.

How well is public education doing in producing such people?

While increasing numbers of high school graduates can barely read their diplomas, the wrath of teachers unions and agencies of the Clinton Administration bankrupted a company that had the *nerve* to produce an innovative way of teaching phonics. It was the elimination of phonics by liberal educators some 40 years ago that triggered the long decline in literacy rates.

Lower reading skills and comprehension also contributed to degradation of mathematics, science and other technical subjects.

> Only 7 percent of U.S. high school graduates are prepared for college-level science courses.
>
> CNN Factoid

As to instilling a strong work ethic, in great numbers of schools homework was all but eliminated, classroom hours were cut back, achievement standards were reduced and tens of thousands of "students" were simply handed off to the next grade level when they failed to achieve passing grades.

Meantime, controversy broke out over new national standards for history textbooks that would eliminate mention of Thomas

Edison, the Wright Brothers and other great American achievers, but require the study of civil rights pioneers, mistreatment of Native Americans and the evils of McCarthyism.

In an environment in which there is a growing shortage of well-qualified people, some regulatory burdens that stifle job creation may become unnecessary.

Companies are discovering that severely handicapped people can become their *best* employees, making the investment in wheelchair ramps well worth it. Unable to find enough well-qualified people, why *wouldn't* a company want to invest in a day-care program, set up a job-sharing system and take other steps to accommodate people with conflicting work-and-home priorities?

> Indeed, some 37 percent of the companies studied report that they have had trouble recruiting technical staff the past few years. And 30 percent have had difficulties recruiting skilled labor. As an example, New York-based Chemical Bank has had to interview 40 job applicants for every 1 found suitable for training as a bank teller. And NYNEX has had to test 60,000 applicants to fill 3,000 open positions.
>
> U.S. Labor Department/Hudson Institute
> *Workforce 2000 Study*

Personal choices: What will you do about your own level of education and job skills? What will you advise your children to do? If the school board wants to raise taxes to improve the quality of education *and has a good plan to do it,* how will you vote?

Your willingness to help overcome the "educational gap" will go a long way toward answering these personal-choice questions.

It goes like this:

> When businesses must compete with each other for a limited supply of well-qualified workers, there should be less need for government regulations that purport to protect employees from "abuse."

> A business is more likely to invest in state-of-the-art equipment when it can find enough skilled people to operate it.

> Willingness to work hard will attain a fresh and less onerous perspective when enough people are willing and able to work "smart."

2. *The Instability of Large Institutions*

More than any other single factor, it is intense competition — or the *fear* of it — that has brought about the second of the five "Continuous White Water" trends: the instability of large institutions.

In olden days, we had two good rules of thumb: (1) the larger the institution, the more stable it is likely to be and (2) the higher you go in a large organization the more likely it is that you will enjoy great job security.

Today, both thumbs have been amputated.

Whole industries have been so shaken by change that what once were bedrocks of security for shareholders and employees alike too often have turned into "silt fines" washed down-river by all that continuous white water.

Some of the biggest names in the airline industry are now memories, including Pan Am and Eastern, while others are battling mightily just to survive.

Fortune magazine listed the 100 largest industrial companies in 1956. By the mid-1990s, more than two-thirds of those companies had disappeared from the list with some still on the list struggling to stay profitable.

For most of the past two centuries or so, people who worked for banks accepted relatively low pay in exchange for prestigious titles and incomparable job security. By the end of the 1980s, we had 12,000 banks and related financial institutions in the United States, compared to just 20 in Japan.

How about a career in banking today? Not only is the pay still relatively low, but rock-solid job security is out the window and those high-sounding titles aren't as plentiful either.

Even the utility industry, once the stuffy epitome of tradition and intransigence, has turned into a battleground on which a former brotherhood of cooperating companies is fighting over territorial and technological turf.

Colleges and universities, also among the traditional bedrocks, now are less stable than ever. Although tenure still protects some professorial sloths, the job-life expectancy of a university president has plunged to an average of less than three and a half years.

To be the CEO of a large company once not only offered great prestige but great job security as well. Now the CEO is as likely to be targeted and temporary as to be top-drawer and tenured. There are, of course, enormous amounts of money in the forms of pay, perks and golden parachutes for those willing to take the risk.

While a toppled senior executive usually is splashed with monetary balm to heal a wounded ego, people at the other end of the spectrum do not fare nearly so well.

Instead of cushy retirements or lucrative contract buyouts, professionals and middle-managers often face packages far short of what's needed to make ends meet between jobs. "Joe Lunchbox," on the other hand, is more likely to be escorted to the gate by security guards and given minimum severance pay.

What the instability of large institutions brings to the 1990s is an enormous slice of the populace with shattered dreams, especially those who, through personal choices, managed to rack up far more debt than savings for the rainy day that turned into a monsoon.

What does all this mean? For one thing, of the millions who lost their jobs due to the instability and precipitous decline of large institutions in the first half of the 1990s, only about one in four will ever be called back.

Even the big, *profitable* companies are catching the fever and chopping employees in droves. Procter & Gamble, to cite a classic example, enjoyed an increase in net earnings of more than a *half a billion dollars* from 1992 to 1993, but found it could boost profits by *another* half a billion by closing 30 of its 147 plants and chopping 13,000 employees, including 15 percent of Cleveland's entire non-manufacturing workforce.

There are at least two other distressing tendencies resulting from the instability of large companies:

• Early-retirement windows provide handy exits for a company's *best*-performing people. Those with talents and skills in great demand often are quick to take the money and run. Those with poor to mediocre work performance and qualifications, and who would have a lot of trouble finding a job elsewhere, tend to cling to the company as long as possible. Too often, these are people with big debt and small savings who are least able to handle loss of a job.

• "Corporate politics" often enters into downsizing efforts when executives and managers become tempted to get rid of peak-performers who may pose a threat to their own survival. Old adage:

> First-rate managers hire and retain first-rate people,
> Second-rate managers hire and retain third-rate people.

Finally, the largest and traditionally most stable institution in the world — the U.S. Government — no longer can be counted on to provide the kind of legendary job security that once required phenomenal effort to lose a Civil Service job (political appointments never were that secure, especially when an incumbent chief bureaucrat is caught belonging to the wrong political party).

Enormous downsizing of the military to one side, taxpayers personally experiencing "continuous white water" will grow more and more intolerant of a bureaucracy in which people receive relatively fat compensation for jobs that are relatively unproductive and risk-free.

Demands for better public service costing fewer tax dollars has already shaken many state and municipal governments with an ever-louder cry for privatizing everything from garbage collection to public schools to prisons.

As for *starting* a career in government service:

> Unprecedented numbers of government employees will be fired. Civil service pay will be cut one or more times. The economies of Washington, D.C. and most state capitals will suffer more than usual as spending is slashed and government work is reduced.

> James Davidson & William Rees-Mogg
> *The Great Reckoning*

There are key messages here for young people contemplating careers with large companies or governmental agencies, and older people wondering what the future in such organizations will bring:

• *Never count on anything beyond what you are legally owed by your employer.* Vested pensions, funds in a 401K, accrued vacation pay, etc., should be secure. But be wary of even those "entitlements," especially if your employer is in financial trouble.

• *Cut expenses and postpone major purchases.* Do all you can to accumulate in a *secure* account or investment instrument enough liquid assets to enable you and your family to survive for a year or more in the event you suddenly lose your job.

• *Be a reliable, top-producing employee.* You should be among the last on the list in a cutback. But don't assume good performance will give you protection.

• *Act as though you plan to stay until retirement.* But update your resume and keep an eye open for better situations, including greater job security.

• *Consider your job temporary.* Focus on employability, not on survivability. How qualified are you to get a job elsewhere?

• *Diversify your income.* If you and your spouse work for the same firm, decide whether one of you should pursue a job in another organization to avoid the axe falling on *both* of you. Look for *proven* ways to earn income on the side, then use such extra income to pay off debts, bolster savings and lessen long-term dependency on paychecks.

Large institutions haven't cornered the market on instability. Many small or mid-size companies, non-profit organizations and governmental agencies are showing similar patterns of behavior. In fact, working for smaller organizations may offer even *less* security since they may not have the resources to make it through tough times.

The good news is that, overall, big institutions may be shrinking but many smaller organizations are growing, some at phenomenal rates. In fact, most of the opportunities to make money in the future will be found in small to mid-size organizations.

All of which points to:

3. *Reinvention of the Workplace*

There's much more to the instability of large institutions than mergers, takeovers, bankruptcies and massive cuts in workforces. The nature of organizational design, individual jobs and the way people relate to each other, is going through enormous change as well.

Large or small, private or public, organizations are reinventing the workplace to avert instability and beat intense competition.

Hierarchical management is being replaced with empowered work teams. Front-line employees are given more and more accountability for results. Traditional chains of command are eliminated. Compensation systems are redesigned, tying rewards to performance rather than years of service and the cost of living.

And whole categories of jobs are eliminated through a process summed up by a single word. Coined in 1967 to describe diversion of money into high-yielding direct investments, this little-known word has come to mean much more:

> dis · in · ter · me · di · a · tion \ noun: the elimination of employees between the customer and the computer.

The classic example of disintermediation is the automated teller machine. Stick your card in the slot, hit some buttons, bypass all the employees, go straight into the bank's computer system and make a transaction. Automated phone systems, direct ordering of products on the Internet and even robotic stock-picking machines in distribution centers are all forms of disintermediation.

And so, the 1990s is the decade of the disposable employee:

> I don't care how many years of your life you've given to this organization. If you can't handle an increased workload, there are plenty of people willing to step in and do it — probably for a lot less than we're paying you.

Not only are employees expected to do more work, often for the same compensation, but the 1990s brought more and more people onto the scene who are not regular, full-time employees.

Due in large part to soaring health-care costs and inexorable escalation of government regulations, more and more companies cut deeper into the full-time workforce and "farmed out" some of their less-critical responsibilities to independent contractors.

A concept called the "Shamrock Organization" offers a model in which work is accomplished by three kinds of people.

About a third of the work is done by regular, full-time employees. Roughly another third is done by contract specialists on a full or part-time basis. The rest is "outsourced" to vendors, many of them running businesses out of their homes.

The key to deploying the workforce now and in the future is flexibility. The more that government imposes regulations making it harder for businesses to be flexible with employees, the more businesses will try to avoid hiring regular, full-time people.

Where jobs are concerned, the good news of the 1990s and beyond is that millions of new ones will be created. The bad news is that (1) they will be lower level jobs with less growth potential due to disintermediation, work teams, delayering and flattened organizations, and (2) a larger percentage of the new jobs will be temporary.

The first half of the 1990s underscored the problem for people seeking good, relatively secure jobs. Percentagewise, regular, fulltime jobs grew in the low single digits, but temporary jobs soared to a growth rate of more than 20 percent!

> Although most of Corporate America is hesitant to admit it because of potential political liabilities, the hard truth is that it is becoming standard management practice in U.S. corporations to cut permanent staff to the absolute minimum number of persons required to continue profitable operations while utilizing a variety of innovative, non-permanent employment relationships to cope efficiently with fluctuating workloads. This strategy is most often referred to in management circles as the "core-staff concept."
>
> Dan Lacey, editor of *Workplace Trends,*
> in testimony before the
> Joint Economic Committee of Congress

Not only do employers save on benefits by hiring temporaries, but they can pay them less ($8.25 an hour vs. $10.80 on average for all occupations as of the mid-1990s) and can avert pay hikes by simply replacing higher-paid temps with people willing to work for less.

Not only are temporary employees easier to get rid of, they also give management a good way to "audition" people for regular jobs, averting the paperwork, expense and unpleasantries of having to fire people who looked good in their interviews but who didn't perform up to expectations.

Besides mergers, consolidations and bankruptcies, the delayering of Corporate America will continue to have an enormous impact on people in white collar jobs. Downturns in the economy can make matters even more uncomfortable, as evidenced by the recession of the early 1990s:

...The white collar workforce is feeling more of the
relative pain caused by this recession than in previous
recessions. For example, in past recessions the white
collar workforce has often experienced small or flat job
growth. However, the current recession is the first time
since the Great Depression that the white collar employment has declined by a statistically significant amount.

Dr. Richard S. Belous
National Planning Association

The most vulnerable of white-collar jobs are middle managers.
While executives are imperiled by demands for greater and better
performance, and people around the bottom of the corporate ladder are
threatened by automation, out-sourcing and shifting work to temporaries, middle managers frequently face total elimination of their jobs.

Almost one-third of middle management has disappeared. Those who remain are more likely to stay
longer. In fact, it has been estimated that by the
late 1990s, there will be more than 30 candidates
for each middle management opening.

Dean R. Spitzer, Ph.D.
SuperMotivation

Not only middle managers, but headquarters staffs in general proliferated in the 40 years that followed World War II — in
corporations, the military, government and other institutions.

By the 1990s, what many big organizations struggling to
survive or recover had in common were workforces with operations
and production people in the *minority*.

IBM, for example, began the decade with more than 90 percent
of its U.S. workers having little or nothing to do with production or
operations, thanks in part to legions of planners and paper-shufflers in
the U.S. and most manufacturing jobs having been sent overseas.

Most school district employees used to be teachers. By the
1990s, teachers often were in the minority with Denver, for example,
having only 24 percent of its workers presiding over classrooms.

And when the Cold War ended, the U.S. military had far more
generals and admirals than it did at the height of World War II when
there were six times as many troops.

The implications of delayering and staff cuts are frightening to
anyone looking for career success by climbing a towering organizational ladder. What used to feature many rungs that could be climbed

rapidly has been turned into a mile-wide ladder that's every bit as high but with only a few rungs that, for many, will be out of reach.

While the brightest and best eventually will struggle to the top of such a ladder, traditional career progression will elude those expecting promotions from specialist to supervisor to assistant manager to manager and so on.

What fills the void when entire layers of an organization are removed? From the organization's viewpoint, it should mean *more* people empowered to produce more and better work.

> Layers insulate. They slow things down. They garble. Leaders in highly layered organizations are like people who wear several sweaters outside on a freezing winter day. They remain warm and comfortable, but are blissfully ignorant of the realities of their environment. They couldn't be further from what's going on.
>
> Jack Welch, CEO
> General Electric

Replacing supervisors and managers with empowered teams, requiring front-line workers to assume responsibilities that once rested with supervisors, and rotating people among a variety of jobs, are the principal delayering tools of the 1990s and beyond.

From the individual employee's standpoint, this often will mean harder work but a greater variety of tasks. It also will mean results-oriented compensation frequently based on *team* rather than individual performance.

For people uprooted from traditional workplaces, career survival will depend on ability and willingness to make personal changes.

As with anything else in life, the people who do the best job of changing with the times and with organizational needs will be the ones who will do better than those with their heads stuck in the past.

Some implications of the re-invented workplace:

• A *"traditional education" is less likely to be a good admission ticket.* Deep but narrow specialization was much sought-after when there were lots of jobs demanding specialization. No longer.

A good *general* education that includes sufficient depth in more than one area of specialization attractive to prospective employers will work best for most young people wondering how on earth they're going to *find* a job after graduation.

A blending of *relevant* "hard skills" and *relevant* "soft skills" could be ideal. Examples: a major in biotechnology with a minor in business communication; or a major in marketing and a minor in the Russian language.

Those hoping to land good corporate jobs with a major in such fields as philosophy, speech communication and ethnic studies may want to figure on spending at least some of their career years flipping burgers or waxing eloquent in the detailing bay of a car wash.

• *The ability to get along with people and communicate well will become more important to career success.* Simply mastering a single technical skill won't be enough. For example, the only way six or so heads can be better than one on an empowered work team is for team members to have good communication skills and work well together.

• *Upward mobility will require outward mobility.* With fewer rungs of the career ladder to climb, those who are turned on by bigger job titles, faster pay raises and more responsibility should figure on changing places of employment more often.

This could have substantial implications when deciding whether to rent or to buy a house or condo, especially since lucrative corporate relocation packages are on the wane and the inability to sell a home in a weak real estate market may be a huge economic millstone.

Outward mobility also may put an extra strain on a marriage, especially if *both* partners are career-oriented, are seeking advancement and are bringing home paychecks that contribute substantially to their lifestyles.

4. We're Awash in Professionals

The special collections room of a big-city's main library holds a telling commentary on the times.

In the Yellow Pages of the city's 1960 telephone directory, there were three pages of attorneys — all listed in discreet light-face type. Ten years later, the lawyers had managed to spill onto a fourth page.

By 1980, the advent of the so-called Decade of Greed and Excess, the number of pages of legal-eagles had proliferated to 14, thanks in part to the appearance of small display ads.

Anyone who cheered when the dinosaur ate the lawyer in the hit film "Jurassic Park" would become apoplectic adding up the pages of attorneys in the 1997 edition of same city's phone book.

Forty? Seventy? Ninety? Try 116, including full-page ads with blood-red type that seem to cry out:

> Attention all victims, get your due!
> Stop in for a free visit and then let's sue!

While adding up the pages of lawyers in one city's phone book is an unscientific measurement of career potential in the legal profession, it has to be, at the least, an interesting commentary on the 1990s — especially when the 1996 directory offered 24 *fewer* pages of doctors than lawyers.

Let's leave to the imagination the implications of having more clamor for legal services than medical services, but consider some other indicators of what's ahead:

• The number of lawyers in the United States is expected to top *one million* by 2000.

• We have far more lawyers per 10,000 population than scientists and engineers. The Japanese have far more scientists and engineers than lawyers.

• As the most litigious nation on earth, we either are going to find a way to unburden ourselves of tens of billions of dollars worth of unproductive legal costs or we will be unable to compete effectively in the global marketplace.

The willingness of the U.S. political system to make work for hundreds of thousands of new lawyers has been advanced for many years by large numbers of lawyers in Congress and state legislatures.

The question is whether public demand for profound changes in our legal system will be strong enough to force the U.S. to adopt the far-less-predatory practices of the industrialized nations with which we must compete. If so, many thousands of lawyers may face a choice between changing careers or pricing their services somewhere between plumbers and manicurists.

> Attorneys file 18 million civil lawsuits in the U.S. each year, causing a drag on the economy. In fact, the mere filing of lawsuits has forced industrial plants to shut down, doctors to abandon their practices, playgrounds to close and dads to stop coaching Little League. The defendants decided they simply could not afford to fight all the lawsuits, even though they might well win.

> Parade Magazine

Tort reform is among imperatives if we are to keep our health-care system from bankrupting us, and that prospect offers a cheery financial outlook for neither lawyers nor health-care professionals in general and doctors in particular.

While medical malpractice has been a boon mostly to lawyers, it has also enhanced the incomes of many doctors and other health-care professionals.

In essence, lawyers can make money suing doctors and doctors can make money practicing defensive medicine, prescribing all kinds of tests to reduce the probability of being sued. Stub your toe? Better schedule a CATscan just to be on the safe side. Want a wart removed? Better give you an MRI and a full round of blood tests just to make sure there won't be complications.

Two other ominous factors have come on the scene for what have been our two most lucrative professions: para-professionals and do-it-yourselfers.

> Emerging Medicine/Law Clinics: Not staffed with full-fledged M.D.'s or lawyers, but associates who know the system well enough to give first aid/fast help—from injections and prescriptions to advice.
>
> Faith Popcorn
> *The Popcorn Report*

Office supply stores now carry do-it-yourself legal forms and there are scores of computer software packages to prepare wills and trusts and deeds and, in some states, even lawsuits.

Family medical guides offer easy-to-understand flow charts for self-diagnosis with enough "be-sure-to-see-your-doctor-if..." notices to discourage readers from suing the publishers.

It's hard to argue that, like lawyers, the U.S. has too many doctors. Many rural areas have a chronic shortage of doctors, while doctors in urban areas are spending more and more on advertising to drum up patients.

> So if you're suffering discomfort when you sit down, just pick up your phone right now and call 1-800-4MD-TUSH.
>
> TV commercial advertising
> a proctology clinic

Given the condition of the uppermost professions, the 1990s bring practitioners and aspirants face to face with daunting questions:

• *Can we handle a million lawyers?* If so, what impact will there be on the economy? If not, could you make good money—or even a decent living—as an attorney?

• *Is the additional education to become a professional worth it?* Many are asking the question as hundreds of doctors quit their practices because of lawsuits, thousands of others open sideline businesses to diversify their incomes, and government piles more and more regulations onto the practice of medicine. Is it worth eight, 10, 12 years of your life and more than $150,000 of investment to become a doctor? Or how about years of law school at a cost of tens of thousands of dollars to become a lawyer?

• *Do you have what it takes?* Recognizing that the best people of any profession are very likely to do well in it, do you really have what it takes to be among the best?

Law and medicine aren't the only professions that will undergo great change and mounting challenges as the decade of the 1990s winds down. How about a career in accounting?

> Over the last five years, the staid accounting profession has been transformed into a Darwinian jungle. The major accounting firms are reeling from a sharp rise in competition, shrinking audit business in the wake of client mergers, waves of litigation from disgruntled clients, and unprecedented layoffs and partner defections. Accountants are leaving the business in droves. Those who remain are finding that the law of survival of the fittest prevails over generally accepted behavioral principles.
>
> Lee Berton
> *The Wall Street Journal*

For years, the best and the brightest gravitated to what used to be the "Big Eight" accounting firms. Of all the big partner names attached to those firms, few are left standing end-to-end.

With better and simpler tax-preparation and general accounting software becoming available to individual taxpayers and businesses of all sizes, a major unanswered question is whether legislative bodies can create complication and confusion faster than software suppliers can create simplification and user-friendliness.

That question, though, will be moot if political movements lead to massive reform of the income tax system or total elimination of it.

Among what also can be considered the "hard-skill" professions, engineers are likely to fare the best as we head toward the New Millennium. Starting salaries for graduate engineers continued to show modest increases in the first half of the 1990s, while some other professions remained flat or, like medicine, declined.

While thousands of engineers lost their jobs in the wind-down of the defense industry, the skills and abilities of first-rate engineers and other technical people have become supremely important for companies seeking to re-emerge. Whether it's General Dynamics adjusting to the post-Cold War era or Chrysler Corporation striving for leadership in the hotly competitive automobile market, engineering talent will be of prime importance.

And, of course, engineering and design will make or break thousands of newer, smaller companies ascending the growth curve.

Teaching, which is the *highest* paid profession in Japan and the *lowest* paid profession in the United States, will have to play a major part in any sort of national economic renaissance.

Young people in Japan leave school ready to go to work with a minimum of training by their employers. Corporate America, on the other hand, spends more money on training employees to be employable and productive than American government spends on educating them from kindergarten through high school.

There is a huge need for what first-rate teachers, trainers and educators are able to contribute to our nation's economic well-being. And yet, no surprise: teaching does *not* draw our brightest and best students. A single outstanding teacher can sow seeds of greatness in even the most culturally and educationally deprived students. The problem is that we have far more poor teachers than truly outstanding teachers and each day in America we have to live with the results:

> A poor surgeon hurts one person at a time. A poor teacher hurts 30.
>
> Ernest Boyer
> *People magazine*

Clearly, we need more first-rate teachers. But when will the public and private sectors be ready to pay what's needed to get them?

The safest of assumptions for anyone considering the teaching profession is simply this: Your prospects of finding a job and enjoying long-haul career growth will depend on four attributes:

• *You have subject-matter expertise* related to current skills shortages (computers, robotics, basic engineering, mathematics, etc.)

• *You demonstrate superb skills* in transferring technical information to people with limited education.

• *You are personable, upbeat, enthusiastic:* a pump-'em-up-type motivator who can get people to love what you're teaching, and

• *You keep up with constant changes* in your subject-matter areas as well as in the latest teaching techniques.

As much as we need more good teachers, perhaps the most neglected, underpaid, short-handed profession is the one that, in the continuous white water of the 1990s, is needed as never before.

We have an abundance of professionals to deal with the word of law and the word of the accounting standards boards. In many areas of the country, we even have enough people up on the latest word from the medical journals.

What we have an acute shortage of are honorable people to convey the Word of God — deeply caring men and women who can bring home to individuals buffeted by the 1990s the message that there really is a living, loving God who offers hope, shelter from the tumult of the times and strength to overcome whatever bad hand life seems to have dealt.

The need for such people is especially acute in tradition-bound Protestant churches and Jewish synagogues from which people, largely baby-boomers, defected in droves over the past 20 years. A critical factor in such defections most often is the lack of a person in the pulpit who can inspire confidence and commitment.

As elderly clergymen retire, there should be an opportunity for congregational renewal. But when a pastoral search committee spends months trying to find someone of exceptional capability only to have to settle for a person who squeaked through divinity school and comes with an array of personal problems, there's no reason to believe that the decline in membership won't continue.

The shortage is acute on the other side of the spectrum as well. Far from declining in ranks, Catholic churches are growing, but can't find enough people willing to become priests and nuns.

Also growing are congregations led by outstanding spiritual leaders adept at offering relief from the stress of life in the 1990s.

More and more people are seeking affiliation with some kind of organized religion. But the number of theological degrees granted declined through the 1980s, perhaps due to a greater focus of that decade on things material over things spiritual.

Where opportunities in the professions are concerned, none offers so great an opportunity nor so great a challenge than the clergy. For the right person — the one with a love of God as well as a love of people — it also can be the most self-fulfilling of professions.

5. *Crime & Violence Are Daily Threats*

We know we've got a problem when, in spite of thousands of additional police officers, sheriff's deputies and state troopers, crime and violence in major American cities became worse in the 1990s than it was in the roughest of cow towns in the 1870s — even though in those days there was little or no organized law enforcement and virtually every male over 14 carried a gun.

By the mid-1990s, the number of adults in prison, on probation or on parole in the United States topped *four million*. More than half the states in the union don't even have that many people living within their borders! We have a higher percentage of our population in prison than any other nation on earth.

Between 1980 and 1993, the federal prison population tripled and is expected to have quintupled by the end of the 1990s. The annual impact of crime on the U.S. economy exceeds well over half a *trillion* dollars a year. It continues to grow at an alarming rate with more and more criminal bahavior exhibited by younger and younger children.

Not only is there an awesome economic impact but, as we'll see later, there is a substantial effect on people's lives — yet another example of "continuous white water."

Since we're a nation quick to seek out simple answers and fix blame, too easily we point the finger at what has become Public Enemy No. 1, from upscale suburbanites sinking megabucks into alarm systems to inner-city single moms hoping to see their kids alive after a day in a violence-wracked school: *T-e-l-e-v-i-s-i-o-n*.

In 1939, RCA Chairman David Sarnoff predicted that television, coupled with a universal increase in schooling, could propel the American people to "the highest general cultural level of any people in the world." That forecast ranks right alongside British Prime Minister Neville Chamberlain's pronouncement a year earlier that he and Adolf Hitler had achieved "peace for our time."

Twenty-some years after Sarnoff's rosy prediction, the broadcasters who were supposed to be leading us to these new heights of culture got a point-blank assessment of what they had wrought from the chairman of the Federal Communications Commission:

> I invite you to sit down in front of your television set when your station goes on the air and stay there without a book, magazine, newspaper, profit-and-loss sheet or rating book to distract you — and keep your eyes glued to that set until the station signs off. I can assure you that you will observe a vast wasteland.
>
> Newton Minow in 1961 speech to the National Association of Broadcasters

Thirty years after that, with hundreds of additional channels on the air, and cable systems offering enormous menus of free and pay-to-see programming, Minow reflected on what the "vast wasteland" had turned into:

> One evening as I watched, with my remote control in hand, I flipped through the channels and saw a man loading his gun on one channel, a different man aiming a gun on another channel, and another man shooting a gun on a third. And if you don't believe me, try it yourself...In 1961 I worried that my children would not benefit much from television, but (today) I worry that my grandchildren actually will be harmed by it.
>
> Newton Minow in 1991 speech at the Gannet Center, Columbia University

For a large part of the adult population, television programming may be nothing more than passive electronic balm for the functionally brain-dead. But for children, television viewing is a potentially life-ruining experience that can undo even the most positive of upbringings.

Television begins affecting behavior at the age of 14 months. Parents who use television as an electronic baby-sitter and see no harm in letting a few hours of Saturday morning cartoons "keep the kids out of trouble" shouldn't be surprised by early signs of aggressive behavior.

The effects of television are so profound that a school board in Indiana felt compelled to take action when children started crawling into storm drains in search of Teenage Mutant Ninja Turtles.

Children who grew up in front of TV screens, coming to believe that violence is some sort of societal norm, enter their teen years ready to accept the "technical training" that television has to offer — how to load, aim and fire the gun; where to stick the knife to kill a person, how to loop the wire around someone's neck; and exactly what sorts of screams, blood-splatterings and deaths result from each method.

Study after study shows a direct correlation between television and violence. Remote areas of Canada that were free of television also were virtually free of crime and violence. When television was introduced, crime and violence rose to levels prevalent in places where there had been television for many years.

Television is so effective as a training tool for criminals that there have been thousands of cases from coast to coast in which specific crimes have been traced to specific TV shows.

That criminals usually are caught at the end of the show is little deterrent for people who have been "programmed" to believe that crime can be a solution to their problems. It's simply a matter of avoiding the "dumb thing" — often a minor detail — that led to the arrest on TV.

In fact, a study in the mid-1990s found that in 84 percent of programs containing violence, no long-term consequences for the violence were depicted. *Only 4 percent* of the violent programs had anti-violence themes.

In or of itself, there's nothing wrong with the *technology* of television.

Few would argue that programs such as Sesame Street have not had a positive influence on impressionable children. And who would claim that channels such as *Mind Extension University* lead to criminal behavior on the parts of people who have reached their teens or adulthood?

The problem has been in the *process* that results in *programming* that delivers a steady diet of crime, violence and sex, especially in urban areas where violence is the worst and choice among commercial TV channels the greatest.

It goes something like this:

• To pay for programming and to make a profit, TV networks and individual stations must attract advertisers.

• Advertisers want the most for their advertising dollars, so they are willing to pay more to place their messages on programs with a large share of the television audience as measured by ratings.

• To boost ratings and lure more advertising dollars, programming executives concentrate on "what sells," especially when trying to capture market share from competitors.

• If "what sells" is crime, violence and sex, the programs that offer the most crime, violence and sex will make the biggest profit, whether the programs are newscasts or "entertainment."

The greater the public appetite for crime, violence and sex on television, the more crime, violence and sex will be seen on television. And the more that is seen, the easier it is to stimulate the appetite.

As one small example of how the process works, let's say two daytime talk-show hosts are in a ratings battle. They know that the more bizarre, controversial and base the subject matter on their shows, the greater the viewing audience. So they will leave no rock unturned in their effort to find "guests" who will attract the most viewers. When cameras roll, they "have at it" with microphones and vicious questioning and commentary to induce maximum uproar and controversy.

If one talk show increased audience share by interviewing "lesbian hockey players who want to marry their priests," the competition will do whatever it takes to turn up some "transvestite dirt bikers who eat their young."

The process even extends to children's programming. In the course of a Congressional inquiry into violence on television, the producer of a children's show noted there are two versions of each episode produced — a "violent version" for the U.S. market and a "nonviolent version" for distribution overseas. Asked why, the producer pointed out that the violent version would be unacceptable to stations in foreign markets but was necessary in order for the show to attract viewers in the U.S.

In the hotly competitive local news market, whoever combines the fastest and most breath-taking delivery of the most negative and oftentimes violent news *wins*.

The argument that violence on "entertainment" programs isn't harmful because people see as much violence on the news, simply doesn't hold water. Reports of violent crimes on news broadcasts usually reflect upon the tragedy of violent acts. As entertainment, violence tends to be "glamorized," sometimes even depicting people finding blessed relief from whatever bothers them by cutting someone in half with a machine gun or a chain saw.

What should be apparent to everybody by now is that if we are to see a reduction in the kinds of violence and criminal behavior that add greatly to the stress and uncertainties of the 1990s, there must be less exposure to crime, violence and sex on television. That won't be easy, even with an agreement among the networks to reduce the amount of crime, violence and sex in their programming.

If we wait for the networks to solve the problem, we'll be waiting a long, long time, especially with competition increasing as networks lose market share to a plethora of new independent stations and cable channels.

If there is an ongoing demand for crime, violence and sex on television, someone in the medium will find a way to fill it and the real-life carnage will go on and on.

However, more channels from which to choose doesn't necessarily mean a greater profusion of violence and sex-oriented programming. In fact, the opposite is true when enough voices are raised to create markets for programs that reflect positive moral values.

If we agree television programming is *an* underlying cause of unprecedented crime and violence, and if we also agree outright censorship is not a realistic alternative, how do we solve the problem?

If, right now, parents would assume full responsibility for the viewing habits of their children and would set a good example by reading more and watching less, focusing only on those programs that reflect reasonable standards of human decency, the crime rate in America would begin to return to pre-TV levels.

The odds of *that* happening are even less than a return to censorship laws. There simply are too many dysfunctional families, "latch-key" children fending for themselves after school and parents whose priorities are skewed elsewhere.

What can be done?

• *Put pressure on* legislative bodies, network executives and others to limit crime, sex and violence in programming — especially explicit material that glamorizes violence. Viewers should be able to figure out that a character has been killed or wounded without having to see bloody bullet eruptions across his chest or watch his head explode "in living color."

• *Go after businesses that sponsor* programs devoted to crime, violence and illicit sex. Write letters, organize boycotts, do whatever it legally takes to bring home a message that sponsoring such programming is counterproductive marketing.

• *Keep the heat on local and state political bodies* to do all they can to put a lid on obscene or inflammatory programs on local-origination channels.

Freedom of speech shouldn't be a license for sensuous naked dancing or for Nazi-types preaching hate. If it isn't possible to shut down such programming altogether, lobby for rules requiring cable companies to isolate it on "premium" channels that require an additional charge paid by those who want it.

• *Support development and sale of devices* that make it easier for parents to block access to channels or programs that offer material they consider unfit for their children. Such devices already are on the market but manufacturers should make them standard on all new television sets.

In fact, with most people saying they don't approve of violent and sexually explicit programming, why not make people who want sex and violence pay extra for a device to receive it rather than making people who don't want it pay more for a device to exclude it?

• *Work through parent-teacher groups* and school boards to encourage viewership of programs that contribute to education. Support efforts to bring more educational channels and educational programming into the home.

• *Encourage press coverage* that underscores the undeniable link between television viewership and the rise of crime and violence.

There's much more to fighting crime and violence than cleaning up television programming and encouraging viewership of worthwhile programs.

The criminal justice system in America — the one that assures justice for criminals, often with injustice for their victims — also is in need of reform if we are to reduce the cost and stress of crime.

Maximum sentencing laws, aimed at slowing the revolving door through which convicted criminals too quickly end up back on the streets, have contributed to prisons jammed to capacity. When prisons become overcrowded, other laws kick in that require inmates — some of them potentially violent — to be turned loose.

Part of the problem amounts to ineffective "triage."

> Because of mandatory sentencing laws, federal district judges have no discretion in sentencing. They must send offenders to prison for long terms. Between 1984, when mandatory minimums were first enacted, and 1991, the sentence length for a non-violent offender has increased an average of 48 months. Ironically, mandatory sentencing laws often mean that non-violent offenders receive longer sentences than violent offenders do.
>
> U.S. Rep. Don Edwards (D-Calif.)
> House Judiciary Committee

The odds of a "white-collar criminal" mending his or her ways after a short sentence is greater than someone convicted of a violent crime — especially if prison is perceived by the white-collar criminal as something awful and by the violent criminal as little more than a refresher course in criminal behavior in a setting that "ain't as bad as the neighborhood I come from."

To what extent is prison a deterrent to future criminal acts? When 70 to 80 percent of state-prison convicts end up back in prison within two years of parole, it should be obvious the system isn't doing a whole lot to discourage criminal behavior.

One question hotly debated is whether prisons are too hard or too soft. To anyone who has lived comfortably with no intention of ever committing a crime, even the "nicest" of prisons would seem too hard. But to one who has grown up in the worst of circumstances and has been hardened by violence and deprivation, prison life may not seem all that bad. Such a person may view crime as a "no lose" situation:

> If I get away with it, I get to live better. If I don't get away with it, I still get to live better — and have time and peer support to figure out how to get away with it the next time.

Our society's concept of "cruel and unusual punishment" contributes mightily not only to crime, but to the billions of dollars it is costing us each year to run our ever-expanding prison system.

The State of Delaware's flogging law, until declared "cruel and unusual punishment" only a few decades ago, had a recidivism rate that would be the envy of even the best, most rehabilitation-oriented prison in the U.S. today. Of those tied to a post in a public square and subjected to 20 or so lashes, *no one ever came back.* Some may have found other states in which to commit crimes, but most others undoubtedly got the message that no matter how good the hours are, crime doesn't pay — at least not in Delaware.

Is requiring able-bodied men to convert large rocks into small stones the old-fashioned way cruel and unusual punishment? Is imprisonment without TV, air conditioning and wall-to-wall carpet cruel and unusual punishment?

Should prisoners be given law libraries and unlimited time to cook up frivolous lawsuits — such as the inmate who sued because he was denied his choice of crunchy over creamy peanut butter?

Should television be a regular part of prison life, especially with no restrictions on what is watched?

Is the death penalty cruel and unusual? If so, is lethal injection more cruel and unusual than the electric chair? Is keeping someone on death row for 12 years cruel and unusual punishment?

If America's plethora of lawyers extract from American taxpayers about two million dollars per death sentence actually carried out and it costs "only" about $600,000 to keep a person in prison for life, should we save money by scrapping the death penalty?

If we scrap the death penalty and substitute life imprisonment with no parole, would it be more "cruel and unusual" to help the lifer live as long a useless and hopeless life as possible through good diet and regular exercise, or to minimize the cost of incarceration and extend to the lifer the same option available to people outside the prison who have no hope for the future — the option of bringing a *voluntary* (and painless) end to his or her own life?

Should we *encourage* life-without-parole convicts to end their lives early by distributing a portion of the tax dollars saved to their families and, to the extent they have any remorse at all, to the victims of their crimes?

The contribution of crime and violence to the "continuous white water" of the 1990s will go unabated until some powerful steps are taken.

It means doing all we can to eliminate television programming as a prime source of criminal behavior. It also means reforming the criminal justice system.

For Every Action, A Reaction

Do you agree that these are times of "continuous white water?" If so, would it make sense to examine more closely what the five white-water trends mean to you?

To what extent does intense competition put you and those around you at risk? What are you willing to do to measure up to those with whom you will be competing for a better-paying job or in a business of your own? Are you willing to *change?*

> Insanity is the conviction that you can keep doing what you're doing and being who you are and getting different results.
>
> Zig Ziglar

If you have gone through or face wholesale reinvention of the workplace, what are you doing to protect yourself? Are you seeking ways to adapt? Are you looking for other ways to earn a living?

Are you in a profession in which the supply of professionals may far exceed the demand for services? Are you pursuing income diversification strategies? Are you increasing your education and certifications to stay ahead of the competition?

Do not let your chances like sunbeams pass you by,
For you never miss the water till the well runs dry.

Rowland Howard

What are you doing to help fight crime and violence? How many hours of violent, mind-numbing television programs do you watch a week? What do you allow your children to watch? Do you spend more time reading ain't-it-awful stories in newspapers and magazines, or do you spend more time reading positive mental attitude books? What have you come to believe about yourself and the world around you?

If the proper mental pictures are created and constantly maintained, health, wealth, and happiness must follow, for the law of cause and effect is immutable.

Claude M. Bristol
The Magic of Believing

What people are doing to shelter themselves from continuous white water has produced five other trends.

Chapter 4

An Ongoing Search For Stability

- 5 Counter-Trends & How to Deal With Them:
  1. *Down-sized Dreams & Lower Expectations*
  2. *An Avalanche of Entrepreneurship*
  3. *Bunkerization & Balkanization*
  4. *More Demands for Solutions*
  5. *Return to Many "Traditional" Values*

The more *continuous white water,* the more you are likely to seek a greater sense of stability in your life.

Fortunately, life doesn't come with guarantees. If it did, you'd be bored stiff. You can, however, bring *relative* stability to your life, including a greater sense of security.

Many believe the way to do that is through power and control over other people. If you believe that, look deeper. It is power *within* yourself and control *over* yourself that is the secret — doing all you can to become a *better you.*

Will greater power within yourself eliminate all of the "white water" in your life? No. Will it keep the white water from being "continuous?" Absolutely.

A stable family life, for example, can do much to offset white water churning in your career. Do you achieve it by gaining power and control over members of your family? In the long run, no. But it's amazing what will happen in your family when you become a better you and your spouse and children do likewise.

Another important key to increasing stability is a good career and personal plan. Part 2 of this book will show you how to do it.

Here are two essential points to put your *ongoing search for stability* into perspective:

• What is relative stability to one may be chaos to another. One person comes home from a hard day's work and becomes "spastic" over the tranquility-shattering sound of a dripping faucet. Another finds blessed relief by returning to a houseful of rambunctious children and barking dogs.

• It's not security, it's *relative* security. Relative to what? Relative to what is *possible* for you to achieve in life once you have become a *possibility thinker* and stretch *what* is possible as *far* as possible.

Here are five of the most important trends that represent an "ongoing search for stability." Within them, you can find many opportunities and seeds of success. You also can find some *barriers* to success, especially in the first of the five:

1. Down-sized Dreams & Lowered Expectations

A traditional success story:

> Factory worker with high school diploma toils for 25 years so he can put his children through college. Earning top dollar as a journeyman in a union shop, he makes sacrifices so his children can become well-paid professionals and never have to work on an assembly line.
>
> His wife gets a job at a restaurant to help meet tuition payments and save for retirement.
>
> The children get good grades in college, have jobs awaiting them upon graduation, move into nice apartments and are paid as much or more than their father is making after 25 years at the factory.
>
> Mother and father work another 20 years and, financially secure thanks to savings, a good pension plan, Social Security and, above all, the ongoing pursuit of their dreams, enjoy a happy life of fishing, knitting and grandchidren.

Same story, 1990s version:

> Factory worker with high school diploma works hard for 25 years so his children can go to college. Threatened by fierce competition and with the union unlikely to call a strike in a time of high unemployment, the factory owners hammer out a new contract cutting pay and benefits, and getting dad to work longer hours.

Mom loses her job, along with good tips, when the restaurant closes due to three new fast-food places opening
nearby. She goes to work for one of them at minimum
wage (no tips) and dad gets a night job driving a cab.

The children also get jobs at fast-food places to help
pay tuition, which is increasing between 5 and 10 percent a year. The parents deplete their savings and the
children get student loans to meet expenses.

The children do fairly well despite working nights. On
graduation, they move back in with their parents and,
armed with brand new college degrees, spend months
searching for entry-level jobs in their fields while continuing to work at fast-food restaurants.

The children finally start their careers after accepting
jobs that pay much less than expected. Unable to afford
apartments, they stay with their parents and begin
years of monthly payments on their student loans.

The parents, meantime, with savings gone, paychecks
lower, medical expenses rising steadily, cuts made in the
factory's pension plan and rumors that the factory may
shut down, wonder whether there will be an opportunity
for any sort of retirement.

Big dreams? They'll settle for survival.

The latter scenario is bleak, to be sure. Sadly, it has become
reality for many Americans.

Putting children through college long has been woven into the
fabric of The American Dream. Statistics do little to keep that fabric
clean and bright:

• By the year 2000, the *average* cost of a college education will
be around $100,000. The top-rated private institutions will charge as
much as $300,000.

• 86 percent of all parents in the U.S. want their children to go
to college, but only 54 percent are saving *anything* to help pay for it.

• Of the occupations expected to grow the fastest in the decade to come, 80 percent of the new jobs will require no more than a
high school education.

So many millions of Americans are trying to fulfill the dream of
a college degree during these times of continuous white water that
graduation day often is *dreaded* more than anxiously awaited.

> Your competition for a good job not only will be from fellow graduates, but from the graduates of last year's class who still haven't found jobs in their fields of study.
>
> Wake-up call by a career counselor

When resources can be found, a common way to avoid graduating into unemployment is to postpone the experience by going to graduate school. Not only does this way give hope that the job picture will improve in another year or two, but additional education is likely to increase the prospect of finding a job — perhaps even a *good* job.

That there are too many college graduates chasing too few jobs requiring a college education is becoming more obvious every June. Yet too few parents and their children are pausing to make a reality check before mailing transcripts to admissions offices.

For many parents, children in college are status symbols. To many children who grew up on 20-30 hours of television a week and haven't a clue what they want to do with their lives, college becomes an escape more than an important element of *potential* success.

Tens of thousands of high school graduates head to college each fall, woefully unprepared and unmotivated for four or more years of productive work. Elective courses often are chosen because they are easy, not because they add an important ingredient to the student's future. Forced enrollments in remedial math, remedial English and remedial science increase as fewer and fewer enter college meeting even minimum qualifications for achievement in those areas.

When it comes to learning, productivity often is low.

> Why don't college students learn more? Because they enroll in college for a variety of reasons besides a passion for education.They want to get away from their parents, to party with friends, to participate in varsity or intramural athletics, to work on the student newspaper, to indulge a substance-abuse problem, to explore sexual relationships, to stage protests against the college administration — or just to postpone an eventual full-time job.
>
> Jackson Toby
> Professor of Sociology
> Rutgers University

If parents at the "sending end" don't have reason to question an investment in a college education, employers at the "receiving end" do. It's costing employers more and more to prepare their new hires for entry-level positions.

Expectations for good jobs at high starting salaries have been falling steadily while college enrollments have continued to rise.

What can people look forward to after working 45 or so years?

According to a U.S. Department of Health, Welfare and Education Department study, for every 100 Americans who started their careers 45 or so years ago, here's their situation when they are due to turn 65 in the 1990s: 29 will have died, 13 will be making $5,200 per year or less, 55 will be making between $5,200 and $33,000 with a median of $7,900 per year and 3 will be relatively well off with incomes of $33,000 or more.

> Planning for retirement is such a daunting process that, apparently, millions of people aren't doing it, according to a study by Merrill Lynch & Co. And a separate study, done for Oppenheimer Funds, the mutual fund company, concluded that in retirement most Americans will have only one-third to one-half of the income they will need to live as well as they did before they quit working.
>
> Jeff Brown
> Knight-Ridder Newspapers

Once upon a time, "The American Dream" was to *have it all* — wealth, health, freedom of choice and the joys of sharing it with others in positive ways. In the 1980s, most of the dreams to *have it all* were appended with *right now!*

Dreams are kept alive by hopes and hopes are kept alive by a burgeoning number of people who are fulfilling their dreams by "making it."

When the get-rich-quick stories of the 1980s faded — or ended abruptly at highly publicized trials in which some of the "role models" traded pinstripes for prison stripes — the *right now* part of the dream began passing from the scene.

For many, if not most, people, dreams of *having it all* are sinking fast into a sea of murky economic forecasts and all-too-many painful job-related experiences.

To the extent that fulfillment of dreams is tied to successful careers, there's also the harsh reality of "topping out" at an earlier age.

> Topping out is the day you look in the mirror and say to yourself, "this is all there is." The promotions have stopped. You're not going to get a better job.
>
> Jane Bryant Quinn
> *Newsweek*

As rungs are chopped out of career ladders, management positions are combined and teams of employees are empowered to make decisions once the province of higher-ups, people depending on careers to fulfill their dreams are topping out earlier in life.

Meanwhile, the one-career/one-company paradigm has become almost non-existent. To fulfill big dreams by working for other people most likely will take five or more changes of employers, periods of unemployment and much retraining and additional education.

As if it isn't stressful enough for *one* breadwinner to strive for having it all under such circumstances, the pressure on a *two*-breadwinner family can produce the kinds of stress that bring a couple face to face with determining whether fulfilling big dreams is worth the price — perhaps even the "price" of staying together.

> Americans have re-evaluated the relationship between work and leisure, and for the largest share leisure now represents a higher personal priority than work.
>
> The Roper Organization
> *Public Pulse*

Does all this mean that the American dream is dead? Not at all. It depends on what is meant by having it all, and how to have it. There are three choices:

• *Redefine having it all* by lowering expectations, down-sizing the dream or redirecting the dream by focusing on the non-material aspects of life.

> We'll never be rich, but somehow we'll make enough money to get by. We have our health, we have each other, we have faith and we will find creative ways to enjoy life without living in a big house, taking expensive vacations or driving fancy cars.

• *Overcome all obstacles* and have it all through traditional career success.

> No matter what it takes, I will make it to the top in order that we can fulfill our biggest dreams. Whatever the sacrifice, we must make it. Whatever the hours I must work and be away from home, I'll do it. I will make it, for I owe it to myself and my family to be a big success.

• *Look beyond traditional ways* and have it all by finding a new vehicle through which big dreams can be fulfilled:

> We'll begin by looking at every option, particularly the
> non-traditional ones. We'll examine the lives and the
> stories of those who, in spite of the times, have found
> ways to "have it all." We'll choose a new vehicle, well-
> suited to ourselves and our circumstances, and learn
> from people who have made the most of that vehicle
> Then we'll push forward with determination and unity of
> effort — and win!

Yes, you can lessen the gloomier realities of life by downsizing or redefining your dream.

But it's also still possible to *have it all* — if you're willing to abandon traditional thinking.

To fulfill a big dream through a job — trading your time for an employer's dollars — you'll have to go well beyond keeping your nose clean 40 hours a week. You must have outstanding qualifications continually updated, you must be willing to make considerable sacrifices, including some to virtually all of your family life.

If you reach the uppermost rungs of a corporate ladder, you may achieve *financial* security, but never *job* security. And if you spend 40-plus years on and off the lower rungs of various corporate ladders, you'll probably be among the growing majority that *plan* to work past retirement age or won't have a choice.

Does all this mean you'd do well to downsize your dreams and lower your expectations? Certainly not! Opportunities to fulfill big dreams continue to emerge — if you're willing to dream big, cast off the old paradigms and grow into an exciting new (1) *cyberworld* in which (2) *terabytes* of information move in (3) *femtoseconds*.

If you're not totally confused or intimidated by terms (1), (2) and (3) and are willing to take advantage of dynamic changes and new trends, you may be able to make those big dreams come true. If not, you may be left holding a "Work for Food" sign in a gutter along the Information Superhighway.

> A fast-changing society poses major dangers for people
> who have difficulty adjusting to new situations, but it is
> a wonderland for entrepreneurs — those imaginative
> and energetic self-starters who can recognize emerging
> needs and create ways to fill them.
>
> Edwin Cornish
> World Future Society

Which leads to the second of the five *Ongoing Search for Stability* trends:

2. An Avalanche of Entrepreneurship

Being in business for yourself long has been at the forefront of the American Dream. It fits with the country's tradition of individualism, and it underscores the great truth that working for yourself to fulfill *your* dreams is more likely to produce success than working for other people to help fulfill *their* dreams.

However, there are harsh realities to contend with when going into business for yourself:

• If you're like most people, you'll choose a business that, at least for the first year or several, involves trading more of your time for fewer bottom-line dollars than would be the case if you had kept working for someone else.

> First you trade your time for no dollars to get started and drum up business. Then you trade your time for some dollars on the business you drummed up. Then you try to collect payment on services rendered, all the while trading more time for no dollars to drum up more business.
>
> Consultant after one year in business

• Overall, the odds of succeeding in a new business are against you. Some 80 percent of all small businesses fail within the first 18 months.

> Is the American Dream owning your own small business? I did that. Made a million dollars. And it cost me $1.2 million to do it!
>
> Burke Hedges
> *Who Stole the American Dream?*

Not only do 80 percent of the startups shut down within the first year and a half, but the great majority of the survivors are gone within the next few years.

There are many reasons why the failure rate is so high: lack of a good business plan, offering products or services for which there is a limited market, naivete as to what it really takes to make it on your own and lacking expertise in a newly chosen field. And then there are such things as being unable to tap into a support system that helps you avoid mistakes, being unable to hold out financially for the three to five years it usually takes to begin making a decent profit, expanding too rapidly at the first signs of success, etc.

What is the underlying reason so many small businesses fold so quickly? It's simply that, in pursuing the age-old nostrum that "you have to spend money to make money," the *spending* part quickly overwhelms the *making* part.

> When the draft of your boat exceeds the depth
> of the channel, you are most assuredly aground.
>
> Sign in the Pilot House
> Of a Mississippi River Towboat

If you are planning a traditional business, the startup and general operating costs can be awesome, especially if dedicated space is involved (rent or mortgage payments, electric bills, municipal fees and permits, liability insurance, security systems, signage, furnishings and equipment, etc.).

If there are employees to be hired, costs mount from wages and salaries, Social Security and other taxes, worker's compensation and other insurance premiums, boundless government regulations, restrictions and requirements with associated paperwork, etc.

Being unable to meet a payroll can be the worst of all experiences for an entrepreneur. But if you shift the question from one of hiring people to one of how best to acquire additional help, your odds of success can improve.

Engaging temporaries through a service that handles the paperwork and headaches, leasing employees, developing a network of people with whom you can trade services and getting family members to help out are among the ways to avoid — or at least postpone — the day when it may become necessary to take on a payroll of your own.

But your greatest opportunity to cut costs both initially and over time, may be to join the millions of people in the 1990s who are trying to improve the odds for success by running businesses from their own homes.

Technology and current tax laws make at-home businesses very attractive indeed — the "officeless office" when services are involved, and the "storeless store" where products are concerned.

Not only does a business at home avoid the considerable expense of setting up shop elsewhere, but federal tax laws allow deductions for properly allocated residential space that's used exclusively for business. This avoids business expense while saving on household and transportation expenses.

Rapid advances in technology, along with declining costs of acquiring it, have helped create a burgeoning cottage industry. Even large corporations are recognizing the advantage of letting employees work part of the time (or even all of the time) out of their homes.

Computer networks, FAX machines and other modern devices, along with low-cost and highly efficient courier services, make it easy to connect employees to the workplace and help at-home entrepreneurs serve clients and customers well. And in most cities, new services are springing up — some open 24 hours — that provide a full range of support services, including desk space and computer time.

In fact, the more that big organizations eliminate the personalized service of employees through disintermediation, the more opportunity is created for entrepreneurs to make money by offering personalized service to people frustrated by dealing with machines. There's money to be made from a tongue-in-cheek word coined here:

> an·ti·dis·in·ter·me·di·a·tion·ism \ *noun:* rebellion by customers fed up with automated systems devoid of contact with human beings.

As of 1997, more than 40 million Americans work full or part-time out of their homes. About 16 million are on payrolls, half of them home-based by companies ("telecommuters") and the other half burning midnight oil in at-home offices. The other 25-plus-million run businesses from their homes, about half depending on their businesses as primary sources of income and the rest supplementing their incomes with part-time businesses.

The growth is accelerating due to technology and entrepreneurship, the cost advantages of being home-based, and the attraction of being close to family, especially if child care is involved.

Surveys of two-career households show the No. 1 dream of couples who go running off in different directions each day is a business where they can work together and *be* together.

Even greater growth is likely in part-time businesses run from the home — especially a concept that can leave people much better off than spending 45-plus years of their lives working for bosses.

How can people become secure while rafting through the continuous white water of the 1990s and beyond?

At a time when the emerging generation of Americans will, on average, end up worse off financially than their parents, how can anyone who won't inherit a fortune from better-off forebears even *hope* to fulfill big dreams? If you have a big dream, the fulfillment of which requires wealth and financial freedom, you have a limited number of fundamental options.

• *What is the best way to become wealthy?*

> Win millions playing Lotto, break the bank in a casino, hit the big one at the track, etc.

Gambling is a heavy tax levied upon fools. Besides, your odds of success are about the same as being hit by lightning, then being invited on Larry King Live to tell about it.

> Play the markets: stocks, bonds, commodities and such.

To become rich on investments requires having enough money to invest in the first place and not many people do. With low interest rates on "safe" investments and throwing darts at stock listings often yielding better results than some of the country's best stock-pickers, how productive would it be to bet the family bundle on speculative investments?

> Sue somebody.

Lots of people are doing it nowadays, but it usually requires you to suffer and not everyone is up to it. The more you suffer, the more you might win in a lawsuit. Of course, your lawyer is going to walk away with a big chunk of the money without having to suffer nearly as much as you will. And if your suffering isn't genuine, you may get a chance to trade lots of your time for a few dollars making license plates.

> Work for it.

Aha! This option always has been the most obvious and most likely avenue to wealth, despite all the great efforts to avoid it.

• *If you agree that working for it is the best choice, then you are faced with two more choices:*

> Work for someone else.

We've already hammered on this one but, for the record, it can lead to financial freedom. Just be exceptionally good at what you do, be prepared to change jobs several times to get to the top and put a big hunk of your earnings into a good investment strategy to cushion against downsizing, a takeover, etc.

> Work for yourself.

In spite of the high failure rates of new businesses, the odds of becoming wealthy — a goal actually achieved by fewer than 2 percent of the population — are higher working for yourself than for someone else. And if you can start your business part-time while still having the security of a paycheck, not only are your odds improved, but your risks are reduced as well.

• *If you chose working for yourself, then you must choose from among several economic sectors. Which one is the most likely to yield success?*

> Agriculture.

Forget it. Millions have gotten out of farming and many of those who are left would love to sell you their farms.

> Manufacturing & Inventing.

Although there have been people who have started in their garages and gone on to run mighty factories, the odds of taking that route to wealth are pretty slim. What bank in its right mind would bankroll a manufacturing plant for someone who hasn't already demonstrated success as a manufacturer? There's little chance of parlaying a family aluminum smelter into financial freedom. And if you're clever enough to invent something that can become a marketplace hit, the odds are you won't also be clever enough to manufacture it. Best bet: Invent something and get someone else to manufacture it.

> Real Estate & Construction.

From 1980 to 1995, this sector helped more people become broke than any other. Property values plummeted. Loan defaults toppled banks, bankrupted thousands of developers and dumped so much debt on investors and taxpayers that the dollars would stack from the front steps of the Resolution Trust Corporation to the moon. Some see an opportunity to make big money on a comeback in real estate and a boom in construction, the latter enhanced by government spending on roads, bridges and the like. Others say the real estate market will be soft and more and more brokers will be scrambling for commissions on property selling at 80 cents (or less) in 1980s dollars. If you like it, try it. But you may not like the results.

> Services.

American history is a succession of economic eras — from agriculture in the 1700s and 1800s to manufacturing in the 1800s and 1900s, and on to the "Service Economy" of the late 1900s. More fortunes were created in the 1980s, finding better services to provide and better ways to provide them, than in any other sector. From easy-access computer networks to overnight package delivery to 24-hour banking to horoscopes via 900-number, there were and will continue to be ways to make good money in providing services. But competition has

has become fierce. Spend lots of time and money on coming up with a new service, and the fickle consumer may or may not respond to it. If the new service is a success, people and organizations with more resources than you have will be there in a heartbeat to compete with you. But providing services still is a better bet than trying to become financially free through farming, manufacturing, inventing, construction or real estate. If that's your passion, go for it — but in the process pay heed to the hottest sector of the 1990s:

> Distribution.

It used to be that 85 percent of the cost of a product was in making it and the rest of the cost was in distributing it. Manufacturing has become so efficient (and competitive) that the percentages are now reversed — 15 percent is in manufacturing and 85 percent is in distribution. That creates an enormous opportunity for people who can find better ways to bring products and services to consumers. More fortunes are being made in the Distribution sector than in any other and that trend will continue well into the New Millennium.

• *If, up to now, you decided the best vehicle to reach financial freedom would involve working for yourself in the distribution sector, then which of several choices on how to do that will work best for you?*

> Open a traditional retail outlet.

Decide on a line of merchandise that is likely to sell, then find a good location that isn't awash in competition. Rent a store front, buy inventory, do some advertising, hire a clerk or two. The odds of this one leading to financial success are about even with starting a family farm. Retail stores are closing in droves.

> Buy someone else's traditional retail outlet.

Watch it! If you're buying someone else's successful retail outlet, you may pay top dollar for walls on which the seller sees the handwriting but you don't. Think of how many popular restaurants you have been to that changed hands, then went out of business. Some of the most successful retail entrepreneurs, whether their products and services involve prepared foods or women's clothing or slot-car racing, made big money by knowing when to get out as well as when to get in. And if you're buying someone else's *unsuccessful* retail outlet, make sure your turnaround strategy makes *more* sense than the fire-sale price you're thinking about paying.

> Buy a Franchise.

It may come as a surprise, but more than 25 percent of all U.S. businesses are franchises. That means someone else owns the name, cooked up the formula for success and, hopefully, provides top-notch training and support as part of the package. The odds of success are much greater with a first-rate franchise than starting from scratch or buying what may be someone else's headaches. But franchises cost money and, like owning your own retail outlet, are run by trading time for dollars.

> Start your Own Franchise.

Many fortunes have been made by the people clever enough to do this well. But the combination of skills needed to create a new business and turn it into a successful franchising operation are rarely found in the same body. Remember that Ray Kroc was not the founder of McDonalds. He bought the business from two guys who knew how to make and sell hamburgers, then turned it into the most successful franchise on the planet.

> Go Into Network Marketing.

This may be the best choice for people short on marketing skills or who are unwilling or unable to take large financial risks. The sad fact, though, is that most people who get into network marketing do not become financially free. They may get into a network with low potential for success. Or they may get into a high-potential network, then don't treat it like a serious business, mainly because they haven't got that much money invested in it and may be making enough at a job to get by. But for people who do get into a good network and who do treat it like a serious business and who do make the commitment of time and energy, the odds of becoming wealthy are very good.

• *If you've decided to work for yourself in the distribution sector of the economy with network marketing as the vehicle, there is a set of four choices to consider in seeking the best probability of success:*

> Start your own network.

There's no doubt that this option could produce the greatest financial return. But like starting your own franchising business, it will take a lot more up-front money, a combination of product and networking expertise, and a considerable risk. Hundreds of people try it every year, and the failure rate is about the same as new businesses generally — 80 percent.

> Get in on someone else's new network.

Careful! Many startup networks make get-rich-quick promises based on being "a big ground-floor opportunity." Check out the company very carefully. Will it be one of the 90 percent that will disappear (with your money) in a year or so? If the product or service is new, look at its potential in the marketplace in light of both usefulness to the consumer and by what other means it's being distributed. If you're finding it hard to justify joining the network, how hard will it be for you to get other people to sign up? Remember the adage: "If it *sounds* too good to be true, it probably is.

> Join an established network with a narrow product line.

There are some successful networks that have helped many thousands of people earn extra income working out of their homes. Financial freedom came more readily to those who got in early or latecomers who possess the sales skills to move large volumes of a limited number of products. If you're con-sidering this kind of network, pay close attention to its annual growth rate — not only in gross sales, but in the number of distributors signing up and the number attaining substantial incomes. Be especially wary of inventory requirements. Some established networks offering a limited range of products or services require or "strongly suggest" a major up-front invest-ment in inventory. Too often, the newcomer ends up with a garage full of products that are much harder to sell than imagined, especially if there isn't widespread demand for the products and the products are readily available from a wide variety of other sources.

> Join an established network with a wide product line.

When a network marketing company offers so many products and services that its distributors can meet much of their mini-mum sales bonus requirements simply by changing their own buying habits rather than having to sell large amounts of products to others, the probability of success is improved. In a time when people are bombarded by telemarketing, "blitzkrieg" advertising and a deluge of catalogs, there's a special appeal to acquiring what you need from people you trust — especially yourself. There are very few such networks in existence. The oldest and largest is Amway Corporation which started out as a door-to-door soap-selling operation and now is a fast-growing, world-wide network offering more than 80 percent of all the products and services the average household buys.

Network marketing has become the single-most exciting non-traditional business concept of the 1990s.

If you find a *good* network and are willing to do the business right, network marketing can provide blessed relief from *continuous white water.* It also can be the single most effective vehicle to fulfill the *ongoing search for stability* sought after by millions who have been battered by rising levels of change and uncertainty.

If you are among those who want to overcome the turbulence of the 1990s and rebuild faded dreams, here are 17 advantages that network marketing may offer you:

1.   Unlike most of Corporate America, you become successful by *cooperating* with other people rather than competing with them.

2. You can build your network on a part-time basis while continuing a traditional job, avoiding the all-or-nothing risk of quitting a job to start a traditional business.

3.   As your own boss, you can't be fired.

4.   With no such thing as a secure job, you can diversify your income and reduce the impact of a future job loss.

5. If you love a job that pays poorly — the ministry, teaching, working for a charity, etc. — network marketing can give you income to continue doing what you love to do.

6. Your startup costs should be very small compared to opening a traditional business or buying a franchise.

7. You run your business out of your home with no need to invest in office space and employees — until it makes sense to do so.

8. The best networks provide you, at minimum cost, a wealth of motivation and education to help you become successful.

9. As an independent distributor, you can choose how much time and effort you want to put into the business.

10.   Relationships with family and friends can be strengthened by working together toward mutual success.

11. A huge investment in a college education isn't a prerequisite for success, because your *ability to learn* is more important than a certificate attesting to what you're supposed to have already learned.

12.   The concept can enable you to make money by "duplicating yourself" rather than trading time for dollars.

13.   In a good network, the people above you have a vested interest in your success, for the more money they can help you make, the more money they will make.

14.   In networks without geographical limits, you can make money anywhere the corporate sponsor does business.

15.   Your success is totally dependent on your own performance, not on "politics" or getting "lucky."

16.   You are likely to get far more personal recognition for your achievements than in a traditional job or a traditional business.

17. Once having built a successful network, you can opt for leisure and *still have a growing residual income.*

As alluring as all those advantages may appear to be, there are some potential downsides to network marketing that you should be aware of.

Perhaps the biggest concern is that many people go into network marketing looking for big bucks in a matter of weeks. Like any business, network marketing tends to be "back-end loaded." You can expect to lose money or see scant returns at the front end.

If someone promises you big bucks at the front end, be wary. "Get-rich-quick" schemes almost never work for the people lured into them. Network marketing plans promising quick returns inevitably focus on selling distributorships rather than products and services, a characteristic of an illegal pyramid.

Like any business, you also should approach a network marketing "opportunity" with caution. If you expect lots of money without hard work, you're setting yourself up for disappointment.

There are a few excellent programs, some number of feasible ones and an awful lot of schemes and scams. Check them out. Look at histories, who is running the organization, financial strength, whether their products and services are in great demand and the extent to which they amply reward people who produce results.

And never let yourself be *pressured* into a network marketing program, no matter *how* good a deal it seems to be.

In examining the questions and the choices associated with the avalanche of entrepreneurship, the second of the ongoing search for stability trends, you may think by now that working for yourself through a network marketing organization that offers a vast product line is the key to success for everyone. It isn't.

There are *many* avenues to financial freedom to be found among the various choices offered here. The key question is simply this: At a time of great insecurity in the workplace and overall economic uncertainty, what could you do that would give you the best opportunity to become financially free?

Only you can answer that question. And there are three more trends that may be factors in the answer you develop.

3. Bunkerization & Balkanization

When psychologist Abraham Maslow developed his "Hierarchy of Needs," he placed on the bottom tiers of the pyramid the needs associated with survival, such as food, shelter, safety and security. Until those needs are met, he pointed out, people can't meet higher human needs such as love and, ultimately, self-actualization — being all you can be.

In the 1980s, many people focused on an upper tier of the pyramid that Maslow called "Ego Needs." Status and conspicuous consumption reigned supreme.

With economic hard times, rising crime and violence, and both haves and have-nots having less, the focus has shifted to "downscaling" — survival more than "thrival."

> We no longer put our logo prominently on our merchandise. Our market studies showed that people are concerned that it might send the wrong signals. One of our customers said it could be an open invitation to a mugger.
>
> Salesperson in a Gucci shop

The 1990s became the Decade of the Bunker. For many, the ongoing search for stability led to fortified environments in which they could feel safe.

Bunkerization is nothing new. People in big-city apartments started adding extra locks and deadbolts years ago. But rising levels of fear bring more and more effort to create living space to which people can retreat and feel secure.

Sales of guns are setting records in many areas. The lock-and-burglar-bar business is booming. Alarm systems are becoming household necessities with demand for greater and greater sophistication. Martial arts classes are more popular than ever, and women are carrying Mace and learning how to kick attackers where it hurts.

People also are spending more *time* in their bunkers, "entertaining" themselves with television, which constantly reinforces... guess what? The need to stay in the bunker and add more layers of fortification!

Drive-by shootings cause some people to stop going out at night, short of an emergency. Companies demanding more overtime work are finding concomitant demands from their late-staying employees: Give us armed security escorts so we can make it to our cars without being attacked.

Fleeing a crime-ridden inner city and settling into a small, quiet town where "people don't bother locking their doors" is no longer a sure-fire substitute for a fortified bunker. Drug dealers, rapists and serial killers have discovered small towns, too — especially ones with a single overweight cop in his sixties who goes off duty at 5 p.m.

America is running out of places to hide. Perhaps the last great place to find relative peace and security in the continental United States is the Rocky Mountains region from Montana south through New Mexico.

Lured by "wide open spaces" and job opportunities in fast-growing high-technology companies that set up shop there because they can attract first-rate employees, people flock to the region to find "the good life."

Yes, but...

Like previous migrations, it's only a matter of time before that region, too, is plagued with the very problems that caused people to flock there in the first place.

Old-timers begin resenting the newcomers. The newcomers try to impose different values on the old-timers. The children of the newcomers grow up watching the same violent TV programming that saturates the inner city. Once-plentiful jobs become scarce. An "under-class" develops. The great regional bunker starts to have the same problems as everywhere else.

Where else is there to go? Alaska? Crime and unemployment are up in Alaska, too. And not everyone is hardy enough to freeze in the dark for six months out of every 12.

So we build communal bunkers. Upscale families seek shelter in condominiums with well-trained security staffs. Real estate agents specializing in condominium sales recognize security as an alluring feature, especially when dealing with prospects who have gone through a home invasion or other forms of neighborhood crime.

The number of "gated" communities is also on the rise. A fortified bunker inside a fenced community with a single guarded gate has great sales appeal, especially when there's a first-rate police force patrolling the surrounding area.

Faith Popcorn, who coined the word "cocooning" in the late 1970s, describes new heights — or depths — of security consciousness in her must-read book:

> We are going into emotional as well as physical with-drawal. Our answering machines were screening all our calls. If anything, the early 90s have brought us into a time of heavy-duty Burrowing, digging in deeper, build-ing ourselves a bunker — Cocooning for our lives.

> Faith Popcorn
> *The Popcorn Report*

Is bunkerization, cocooning or burrowing the way to meet your safety and security needs? Will sitting with a shotgun across your lap behind triple-locked doors in a "home" with an alarm system that dials the police department automatically make you *that* much more secure?

Following World War I, the French tried to build the ultimate *national* bunker. It was called the Maginot Line and was an extremely expensive string of fortifications using the most sophisticated weapons of the day to keep the Germans from paying a return visit to French soil.

The result forever is carved in history. The Germans simply bypassed the Maginot Line, captured Paris and, with the Maginot Line's big guns all pointed east, attacked the bunkerized defenders from the rear.

There is an equal folly in overdoing household security measures, for the fear that prompts the measures is often more dangerous than measures themselves.

Example: Husband travels a lot. Wife is so fearful of being attacked while husband is away that he buys her a gun and teaches her how to use it. Consumed by fear upon hearing a noise downstairs during one of her husband's trips, wife grabs gun and fires at shadowy figure on the stairs. Wife kills husband who had returned early.

Attack dogs can be effective unless, of course, they attack you — or a friend, or a playful small child who didn't understand what the dog was trained to do, or the long-suffering postal delivery person who never did become immune to dog bites.

The companion behavior of Bunkerization is Balkanization — breaking territories and peoples into smaller groups often hostile to one another.

It's a sad fact of human behavior that when people feel deprived or threatened or see themselves as victims, they tend to seek acceptance, security and status by joining a group that espouses anything that would seem to provide protection and feelings of greater self-worth. Under such circumstances, people can be attracted easily to organizations that will help them feel superior to whatever group offends them.

Whether it's members of an ethnic group banding together to the exclusion of other kinds of people, or members of a hate group who think they can find a better life by ridding the world of one or more ethnic groups, the effect is to build walls, to cast blame and, ultimately, to generate grief.

The mascot of Balkanization is the scapegoat. To the Nazis, the grand scapegoat is the Jew. To the Ku Klux Klan, the scapegoat is the African-American. To the French revolutionaries, the scapegoats were the aristocrats.

From the beginning of civilization, people have tried to feel better about themselves by denigrating those who are "different." The result can be anything from the tragedy of a holocaust to the silliness of social snobbery.

Humorist Russell Baker once described a vacation island in Maine on which a distinct pecking order allowed owners to feel superior to renters, people who rented for the season to feel superior to those who rented by the month, etc. At the bottom were the "dreadful" people who came over on the ferry to visit (and spend money) for only part of a day.

Street gangs long have provided early-life experiences in Balkanization, especially in U.S. cities. Raised largely by themselves in neighborhoods where many see life as cheap, young people seek safety and acceptance within the "security" of a gang. They're willing to trade freedom and relative safety for a sense of belonging and an opportunity to feel superior and, somehow, "get even."

> ...a 19-year-old member of the Latin Counts in Detroit says he spends his time "chillin' and hanging" with the Counts when he's not in jail. He's spent two years behind bars, but that hasn't made him turn away from the gang... (He) began carrying a gun when he was 9 and became a full-fledged Count at the age of 13. He has watched three good friends...die in street wars."
>
> Barbara Kantrowitz
> *Newsweek*

Some 80 percent of America's children return to empty homes after school, up more than a third from 1970. With many of them being raised by single moms working one or two jobs to make ends meet, is it any surprise that it is street gangs, not parents, who keep the kids occupied after school and provide role models?

There are some bright spots in all of this. Instead of trying to break up the gangs altogether, several innovative programs in urban areas are finding success by turning gangs toward positive agendas such as athletics, entrepreneurship and a resumption of education.

At least one gang, once reviled, even has taken on surprising touches of respectability.

> We had just closed a big bond deal over dinner at the Jockey Club in New York when one of the hosts announced a late-night excursion to a notorious Greenwich Village disco called Limelight. Seems they were having a "benefit concert" for the Hell's Angels Motorcycle Gang. So a bunch of us, dressed in our corporate three-piece-suits, piled into a big black limo and headed off for what turned out to be an incredible evening. Hundreds of motorcycles were lined up in front of the place and as we worked our way through the crowd, I encountered a huge bearded guy with tattoos, a cut-off denim jacket and a Harley hat. I didn't see him coming and he didn't

see me and he got the best of the collision. As I fell, he grabbed my arm and pulled me back up. "Excuse me, sir!" he said, totally embarrassed. "Are you all right?" The evening was upbeat from there. Somehow, thousands of every different kind of humanity were having a good time together. When it was over, the Hell's Angels gave most of the money to charity.

Police Athletic League chapters, Boys Clubs, scouts and many other organizations are making headway in some cities, helping defuse neighborhood gangs. But it will take fundamental changes in society itself — each one of us — if a pandemic scourge of violence is to be reversed.

Perhaps the biggest cause of violence is "tolerance." Too often, we tolerate anti-social behavior at home, in school, in the workplace and on the street. Many are unwilling to become involved, mostly from fear of the inconvenience that involvement may bring.

We tolerate the ongoing stream of violence that comes into our homes through the air, via cable and on tape. We tolerate petty shoplifting because, after all, the shopkeeper "can afford the loss." We tolerate sex among teen-agers because "everybody's doing it so it must be okay. Just practice 'safe' sex." We tolerate zealots who ban prayer and Christmas pageants from our schools but allow foul language and satanic Halloween revelry to go unchecked.

When a member of our own minority group (with Balkanization, there no longer is a *majority* of anyone), murders someone from another minority group, there are those who even tolerate *that,* offering shelter, acquiescence or well-aimed bottles thrown at the police.

The problems of Balkanization are worldwide, not limited to the United States. While the U.S. has more than its share of strife with a government that's relatively stable, many other countries have more than their share of strife under governments that are dreadfully unstable.

There are today just eight states on earth which both existed in 1914 and have not had their form of government changed by violence since then. These are the United Kingdom, four present or former members of the Commonwealth, the United States, Sweden and Switzerland.

Sen. Daniel Patrick Moynihan
Pandemonium: Ethnicity in International Politics

Could violence and divisiveness in the U.S. ever reach the point where the world's longest-running democracy falls apart? Probably not. But within our cities, there are a few similarities to this fictional version of a world-news story that has become all-too familiar:

> For many years, a powerful national government prevented upheaval among what used to be a hodge-podge of small independent states. Within months of the government's fall, ancient rivalries were renewed by power-hungry people, much to the dismay of those who had learned to live well together, even to intermarry.
>
> The worst conflict, a bloody civil war, broke out between Tumultia in the north and Bashnos-Mobrulvia in the south. Thousands died in the fighting until, with U.N. intervention, the land was partitioned into small states that were like ethnic enclaves.
>
> With the Tumultians held at bay by U.N. forces, the Bashnoses and the Mobrulvians began arguing over who had the greater right to govern. Warlords cut off food supplies. People starved. But thanks to secret arms deals and intense ethnic pride, the Mobrulvians slaughtered the Bashnoses.
>
> Two days after the victory celebration, the Mobbites got into an argument with the Rulvians over what to call the main street in the capital. Fighting broke out again. Total defeat of the Mobbites brought much exhilaration among the Rulvians, for surely now, peace finally had come to the land. But when the Rulas tribe took control of the central water supply, the Vian clan armed itself and launched a bloody attack, wiping out the entire Rulas army.
>
> Recent news dispatches from what's left of the country report that an attempt to design a new flag resulted in an outbreak of violence between the Vi's and the An's. Now out of ammunition, the two factions are holed up in their respective caves. Every night they send out raiding parties to beat each other with clubs.

Will Bunkerization and Balkanization bring relative stability in our lives? In an increasingly violent and fractionalized society, they may seem to — at least in the short run.

But can a nation of diverse people, a society that is a cultural mosaic, *ever* offer peace and stability if more and more people surround themselves with people of their own "kind"?

How safe will it be inside our fortified bunkers when we can't even live harmoniously as families? Sometimes, we can't even *move into* the bunker without hurting ourselves and each other:

> Police Say Groom Shoots Bride
> During Wedding-Day Food Fight
>
> Newspaper headline

Where should we draw the line between protecting ourselves and reaching out to others?

Some thoughts for the late 1990s and the New Millennium:

• Take security precautions appropriate to the area in which you live. If you live in the South Bronx or downtown Washington, you may *need* something that looks like a fortified bunker. In most other areas, good locks, adequate lighting and a way to gain fast access to the police should provide enough in-home security. A good combination intrusion and fire alarm also may be a prudent investment. Be cautious, but don't live a life of fear.

> Fear is an acronym. It stands for False Evidence
> Appearing Real. The antidote for fear is faith.

• Work on relationships. Much of the harm done to people is inflicted by people whom they know or are related to. If you are hot-tempered or stressed-out, seek counseling. These days, flipping your lid over virtually *anything* can get you killed or beaten to a pulp.

> A person who makes many friends rarely has enemies.

• Think through a decision to increase safety and security by moving to another area. When asked if they could simply pull up stakes and leave New York City, a poll showed 45 percent of all New Yorkers would. But what if they did? Would most be more secure? Or, would they simply transplant into their new locations many of the same problems that prompted them to leave New York?

> In 1940, an American college professor was so fearful of all the violence and insecurity in the world that he sold everything and moved his whole family to a remote, far-away island. It was a quiet, peaceful little island in the Pacific Ocean — an island called Guadalcanal.

• Recognize that working with authorities and others to improve your neighborhood will give you far greater security than topping your hedges with razor wire. Support crime watch programs. Support opportunities for young people to find positive alternatives to crime and violence. Get to know the police who patrol your area. Let them know you *appreciate* their efforts to keep the neighborhood safe.

> You can increase your safety a little by working with a screwdriver to change your locks.You can increase your safety a lot by working with other people to change the nature of your neighborhood.

• If your area is plagued with frequent street crime, minimize night-time trips and protect family members and neighbors by arranging for escorts. Invest in a steering wheel locking device and a good car alarm that can be set off by a controller you carry with you.

> It was late and I would have gladly had someone walk her to her car. Even the security guard at the front entrance asked her if she wanted him to find someone to escort her, but she thanked him and said it wasn't that dark out and that she was in a hurry to get home.
>
> Employer of a murder victim

• Defend yourself and your family. You have a right to bear arms, but a moral and legal responsibility to do so safely. There are guns in half the households in the U.S. and if you're already a gun owner, make sure you don't *add* to the peril. Keep firearms in a place where even an experienced burglar couldn't find them. Criminals already have too many arms and too much ammunition.

> He was so proud of his gun collection. The souvenirs from the war covered an entire wall, but the newer ones were kept securely locked in a gun cabinet. We came home late from a party one night to find the back door broken open. Every one of the guns was gone, even the ones that were locked up. That's all they took — just the guns and a lot of bullets that were kept in the cabinet. And, of course, they've never been caught.
>
> Wife of a former gun collector

• If you decide to have a gun that you're willing to use as protection, make sure you obey the law and know what you're doing.

Take a safety course, then practice on an authorized firing range at least twice a year. If you have children, make sure there's no way they can get hold of firearms. Live up to your responsibilities!

> The existence of police does not relieve individuals of all responsibility for self-protection... Ninety percent of violent crimes are committed by persons not carrying handguns. This is one reason why the mere brandishing of a gun by a potential victim of violence often is a sufficient response to a would-be attacker.
>
> George F. Will
> *Newsweek*

• Take stock of the people you relate to. Perhaps without realizing it, you have begun to Balkanize. How many of your friends are from different ethnic groups? Are you uncomfortable when talking with someone of a different race or national origin? Consider joining an organization that helps bring diverse people together or that promotes multiculturalism.

> If any one word characterizes American Society, it is diversity. The American experiment is, in a fundamental sense, a test of whether a common political culture can succeed based on the principle that freedom, justice and equality are the inherent rights of all human beings. In spite of enormous strides, we find ourselves struggling daily with this test.
>
> The National Conference

• If you consider yourself in the "majority" of Americans, to what extent do you harbor prejudices toward members of minority groups? Everyone has some degree of prejudice based on their perceptions of others, which may be rooted in pure fantasy or a broad extension of a few isolated facts. Will prejudice help make you more successful in life? Will your prejudices make you a happier person?

> I am free of all prejudices. I hate everyone equally.
>
> W.C. Fields

• If you're in a minority group, where should you draw the line between feeling good about your heritage and demanding that others feel as good about it as you do?

Will you do better in life by building understanding among all cultures and backgrounds or by demanding that your particular group be given special status? Would you build more bridges or more walls by earning a degree in studies of your own ethnic group? Or would you be better off taking some courses on your heritage but getting top grades in a mainstream field, then going on to become a success in society and a role model for your ethnic group?

> A lot of people I know call themselves (Ethnic)-Americans. I don't see it that way. I'm proud to be an American-(Ethnic). First and foremost I'm an American and then I'm an (Ethnic).
>
> A woman of great wisdom

• What are you doing to help instill in yourself and others — especially the next generation of Americans — the idea that we *all* lose if our country turns into a Balkanized society?

What are you teaching your children about understanding and respecting people who are different? What language do they hear you using when you refer to people of diversity? Do you support efforts to help young people build bridges rather than walls? If your small child wanted to invite a friend of a different race or creed to your home after school, how would you handle it?

> Children are born without prejudice. When they are very young, they will play well together, whatever the color of their skin or their religion or their national origin. They learn prejudice from their parents and from older children who learned it from their parents.

Bunkerization and Balkanization make the human condition worse, not better. Don't look to either of these negative behaviors as the key to your ongoing search for stability.

> We have to start thinking of America as a family. We have to stop screeching at each other, stop hurting each other, and instead start caring for, sacrificing for, and sharing with each other. We have to stop constantly criticizing, which is the way of the malcontent, and instead get back to the can-do attitude that made America.
>
> Gen. Colin Powell
> *My American Journey*

4. More Demands for Solutions

At a time when one out of three high-school students expect their lives to be cut short by gunfire...

And when a third of all babies born in the U.S. are at risk...

And when a smaller percentage of Americans are seeing hope of a secure retirement...

And when the per-capita public-debt continues to rise...

And when downsizing and layoffs continue apace...

And when hospitals report record numbers of drug-related visits to their emergency rooms...

And when more and more people are foregoing essential medical treatment in order to buy food...

And when more people feel "wronged" and want to get even...

Some pull blankets over our heads and others cry out:

"Somebody do something! Do anything — even if it's wrong!"

But who is "somebody?" And what should the "somebody" do?

For the millions unwilling to play any sort of role in solving the country's problems, "somebody" obviously means "somebody else."

The broader question, of course, is the extent to which we seek solutions from the somebodies of government, or the somebodies of the private sector, or some combination of the two on which we can agree.

In groping for solutions, we will face many choices and debates. The best choices and the best outcomes of the debates will involve more accountability for personal behavior and less dependence on government for solutions to our problems.

How can you become more a part of the solutions and less a part of the problems? Some suggestions:

• Take charge of your health. Understand that the promise for unlimited "free" health care is an empty one. Your personal choices will be the biggest variable in what you'll pay for health care in the future — financially and otherwise. If you smoke, quit. If you're a fast driver, slow down. If you're overweight, get trim. If you're a couch potato, start a sensible exercise program. Have regular checkups. If you need treatment, don't delay.

> We're more of a "sick care" industry than a health care industry. Americans of all ages and backgrounds must stop turning to the health care industry with cries of "fix me." What we must do is recognize the liberating truth that each of us, to a larger degree than we could ever believe, has the power to shape our own good health.
>
> Frank V. Murphy III, President
> Morton Plant Meese Health System

• Get involved in the political process. Keep up with the issues. Focus on the big-picture and long-term good, rather than narrow self interests and short-term "fixes." Get to know candidates. Support the ones with common sense and integrity. Vote!

> Politics is the science of who gets what, when and why.
>
> Sidney Hillman
> *Political Primer for All Americans*

• Do whatever it takes to assure a quality education for your children. Join the PTA and be active. Run for the school board, or get behind a good person who will. Demand an end to unruly behavior and permissiveness in schools. Fight for the right to have a say over how your hard-earned dollars are used in the educational system.

> ...69 percent (of employers) say the number of high school graduates they have to screen before finding those "who can meet our standards of employment" has risen. For every one acceptable applicant they have to reject five others.
>
> Louis Harris & Associates
> *An Assessment of American Education*

• Adopt a pro-business attitude. Recognize that business is the engine that pulls America's economic train. Government, for the most part, adds heavy cars that slow the engine down. Do all you can to correct what's wrong with business. Champion high standards of business integrity, a strong sense of social consciousness and fair treatment of people. Then, focusing on what's *right* about business, fight for political change that will enable more people to get into business and help business produce more jobs and more prosperity for more people than any governmental welfare system ever devised.

> Business underlies everything in our national life, including our spiritual life. Witness the fact that in the Lord's Prayer the first petition is for daily bread. No one can worship God or love his neighbor on an empty stomach.
>
> Woodrow Wilson

• Support the efforts of non-profit organizations to meet our many social needs. We simply must have the services of a strong, well-managed system of non-profit organizations that almost always can provide a higher level of social services at a lower overall cost than government at any level.

For the first 157 years of our country's history, there *were no* massive government welfare systems and entitlement programs. Support was four layers deep *without* goverment aid. First, we took care of ourselves. To the extent that we couldn't take care of ourselves, our families pitched in. To the extent our families couldn't take care of our problems, the people of our churches helped out.

When even the churches couldn't get the job done, we developed the world's largest and best system of charitable organizations — many spawned and supported by churches, synagogues and mosques.

The search for solutions to our problems will reach the happiest ending when the only role left to government will be to fill those needs we *can't* meet ourselves, absent the unending passel of needs we've been *unwilling* to meet.

More self-reliance. Less government aid. Those tenets lead us to the fifth trend in our quest for stability:

5. *A Return to Many Traditional Values*

For generations, tens of millions of American children took to heart the childhood example of George Washington for whom punishment was preferable to telling a lie.

The great majority of Americans grew up with an innate sense of honesty — the belief, strongly practiced, that it is wrong to lie, cheat or steal.

Simple, basic honesty was a time-honored, traditional American value. Yes, our past is checkered by the corruption of those whose greed overshadowed this simple virture. But for most, during the first 200 years of American history, honesty was and always would be the best policy.

To be a good American was to be a good citizen. Good citizens were scrupulously law-abiding and honest. But today?

> We are a nation of lawbreakers. We exaggerate tax-deductible expenses, lie to customs officials, bet on card games and sports events, disregard jury notices, drive while intoxicated — and hire illegal child-care workers... University of Colorado sociologist Delbert Elliott has tracked a group of young adults since 1976, when they were junior-high and high-school age. The tally thus far: 90% of the group has broken the law at some time.
>
> Stephen J. Adler & Wade Lambert
> *Wall Street Journal*

The antithesis of traditional American values, it seems, is "situational ethics." We break the law or violate the rules when we believe the *situation* makes it right.

We believe it's all right to cheat on taxes because the taxes are too high. And yet, if *no one* had cheated on taxes over the past 25 years or so, the additional annual federal tax revenues would have been enough to have *avoided the entire national debt!*

We believe it's all right to exceed the speed limit because we're in a hurry — or the speed limit isn't high enough for the road we're traveling on or the car we're driving. And yet, we're quick to complain when someone drives too fast through our neighborhoods or our own teen-agers push the family car past the legal limit.

We believe it's all right to help ourselves to the supply cabinet at work or to some of the merchandise our employers sell or manufacture. And yet, we complain bitterly when our salaries are cut or our jobs are lost because excessive costs have more than wiped out the company's profits.

Is it naive to think George Washington's childhood example once again may set a standard for a new generation of Americans? Perhaps. But hope lurks in how we *celebrate* simple acts of honesty that once would have been shrugged off as commonplace.

Example: A homeless family in Buena Vista, California, found a wallet containing credit cards, a thick wad of $100 bills and a $1,500 plane ticket.

How easy it would have been for situational ethics to control their actions: "We're homeless and broke and the person who lost this wallet is well off and probably is covered by insurance. So we'll consider the money a 'gift from God' and go find a nice motel."

Many today would consider that an *honest* response — finders-keepers, don't you know? Some might add a caveat that keeping the money would be okay, but using the credit cards or cashing in the plane ticket would be dishonest.

> All we did was what was right. We could have used that money, even just a little of it. But we weren't brought up that way, and we didn't want our son brought up that way.
>
> Pauline Nichter, homeless
> with husband Tom and son Jason, 11

The Nichters returned the wallet with all its contents and the tourist who lost it rewarded them with only a handshake. A reporter ran across the story and the Nichters' simple, unrewarded act of honesty brought forth an extraordinary outpouring of public support.

Scores of well-wishers gave the Nichters almost $10,000 in cash. A real estate agent gave them free use of an apartment for six months. People donated furniture, young Jason got an ice cream coupon from a boy in another city and employers responded with job opportunities, no doubt anxious to add to their payrolls *anyone* with such a great sense of honesty.

In itself, this story gives little evidence of a wide-spread return to the traditional American value of honesty. But it does show that, no matter how great the personal hardships, there still are people in America who put honesty above gain.

It also suggests a long-held traditional American virtue that thrives even today. We will open our hearts (and even our wallets) to help those who dramatically demonstrate the values and beliefs through which America achieved greatness.

When 83 percent of the undergraduates at one of America's most prestigious universities admit to cheating, how likely is a significant return to basic honesty in American society?

A nationwide survey of children 10-17 commissioned by Newsweek and the Children's Defense Fund turned up two findings that may give at least a little hope:

1. More than two-thirds of the children experienced theft of money or property

2. The children listed, in order, parents, grandparents, places of worship and teachers as having the greatest influences on their lives, with parents having nearly four times the influence over them as TV, movies and music.

This suggests that dishonesty among young people has resulted far more from the negative influence (or lack of positive influence) of parents than from sources most-often blamed, such as television programming.

But if most children have experienced the painful effects of a dishonest act such as the theft of money or property and if most children are influenced far more by their parents, grandparents, places of worship and teachers than they are by their peers and the entertainment industry, it's clear that adults have a great opportunity to re-instill in American youth the traditional value of honesty.

Whether parents *will* exert such influence has a lot to do with the return of another traditional value: a strong family unit.

In what some still regard as the "happy days" of the 1950s, Ozzie and Harriet Nelson represented the "typical American family."

That few families lived Ozzie-and-Harriet lives and lifestyles wasn't as important as what the long-running broadcast series represented: that the great majority of children were born in wedlock, with most growing up in a family that stayed together with the full-time supervision of a mother who didn't work outside the home.

Today, of course, such conditions are rare. Fully a quarter of all American children are born out of wedlock. Of those born to married couples, most will experience marital impermanence — that is, they will be born into a second or third marriage and/or their parents will divorce or separate at some point.

As to the full-time supervision of a parent, that's a relative rarity. In today's "typical American family," both parents work full time. Many pre-schoolers are parked in day-care centers and many in-schoolers spend after-school hours in a hodge-podge of "arrangements" while both parents work.

We now have in America our first-ever generation of children growing up without the full-time attention of at least one parent.

Among the many factors blamed for the near-demise of strong family units are economics and the role of women. The economic question: To what extent do both parents *need* to have full-time jobs in order to "survive" and to what extent do both parents *want* to have full-time jobs in order to enjoy a better lifestyle or find "professional self-fulfillment?" And what is meant by *survival,* anyhow?

> We can't possibly *survive* without at least two cars.

> I'm not going to be able to *survive* in my career unless I keep up with the latest fashions and get my nails done professionally at least once a week.

> There's no way we can *survive* in these times unless we live in a better neighborhood where we can have the right address and meet the right people.

> I can't *survive* without a maid at least twice a week, and whatever would we do if our children had to go to a public school?

Today's economics make it easier to rethink the necessity of *two* full-time jobs while trying to raise school-age children. Consider:

• The second full-time job probably pushes total family income into a higher tax bracket, reducing the overall financial benefit of both parents working.

• The cost of services such as day-care, special transportation, domestic help and the like will continue to go up, including the onus of having to pay Social Security taxes for even a part-time babysitter.

What is the *actual* economic benefit of both parents working? What is the *actual* net income after higher taxes, additional wardrobe costs, a half dozen or so restaurant meals per week, commuting costs and the like?

After being *forced* to live on one income due to the rampant job cuts, some parents have discovered they're almost as well-off financially with one staying home to be a *full-time parent.*

And with more and more at-home businesses and companies getting work done through outsourcing rather than on-site employees, there should be more impetus to rediscover the traditional value of children coming home after school to find a parent willing to look after their needs.

> In keeping with a shift from the frenzied work ethic of the 1980s to more traditional values, the majority of women listed having a happy marriage as more important than a successful career.
>
> *Time* magazine poll

When the stunning news broke that the cartoon character Blondie was going to join America's workforce to find self-fulfillment and help make ends meet in the 1990s, there was an uproar from many who had treasured the idea of at least *one* woman who didn't feel compelled to run off to a job, leaving the children behind.

What emerged from the imagination of cartoonist Dean Young, however, was a good case example of how today's woman *can* contribute to a family's financial well-being while still being supportive of her husband and children. Blondie's catering business makes a *positive* contribution to the whole household, including Dagwood's appetite for outrageous sandwiches.

There are a few other factors that may help people return to more-traditional parenting and family units:

• Split-shift parenting is on the rise, with as many as one in six families having parents whose night shift/day shift work schedules assure one parent being available to the children.

• More men are putting family ahead of careers, turning down promotions, transfers and additional responsibilities — even quitting altogether, such as the executive who shocked the business world by resigning from one of the entertainment industry's top jobs to look after his 9-year-old daughter who was injured in a car crash:

> Personally, I have learned the hard way that it is one grand illusion if you start believing you can be totally dedicated to the demands of your job without short-changing your pressing responsibilities to your family.
>
> Brandon Tartikoff, 42, former CEO of Paramount Pictures Corp.

- Fewer women seem to "want it all," perhaps concluding that the coexistence of a totally fulfilling career with a totally fulfilling motherhood and marriage is more fantasy than fact.
- When the wife's career surpasses the husband's and she has more opportunities than he does, it's becoming more acceptable for *him* to stay home with the kids. For all but the biggest of male egos, the option of being a full-time father (or the parent with the at-home business) may look better than a marginal job that plays a lesser role in the family's economic well-being.

Taxation also has been a major factor in the breakdown of the traditional American family.

> To a very large extent, the economic and personal challenges facing families today are rooted in the consequences of America's system of taxation. The strain of meeting America's crushing tax burden has forced many homemakers into the work force, reducing the amount of time parents spend with their children by approximately one-half.
>
> Contract with the American Family
> Christian Coalition

In looking toward a return to traditional values, it is more likely that "family values" will be manifested in the direction of the traditional "nuclear family" than, to borrow descriptive language from the 1960s, the "family of whatever feels good now."

Young people are marrying later than in decades past. They expect to live longer than their grandparents, who often married in their teens. Frequently, they justify living together on grounds that when they finally *do* get married, it will be "for keeps." So far, however, the divorce statistics don't offer much evidence to support the argument.

Hardship and adversity strengthen the bonds between couples and among family members. The world today lacks the unifying adversity of the Great Depression or World War II. But...

Crime, a rising suicide rate, reduced opportunity for high-paying jobs, rising tax rates and flat or declining living standards could be the sort of adversity that finally tightens the ties that bind.

> This is a generation that hasn't been touched by any larger thing. It hasn't been challenged.
>
> Andrew Kohut
> Times-Mirror Co.

Nowhere is the need felt more than among African-Americans.

A black child has only one chance in five of growing up with two parents.

Newsweek

There seems to be no shortage of motherhood and, concomitantly, no shortage of the sensuous and momentary aspect of fatherhood that causes pregnancy. What's missing is the *responsibility* of fatherhood that follows — the commitment, the care, the love, the leadership, the financial support and the presence of a positive male role model.

In 1960, only 5 percent of America's children were living without a father. By 1995, that total had soared well past 25 percent.

In the 1990s, millions of the children being raised by single working mothers also have fathers who skipped out on their obligations. Among many other things, the 1990s became the Decade of the Deadbeat Dad.

More than half of the 10 million American mothers raising children by themselves receive no child support at all from the children's fathers. Of those who do, 1.4 million don't receive all of the support that is legally due. And of the rest of the single mothers, many would argue that what is legally due is not enough to compensate for the lack of a father in the family.

But as part of our slow but hopefully sure return to traditional values, fatherhood is regaining not only importance but status as well.

It's cool to be a dad.

Wyatt Andrews, CBS News
Father of 3

Men are beginning to accept greater responsibility for the upbringing of children, egged on not only by psychologists and politicians, but the entertainment industry as well. Instead of being portrayed as a mindless boob, now and again we see a sitcom in which the father actually is shown to be a responsible and highly positive role model. Hollywood has unleashed some films that also give a certain amount of status to being a father.

Federal, state and local governments, as well as a variety of non-profit organizations, are closing in on the deadbeat dads, too.

The traditional value of being accountable for our own actions involves much more than holding fathers — and sometimes mothers — accountable for the upbringing of their children.

We have become a nation in which virtually anyone can slip easily into the role of a "victim." A nation of victims is one that has lost its grip on the power and the majesty of self-reliance.

Many politicians, lawyers and pressure groups, such as the American Civil Liberties Union, have vested interests in protecting people from responsibility for their own actions.

One of the best ways to avoid responsibility for even the most heinous of acts is to plead "temporary insanity." There was a time when most people viewed insanity as an ongoing state. Now it's possible for a "normal" person to become insane just long enough to bump off someone who has made life unpleasant — an unwanted spouse, perhaps. By doing the deed in an especially messy way, one can, if caught, line up enough lawyers and psychiatrists to trade all those amps in the electric chair for the courtroom exit or, at worst, a few years at "Happydale."

Absurdities abound in the relentless pursuit of absolution from accountability. Prisoner rights advocates were incensed when California began erecting high-voltage fences around its prisons — even though the electric fences were fenced off by non-electric fences to keep all but the escapees from getting fried.

A drunk driver runs off the road, crashes into a utility pole and sues the utility for not locating the pole properly. A teen who barely made it through high school can't find a job, then blames the school district for not giving him a good education. An unwed mother with five children by four different men blames society for her having to live below the poverty line.

Much of the call for a renewed sense of personal accountability is financial. As payers of ever-higher taxes, more and more Americans are sick and tired of paying for other people's poor choices in life.

> At the personal level, Americans seem to be taking greater responsibility for their actions. They are getting more involved in protecting the environment, taking a balanced approach to key health and safety issues, and even paying down some of the debt they ran up in the 1980s. All this suggests that many Americans are sobering up, financially.
>
> The Roper Organization
> *Public Pulse*

There's another form of accountability that seems to be making a comeback as a traditional American value — accountability to a higher power.

Religion is coming back in a big way. Increasingly, people can't cope with life devoid of a spiritual base and are looking upward as well as inward for relief.

Some 95 percent of the children born after World War II had some sort of religious upbringing, mostly along very structured and traditional lines.

The anti-establishment movement of the 1960s not only fueled a drop in traditional secular values, but traditional religious ones as well. As soon as they could wriggle free from parental control, many teens and young adults joined the exodus from "organized religion."

Cults helped fill the inner void of some. Others experimented with philosophies or sects that would mesh with a new-found sense of situational ethics. Atheism attracted some. But enough stayed with traditional religions to avert wholesale bankruptcies among places of worship.

While some two-thirds of the Baby-Boom generation left the religions of their upbringing, most continued to believe in God, albeit often as personally redefined.

University of California Sociologist Wade Clark Root describes this effect as "believers but not belongers."

Continuous white water is drawing more people not only toward believing but belonging as well. Churches and other religious organizations that package and transmit a powerful message people can relate to are growing. Many tradition-bound congregations continue to decline.

The "graying of America" is contributing to the resurgence of religion, but the value of religious faith as a buffer to modern-day tribulations and as a strong step toward more-fulfilling lives, is applying to people of all ages.

Studies have even demonstrated how strong religious faith and the practice of religions that emphasizes hope can reduce the pressures of daily living to the extent that physical well-being actually is improved.

> Optimistic people are more healthy. If religion is promoting optimism, which is promoting better health, there are a lot of implications there.
>
> Psychologist Shirley Albertson Owens
> Southern California College

Some of the most popular business books of the 1990s are embracing some religious themes and espousing traditional religious principles. In the 1980s, the business press focused on making big bucks. But in the 1990s, the focus is on making money in ways that are honorable and provide fulfillment in helping others.

> The purpose of business is more than making money. My book is about how to create a corporate value system: The CEOs of the future will be those who manage through shared values rather than directives of fear.
>
> Tom's of Maine Co-founder Tom Chappell
> *The Soul of a Business*

By the way: Chappell took time out of his corporate career to earn a degree from the Harvard Divinity School.

If, indeed, the business of America is business, then the themes to be found in America's business press are of special importance:

> The reason business books are changing is that business is changing. The 1980s were the last gasp of a post-war boom that made managers feel smart when they really were mostly lucky.
>
> Michael Hammer, management consultant

To what extent are *you* in step with the trend toward a return to many traditional values? Some questions for you to consider:

• Is there anything you are doing in your career or personal life that you are the least bit ashamed of? If so, what do you intend to do about it? If not, would all of what you are doing get nods of approval from your parents, grandparents and others whose values systems might be more traditional than yours?

> My test is a simple one. If what I'm about to do would not set a good example for my children or would raise moral, ethical or good-taste questions if reported in my home-town newspaper, I don't do it.

• Look back over the past year or so. Make a list of your "technical transgressions" — those things that, technically, are wrong but which "everybody" does. If you can't think of any, remember that the last person completely without sin was nailed to a cross.

> What an eye-opener! In just one day I caught myself driving 10 miles over the speed limit, making a personal call on the company line and trying to save 25 cents on a coupon that had expired. If I am to be truly honest, I must draw the line at little things, for shrugging off the little things eventually will lead to rationalizing choices that could bring grief to me and others I care about.

• If you are an honest person, how *consistent* are you in your honesty? What kinds of support and advice do you give to others? Do you set a good example?

> A co-worker asks me to help cover up a small account-ing error rather than face embarrassment. What should I do? My teen-ager is getting ready for prom night and asks me what the best method is to avoid pregnancy in case the date wants to have sex. What do I say?

• Do you believe there is a power higher than yourself? If so, to what extent are you "plugged into" that power? If not, look around you. Identify the 10 happiest, most self-fulfilled people you know or know of. Do *they* look to a higher power? If so, how do they *connect* to that power?

> Mine is a loving God and His house is a place of joy and of love. My God gives me strength for today and faith in tomorrow. When I face life's inevitable hardships, my God is there for me and so are the people with whom I share this faith. Each day, I give thanks to my God for the many blessings given to me. I can't imagine being without this foundation for my life. I can't imagine facing life without such magnificent support.

• Could you, right now, give a resounding *yes!* to each of the traditional values espoused in this personal creed of a former Ameri-can president?

> I believe in work, for discontent and labor are not often companions.
> I believe in thrift, for to store up a little regularly is to store up character as well.
> I believe in simple living, for simplicity means health and health means happiness.
> I believe in loyalty, for if I am not true to others, I cannot be true to myself.
> I believe in a cheerful countenance, for a sour face is grouchy.
> I believe in holding up my chin, for self-respect com-mands respect from others.
> I believe in bracing up my brother, for an encouraging word may save the day for him.
> I believe in living up to the best that is for me, for to lower the standard is to give up the fight.

This great credo comes from the president remembered most for his silence — Calvin Coolidge. But even if he had shouted it from the rooftops, it would have done little to avert the pitiful decline of moral values in the America of the past few decades.

Perhaps — just perhaps, however — less silence on your part and that of many others will help all of us refocus on those values, so that with the advent of the New Millennium, we will experience together an ever-greater renewal of the American spirit.

> We believe it's time to reclaim America. To take a stand for what's right. To re-establish the fundamental principles upon which this nation is founded; principles such as faith, family, free enterprise, freedom and future. When it's all said and done, it's the Resurrection of the American Spirit.
>
> Dean Sikes
> The Spirit of America Foundation

*   *   *   *   *

10 Precepts for Achieving Ongoing Stability in Life

You've examined five trends that represent an ongoing search for stability. In your quest for a successful life is the need to deal with change. Here are 10 precepts that tie together stability and change:

Stability for most people is preferable to continual change

Change will continue to accelerate, producing ever greater impact

Increasing impact will diminish conventional avenues to self-fulfillment

Self-Fulfillment will come more to those willing to make good choices in life

A choice in life increasingly important is developing an effective personal plan

An effective plan is written, tracked, updated and worthy of support by others

Support by others depends on the quality and strength of relationships

Relationships are strengthened best by developing enduring values

Enduring values increase the ability to handle continual change

Change well-handled produces a sense of ongoing stability.

Onward!

Having...

• Taken a short course in history and learned from the experiences and outcomes of seven decades past;

• Examined the impact of trends creating continuous white water and what needs to be done about them; and,

• Looked at five other trends that may guide you toward an ongoing sense of stability by making good personal choices...

...you now should be ready to develop your own best answers to the questions that *must* be answered well if you are to make a more successful, more joyful, more self-fulfilling journey through life.

Your individual answers and the answers you may choose to develop jointly with a partner on your journey, will determine when, how and whether you are able to continue your journey in that consummately desirable place called "Mecca."

P a r t   2

Your Conquest

Key Questions for Success in Life

- 3 Vital Questions to Complete Your Context
- 5 Crucial Questions for Your Life's Journey
  1. Where Are You Now & Where Do You Want to Be?
  2. Whom Do You Choose to Be for the Journey?
  3. What Will It Take to Reach Your Destination?
  4. How Should You Chart Your Course?
  5. When Will You Know You've Arrived?

*By understanding the context
and knowing the right questions,
you can find the best answers.*

Chapter 5

Start With the Right Questions

- 3 Vital Questions to Complete Your Context
- 5 Crucial Questions for Your Life's Journey

In Part 1 of this book, you sought a better understanding of the times in which we live — a *context* or frame of reference for life in the world around you.

You began by taking a short history lesson, looking into the decades that preceded the 1990s. Each decade successively offered a *legacy* for the ones that followed — legacies that influence your context to this day. Such influence comes not only from your own experiences, but those of older people whose attitudes and beliefs were shaped by the contexts and legacies of decades stretching all the way back to the 1920s, perhaps even earlier.

Then came an exploration of two sets of trends. Five of the trends portend the hard-hitting rigors of *continuous white water;* but the other five reflect the much-cherished relief people seek through an *ongoing search for stability.*

Everything you do in life, you do *in context.* It is *context* that influences each decision you make, right or wrong. It is *context* that surrounds every experience, good or bad. It is *context* that sheds the light of meaning on every outcome of every decision and experience.

Like everyone, you form opinions, beliefs, attitudes and frames of reference from your day-to-day experiences, circumstances, situations, happenings and relationships with other people.

You may find it harder and harder to maintain *any* sort of strong and positive context for your life. Not only has the world become more complex, offering more and more options, but individual value systems — what's acceptable and unacceptable — have been broadened in keeping with a moral and ethical fabric that is vastly different from that which offered a context for past generations.

Perhaps you're among the many who believe they could have

found a more stable, positive context for life years ago. Or, you may be among many who would *never* trade contexts with their parents or grandparents — or among many who are downright unsure.

> Life was simpler when we were young. Myrtie and I dated for three years and saved money so we could get married. We experienced sex for the first time on our wedding night and, in the more than 50 years we've been happily married, couldn't imagine sharing that experience with anyone else. For years, I worked a 48-hour week at the mill and, when necessary, took on odd jobs so Myrtie could stay home and raise the children. Our neighbors were a lot like us. We looked after one another and no one bothered to lock their doors at night. The Church taught us what was really important in life. We could count on the fingers of our hands the number of Sundays we missed and every day we continue to thank God for our many blessings. We never did get a television set because of how much we enjoy each other's company and that of our family, and because of all the wonderful books we still haven't read. If the Lord takes Myrtie first, I'll miss her a lot. But He would watch over me and I would have a big and loving family all around me. Besides, there is a lifetime of wonderful memories that Myrtie and I created together. I don't understand life today. People can't count on each other like they could when we were young. Heck, they can't even manage to stay *married* to each other!

Some questions:

Do you believe there was a more positive and clear-cut context for life 50 or 100 years ago?

Would you have faced fewer big, tough life questions then because there were fewer big, tough choices to make?

For the most part, do you think you would have been happier back then? Would you be happier today if you could find ways to borrow from the past to make life simpler?

Can you and those around you learn to handle today's complexities and *still* enjoy happy, fulfilling lives?

If, like many today, you seek instant gratification in life, would you be better off trying to discover the benefits of *delayed* gratification and self-denial that worked well for many in past generations?

To whatever extent you may feel you've "made a mess of things" up to this point in your life, do you feel a need to seek some kind of *new* direction?

As important as your external context may be, it is *not* the entire context for your journey through life. You also have an *internal* context which may be totally driven by the world around you, may be influenced very little by it, may be somewhere in between or may, like mood swings, go back and forth.

The context for your journey in life is not complete until you have established an *internal context* so powerful that you can overcome every obstacle put in your path by external circumstances.

3 Vital Questions to Complete Your Context

The basis for a strong internal context can be boiled down to three simple words: Want, Way, Work. They are imbedded in Three Vital Questions:

1. What Do You *Want* Out of Life? How could you possibly *succeed* in life if you have no inkling of what you *Want* out of life? To what extent have you *identified exactly* what you *Want?*

> Going through life without knowing what you want is like going to sea without knowing where you're headed.

Winners in life have big *dreams.* Losers, at best, have big *fantasies.* What's the difference?

A big fantasy envisions attaining what you Want without focusing on the Way and Work involved in getting it.

> Some day my ship will come in. It will be filled with much treasure and I'll be set for life!

A big dream envisions not only a major accomplishment that you *Want* in life, but also the *Way* to accomplish it and the *Work* that it will take to accomplish it. Big dreams drive big goals which are accomplished through big effort.

> Ships are passing by here all the time. Some are filled with treasure. I'm going to find out which ship holds the treasure for me, then get in good physical shape and *swim out to it!*

Remember the first of the five *ongoing search for stability trends* — downsized dreams and lower expectations? That's what's happening, but not what successful people are doing.

Dream *big,* like successful people do. Answer the first question thoroughly, deciding what you *Want* out of life, then link your decision to an all-out effort to answer thoroughly the Second Vital Question:

2. What Is the Best *Way* to Get What You *Want?*   Having pinned down what you *Want,* what is the best *Way* to get it? What *Way* are you pursuing now? Is it the *best Way* to get what you *Want?* How are you doing so far? If you're not getting what you *Want,* is it because you haven't found the best *Way* — the right *vehicle?*

> You're about to start a 100-mile road race through the Rocky Mountains. Your only opponent is a three-time European grand prix auto-racing champion. This is the first time you've ever been in a race. You slide behind the wheel of a turbocharged 1997 BMW sports coupe. Your opponent gets into a 1957 Divco milk truck with a cracked cylinder. Who is almost sure to win?

Like the milk truck, you may be in a vehicle that won't get you what you *Want* no matter how good you are or how hard you try. Or, like the turbocharged BMW, you might have found a vehicle that may help you overcome some shortcomings, such as a lack of racing experience.

But there's still *Work* involved, and you must come up with a good answer to the Third Vital Question:

3. Are You Willing & Able to Do the *Work?*   If you know what you *Want* and have found the best *Way* to get it, are you willing to do the *Work?* Do you tend to abandon a *Way* when the *Work* seems too hard? If you're looking for a business opportunity, for example, are you chasing after one get-rich-quick deal after another trying to find a *Way* to get what you *Want* without having to do the *Work?*

> I knew there must be a catch. I *Want* a great lifestyle and freedom to spend time with my family. You told me this business opportunity is the best *Way* to get it. Now you tell me that to get what I *Want,* I'm going to have to *Work!*

Unless you expect to inherit a fortune, the *Way* to get what you *Want* is certain to involve *Work.* And the more you *Want,* the more *Work* is likely to be involved.

If you found the right *Way* to get what you *Want,* are you *really* willing to do the *Work* that's required — to do whatever it takes? If you're in a vehicle that won't get you what you *Want* no matter how hard you *Work,* are you willing to do *whatever it takes* to find a new vehicle with a *Work* plan that's right for you?

The three W's form the core of your internal context. You can strengthen each of the W's with three elements characterized as the ABC's of *Want, Way, Work:*

Attitude. Your attitude as you approach each of the three W's is the mindset through which you can accomplish major goals and make your dreams come true. The more *positive* your attitude, the more you can build...

Belief. To be successful, you must *believe* in yourself and what you're doing. Armed with a positive mental attitude and strong belief, you're ready to make a...

Commitment. The bigger the dreams and goals, the more commitment is required. With *total* commitment you are almost certain to achieve anything that's achievable. With *less than total* commitment, you're almost certain to quit when the going gets tough — or succumb to the trend toward "downsized dreams and lower expectations."

Put together, it looks like this:

THE ABCS OF WANT • WAY • WORK

W A N T	W A Y	W O R K
ATTITUDE Big dreams & goals *can* be fulfilled & I am worthy of earning all that they offer!	**ATTITUDE** The best **Way** to get what I **Want** exists! With an open mind & persistence, I'll find it!	**ATTITUDE** The **Work** not only is worth doing & doing well, but will give me great fulfillment!
BELIEF I have the *potential* to achieve all of my dreams & goals!	**BELIEF** The **Way** I found is *the* best & I have what it takes to make it work for me!	**BELIEF** I am fully capable of doing this **Work** & overcoming every obstacle in my path!
COMMITMENT I *will* achieve my dreams & goals starting with finding the best **Way**!	**COMMITMENT** This *is* the vehicle to get what I **Want** & I will do whatever **Work** is involved!	**COMMITMENT** Believing in the **Way**, I *will* do the **Work** & do it *well*, driven by what I **Want**!

Which is most important to *your* success — Attitude, Belief or Commitment? Or are all three of equal importance?

In your efforts to fulfill your dreams and goals, how would you rate yourself on what you *Want*, the *Way* to get it and the *Work* necessary to make it happen? Where are your strengths and weaknesses within each area? How positive is your *Attitude?* How strong is your *Belief?* How deep is your *Commitment?*

The 10 trends you examined in Part 1 underscore what may be obvious: The *performance bar* you must get over if you are to enjoy at least *material* success has been raised — and no doubt will be raised even more.

If you've cut back on what you *Want,* is it because you can't find the right *Way* to get it? Or is it because you are unwilling or unable, physically or mentally, to do an increased amount of *Work* that may be required?

If you've found a good *Way* to get what you *Want,* should you raise your sights to a bigger dream? Or, as you get what you *Want,* should you back off on the *Work* in order to improve other aspects of your life?

The history lesson and 10 trends found in Part 1 comprise the *external* context for your journey through life. Want, Way, Work provides the core of your *internal* context.

Your choices of how to relate and respond to the external factors and how to change and empower yourself through the internal factors will be made in your answers to:

5 Crucial Questions for Your Life's Journey

No matter how rough things are, no matter how serious your problems may seem to be, no matter how far you may have slipped into despair or how close you already are to true happiness, finding the *best* answers to these five questions can bring you *total* success and self-fulfillment:

1. Where Are You Now and Where Do You Want to Be?
This is the classic planning question, whether for life's journey or for developing a good business strategy. It is the question that must be answered first if the other four questions are to have full value and meaning.

A good answer to this question is essential for identifying the overall context for your life as it is now and a new context for life as you want it to be in the future.

But if you are to take firm, forward steps along the roadway to where you want to be, you must develop a *very* good answer to the Second Crucial Question:

2. Whom Do You Choose to Be for the Journey?
This is the toughest of the five questions. Sadly, many people go through life *never* coming up with a good answer. They stumble along the roadway of life, sometimes reversing course, never quite sure *who* they are, what they want out of life, and what is most and least important.

You have the power to *define yourself* in a way that will make attainable the destination you identified in your answer to the first question. You have the power to change the way you think...to be a victor or victim in life ...to choose how far you want to go in anything you pursue.

But no matter *whom* you choose to be for life's journey, achieving self-fulfillment and *total* success will depend upon your answer to the Third Crucial Question:

3. What Will It Take to Reach Your Destination?

Simply identifying a good destination for life's journey isn't enough. Neither is a good self-definition. The answer to the Third Crucial Question involves five sequential *imperatives* for success.

These five imperatives offer you the *personal power* to get everything you want out of life. And if you're like most people, you will have to strengthen some important personal attributes if you are to harness the power of the five imperatives. You will also have to develop the best possible answer to the Fourth Crucial Question:

4. How Should You Chart Your Course?

The people most successful in life are those who *plan* well. A good answer to this question results in an effective personal plan.

Having answered the first three questions, you're now ready to get specific on such important aspects of planning as your mission in life, your specific vision for the future and your personal goals which, when achieved, will result in sticking to your mission and fulfilling your vision.

Success is measured and underscored by the fifth question:

5. When Will You Know You've Arrived?

This is the confirming question. It also enables you to tap into a system of support that helps secure arrival at your destination through lifelong growth and inner strength.

When you've answered the Fifth Crucial Question well, you've positioned yourself for *ongoing success* and self-fulfillment.

The five crucial questions are the key elements of a process called <u>*Meccanize!*</u>®. Each of the five crucial questions for life's journey contains five elements, giving the process symmetry and helping to make it easy to understand.

No matter how symmetrical and easy to understand, however, the process is *hard*. In the long run, though, success and happiness in life *without* answering these five crucial questions is *even harder.*

That means you've come to a fork in the roadway.

One fork leaves the book at this point and offers the seemingly easier alternative of "winging it" through life. The other fork starts in the next chapter with a process that, if followed, will put you in greater control of your life, give you a firmer fix on where you're going in your life and enable you to take your place among the *less than one percent* of the adult population that has developed a well-conceived, *written* career and personal plan.

When you come to a fork in the road, take one.

Casey Stengel

Do you know people who always seem to "have it all together?" They are the ones who know where they're going and who focus on what's important in getting there. They are successful in their jobs, professions or businesses and, in spite of that, *still* have a good family life with time left to enjoy recreation, hobbies and other such pursuits. They exude self-confidence.

On the other hand, do you know people who lead lives not just of *quiet* desperation, but utter, noisy chaos? They are the ones who either fail at one thing after another or always seem to be hanging onto things by a thread. They go from job to job or business to business, from marriage to marriage or friendship to friendship, and constantly complain about never having time to enjoy *anything* in life. They always seem frazzled and out of breath.

When this latest crisis is over, I'm going to have a nervous breakdown. I earned it, I deserve it and nobody is going to keep me from having it!

Popular sign for the wall

What's the difference? Why is it that some people seem to be in total control of the circumstances in their lives and others allow the circumstances of their lives to be in total control of them?

Quite simply, it's that the people who seem to be in control have developed more and better answers to the Five Crucial Questions than people who are out of control.

They have taken the correct fork in the road.

Chapter 6

The First Crucial Question:

Where Are You Now and Where Do You Want to Be?

• A Roadway Through 5 Cities & 5 States

On the surface, at least, this is the easiest of the five crucial questions. It is, after all, the most basic question in any sort of planning process, whether for a Fortune 500 company, a club, a non-profit social agency, a football team, a family or you personally.

Like everything else in life, this question — at face value — is subject to many interpretations. That's because each person attempting to tackle it will view it in a personalized context.

Your context may involve whatever career or life issue is uppermost in your mind at the moment. It's easy for anyone to see this question in the context of one or more *slices* of life rather than as a framework for life overall.

The context for each slice may be positive or negative, depending on your perspective:

Where Are You Now?	*Where Do You Want to Be?*
Single and lonely	Married and happy
Living in an apartment	Living in a beach house
Trainee welder	Journeyman welder
Business student	CEO of a corporation
A nobody	Leader of a gang
Hopeless duffer	Scratch golfer
English-speaking	Multi-lingual
In prison	Free — to get even
In prison	Free — to make a new life
Stuck in traffic	Commuting by helicopter
Seamstress	Fashion designer
Flat broke	Multimillionaire
Cancer patient	Cured, pursuing a full life

Those are only slices of life — goals, perhaps, viewed as keys to success and happiness. They may be worthy or unworthy, realistic or unrealistic.

Step back, for a moment, and reflect on a broader context for your own life. What do you *want* out of life: Happiness? Contentment? A joy of living? These suggest intangible states of being.

Or, do you identify what you want out of life in more tangible terms: Wealth? A bigger house or a better neighborhood in which to live? Titles? Status?

There are two parts to the first of the five questions for your journey through life: "Where are you now?" and "Where do you want to be?" You may find the first part fairly easy. You may find the second part hard.

• *Where are you now...?*

Your answer may be a matter of deciding how *off* you are — anything from "I'm very well *off*, thank you," to "I'm very badly *off*."

"Well-off" seems like an oxymoron. If you're *well*, how can *off* put you in a positive state? "Well *off* the main highway," for example, could put you in the middle of a swamp. Or how about this: "I'm well-*off* in life but today is one of my *off* days."

If you are doing really, really well, especially in a material sense, should you be regarded as well-*on?*

You also may look at the first part of the question in terms of your general state of mind — anything from being extremely happy to being totally miserable. Or, perhaps you could frame it in institutional terms, such as "in college" or "in mid-career." Or how about psychological terms, such as "mid-life crisis"?

It's possible, of course, to be floundering so much in life that your "Where you are now?" answer may be like many people's today: "I have no clue."

There *are*, sadly, a lot of people who are "lost" in life. Not only have they no idea of where they are going, they have no idea of where they are *now*.

Like everything, the "Where are you now?" part of the question is a matter of perspective — of *context*.

> Many miles off course, a balloonist descends to within shouting distance of a farmer working in a field somewhere in Vermont. The balloonist leans out of the basket and shouts: "Where am I?" The farmer looks up, thinks for a moment and yells back: "Yer in a balloon, ya darn fool!"

And what of the second part of the question:

- ### *Where do you want to be?*

You may see your direction in life as a *continuation* of your "state of *off*." You might say, "I'm well-*off* now and will continue to be" or "I'm not well-*off* now, but I'm going to be well-*off* in the future" or "I'm badly-*off* now and see myself as being worse-*off* in years to come."

While having a grasp of where they are now, many people today haven't a clue as to where they want to be.

They may have vivid dreams of fame and fortune or obscure notions of future happiness. They may be caught up in pure fantasies, envisioning themselves as mega-winners in state lotto games or having their every need met by a Prince Charming or rich widow. They may believe that "the Lord will provide," interpreting that to mean they simply sit back and wait for it all to be handed to them.

How about you? How do *you* answer this two-part question? Do you agree that coming up with the best possible answer is an important first step in becoming happier and more successful in life?

The destination half of the question is vital.

> If a man does not know what harbor he is headed for, no wind is the right wind.

> Seneca, 4 BC

Perhaps answering both parts of the question would come easier if you thought of where you are now in life and where you want to be in the form of a map with a roadway connecting five "cities."

The uppermost city on the roadway is the place called *"Mecca,"* described in this book.

In keeping with the word's second meanings in the English language, "Mecca" is the place most people are likely to *want* to be. It is the culmination of positive life experiences. It is consummate joy of living. It is being all you can be.

At the bottom of the roadway is a city called *Hades Gulch*. It represents consummate misery with little or no hope. Another name for the place would be "Pure Hell."

Moving up the roadway toward "Mecca" from Hades Gulch are three other places describing life overall:

Purgatoria, a place of unhappiness and upheaval that at least offers hope for something better; *Malaisia,* where the inhabitants are getting by but not getting very far in life; and *Fat City,* where there's plenty of material stuff and ego satisfaction but, quite possibly, a feeling that "something is missing."

If you are living in or near the city of "Mecca," a major problem in one part of your life shouldn't send you careening all the way down the roadway to Hades Gulch; unless, of course, there is very little to your life *other than* the part in which you are having the major problem.

For example, the loss of a job can come as a major blow. But, as illustrated on the opening pages, the loss of a job also can be an opportunity to achieve greater happiness. If your whole life is wrapped up in your job, however, such a loss can land you in Hades Gulch.

Similarly, marital difficulties can rob one or both partners of considerable happiness. When the bonds of matrimony become frayed or break altogether, there can be much pain. But while a marriage may be an enormous part of life, it's not the *totality* of life — unless you've chosen to have everything revolve around the relationship.

There are, to be sure, those who seem to have *everything* go wrong in *all* aspects of their lives all at once. Without the positive attitudes to deal with continuous white water, such people join the millions who, tragically, have taken up residency down at the bottom of the roadway in Hades Gulch.

Here is an overview of the five cities and their principal characteristics:

"Mecca"	Self-Actualization "Spiritual" Fulfillment Joy of Living
Fat City	Material Comfort or Success Ego Satisfaction "Conventional" Happiness
Malaisia	Stability / Security Moving in Circles / in a Rut Endurable Pain
Purgatoria	Ongoing Change / Upheaval Hope for Something Better Unhappiness "for Now"
Hades Gulch	Misery Little or no Hope "Life Is Tough, Then You Die"

Before taking a closer look, let's put the concept of the five cities and the roadway that connects them in perspective.

Life is a journey and finding happiness in life has more to do with the journey than with reaching a particular destination. So in viewing the five cities, it's important to understand that "taking up residency" in no way inhibits your journey through life.

Your journey continues no matter what city you're living in. When you move from one city to another, you change residences but your travel through life continues.

Put another way, the cities represent your attitudes or states of mind. Life's journey is one of happiness and self-fulfillment for a resident of "Mecca." If you have taken up residency in Hades Gulch, at the bottom of the roadway, you find life to be full of pain and lacking in purpose.

In an even broader "geographical" context for life's journey, consider each of the five cities as the capital of an attitudinal state that surrounds it. From the bottom of the roadway to the top, here is your guide to the cities and states:

The City of ...	Is the capital of...
Hades Gulch	**The State of Despair**
Purgatoria	**The State of Anxiety**
Malasia	**The State of Mediocrity**
Fat City	**The State of Affluence**
"Mecca"	**The State of Grace**

Now let's take a closer look at the five cities — a "tour," so to speak. We'll see what life is like in each of those places and let you hear from some of the people who live there.

Let's start with:

Hades Gulch (The State of Despair)

The worst part of living in Hades Gulch is that you have little or no hope. There is no best part.

Sadly, millions of people in America live most or parts of their lives in Hades Gulch. If you're one of them, you probably see your life today summed up perfectly by a popular bumper sticker:

Life Is Tough, Then You Die

Most days are bad at best, awful at worst. Nothing seems to go right at work (if you have a job), at home (if you have one) or anywhere else. The future is bleak. When something *does* go right, it only underscores all that is wrong overall.

Where jobs are concerned, Hades Gulch residents not only may include the chronic unemployed but the chronic *overemployed* as well. These are people who work days and nights and weekends just to pay bills or keep up appearances. They have been doing this for so long and getting nowhere for so long that life is one, long, miserable drag.

Hades Gulch is the *ultimate rut.* It's the rut that is hardest to climb out of because the people who live there, seeing little or no hope, have scant reason even to *try* moving on.

Being around citizens of Hades Gulch can make it harder to maintain citizenship in any of the cities higher on the roadway. Denizens of Hades Gulch drag other people down.

Hades Gulchians married to each other replicate the classic observation of crab-fishing: "Catch one crab and put it in your basket and it will climb out. Put a second crab in the basket and neither will climb out, for they constantly pull each other down."

Adapting to the environment in Hades Gulch is a form of masochism. Citizens there can develop a *taste* for suffering, perhaps a certain perverse pleasure in day-to-day pain. Often, they allow plenty of time to reinforce their misery.

> The secret of being miserable is to have the leisure to bother about whether you are happy or not.
>
> George Bernard Shaw

The primary avocation in Hades Gulch is a game called "Ain't It Awful." Even positives can be negatives through awfulizing:

> After all I've done for that rotten company, they give me a lousy 3 percent raise. Oh sure, I didn't get the axe like half the others in the department, but now they want me to do some more work. I told my boss it wasn't fair, and she had the gall to tell me I have a bad attitude!

Dual-income Hades Gulch spouses come home after their bad days (that's just about *every* day) and play a variation on a theme of "Can You Top This?"

> You think you had a bad day! Well, *my* day was so terrible that I have a splitting headache that starts here and goes all the way around to...

People living in Hades Gulch commit most of the domestic violence in America and all of the suicides. There is a great deal of mental illness among the residents. BUT:

Just because you're not violent, suicidal or mentally ill doesn't mean you haven't taken up residency in Hades Gulch. The city also abounds with people who simply have very negative outlooks on life.

And you could be among the many people living farther up the roadway who suddenly land in Hades Gulch following a major shock or setback in an important area of life. It could be the end of a relationship, or the loss of a job or most-dreaded results from a physical exam.

Some such people move back up the roadway on their own and some are helped back by loving residents of the other cities. Some move back quickly, while for others the journey back may take months or years.

The most tragic aspect of living in Hades Gulch is having life end there.

Some people, no matter how much ruin they've brought to their own lives and the lives of others, reach the end believing they were totally blameless for their final misery — that, somehow, it was *other* people, or the world itself, that wronged them.

> ...my trust has been misused by many people. Disloyalty and betrayal have undermined resistance throughout the war. It was therefore not granted to me to lead the people to victory.
>
> Adolf Hitler
> April 1945

Is there anything more tragic than nearing the end of life bitterly blaming others for life's tragic circumstances?

Yes! It's nearing the end of life with the painful realization that the tragedy is, indeed, *of your own making* — that you put *yourself* in Hades Gulch and it's too late to do much about it...that you've frittered life away...that you didn't become all you could be because you didn't even *try*.

> A man once successful in business lost it all by making some bad decisions and having what he regarded as a lot of "bad luck." He lost his fortune, then turned to alcohol and lost everything else — his family, his home and his self-respect. He lived on the streets, begging money to buy cheap wine. Quite ill, he lay in the gutter clutching one final bottle of muscatel. A Rolls-Royce stopped in traffic a few feet from where he lay. A chauffeur was at the wheel and, in the back seat, were a well-dressed couple in happy conversation, apparently heading for the theater. The derelict reflected back on his life and on the gutter in which he lay. Turning his eyes toward the man in the Rolls-Royce, he muttered the saddest words of all: "There but for me go I."

What will be the closing thoughts of *your* life if you are living it in Hades Gulch? What will you look back upon with regret? What words will you use to continue the one sentence — or string of sentences — that begins with the words *"If only I had...?"*

Denial is one of two common characteristics in Hades Gulch.

> There's nothing wrong with me. It's the *world* that's sick. Okay, so I don't walk around with a phoney-baloney smile telling everyone how great things are. The fact is, things *aren't* great and there's no use trying to pretend that they are!

The other common characteristic is a need for help. Fortunately, some recognize that need and go after it, or accept one of the helping hands so often extended by people who care.

There are many good avenues of treatment available and many excellent professionals who can give a big boost back up the roadway. The most powerful help can come from above through prayer, facilitated by caring people who already have found great strength in the spiritual dimension of life.

No one should consign one's self — or be consigned by others — to life in Hades Gulch, no matter what the circumstances!

Where are you now? If you agree that, overall, your life is one of misery and little or no hope, then you are living in Hades Gulch, smack in the middle of the State of Despair. That's the bad news.

The good news is that you can step back and take a hard, fresh, honest look at your life and decide that while Hades Gulch is "where I am now," it's not "where I want to be."

If you don't want to stay there, where *do* you want to be? Onward and upward — *all the way to the top?*

> Was this all life would ever mean to me — working at a job I despised, living with cockroaches, eating vile food — and with no hope for the future?
>
> Dale Carnegie
> Recalling the start of his career

What an improvement in life it would be, just to move up — for now — to the next city and state on the roadway!

Purgatoria *(The State of Anxiety)*

Welcome to Purgatoria. Like Hades Gulch, you may find much "pain and suffering" here. But there are five major differences :

1. If you live in Purgatoria, you *have hope* for something better. If you live in Hades Gulch, you have little or no hope.

2. In Purgatoria, you are *moved to action* by hope and are strengthened by it. You are willing to *work* toward making life better. In Hades Gulch, whatever hope there may be depends on external circumstances such as winning a huge Lotto jackpot. *Not* winning, week after week, reinforces the misery of living in Hades Gulch.

3. Having a good measure of hope, you regard your residency in Purgatoria as temporary. In Hades Gulch, having little or no hope, you probably feel resigned to living there indefinitely.

4. Residency in Purgatoria may have resulted from a conscious decision you've made to pursue a particularly arduous, or even painful, course of action in order to bring about something better in life. If you're living in Hades Gulch, it's *not* because you've made a conscious decision to live there. You may even live there a long time without realizing it.

5. If you are suddenly faced with tragedy — loss of a loved one, a crippling accident, sudden termination of a job or the like — you may land in Hades Gulch. But you'll move up the roadway to Purgatoria the moment you decide to overcome your loss and get going on what ever actions are necessary to recover.

The temporary nature of Purgatoria is underscored by the doctrine of the Roman Catholic Church. Purgatory, according to that doctrine, is a place where, having received the grace of God upon death, a sinner undergoes punishment and atonement in preparation for Heaven.

In a secular sense, Purgatory has come to mean a state of misery or suffering that is temporary. Put another way, Purgatory — or the City of Purgatoria, in this case — is a place of darkness but, like a tunnel, has a light at the end.

People in Purgatoria *know* the light is sunshine. It's the Hades Gulchians who would see it as the headlight of an onrushing locomotive.

If you are like most people, you probably have spent at least *some* parts of your life in the City of Purgatoria and maybe that's where you are now.

You may even have moved to Purgatoria *voluntarily,* perhaps by immersing yourself totally in the pursuit of a goal that you have accepted weeks or months of pain in exchange for significant gain.

Many an Olympic Gold Medal winner spent a *long, long time* in the City of Purgatoria's gyms and practice fields, enduring every hardship just for the *prospect* of winning the gold. The sunlight at the end of the tunnel shines very brightly, indeed!

If you've served in the military, you may have spent some number of weeks in a notorious neighborhood of Purgatoria called

Boot Camp. Or you may have volunteered to live for awhile in an even tougher neighborhood so you could earn greater responsibility and the privilege of leading.

Purgatoria, however, should not turn into a lifelong struggle or even year after year of pain. In the relentless pursuit of something better, there should come a time when the quest itself will produce a sense of self-fulfillment. This is especially true when you measure your progress and feel good about each bit of progress you make.

You haven't lived until you've lived *some* parts of your life in the City of Purgatoria. It's not healthy, though, to live large amounts of your life there.

Whatever Purgatoria's hardships are for you, they should result in an outcome that enables you to pack your emotional bags and move to a higher place on the roadway.

If, like an Olympic athlete, your voluntary residency in Purgatoria could go on for years, the constant striving and continuous improvement should bring the kind of joy that reflects a much higher position on the roadway — perhaps in "Mecca," or a spot just below it.

Marathon runners know this phenomenon as "runner's high." There may be a lot of pain associated with the run and the training that led up to it, but there comes a point when a certain kind of euphoria sets in — an exhilaration from the run itself.

Being in Purgatoria voluntarily is the consummate expression of *no pain, no gain.* If your quest for self-improvement is limited to only those things that are easy or convenient, you haven't decided to take up temporary residence in Purgatoria.

Having the will to endure *voluntarily* the pain of Purgatoria in order to achieve something better requires not only being able to see sunlight at the end of the tunnel, but learning to break goals down into manageable pieces and live one day at a time.

> While serving as chaplain at the U.S. Naval Academy, I remember a young man who came to my office wanting to resign. It was "Plebe Summer" and he had been there about two weeks. "I can't take 300 days of this," he said. I asked him whether he could stand it until tomorrow. He said he could and I told him to come back to see me. The next day I asked him if he could stand it for one more day, explaining to him that he doesn't have to handle all 300 days at once, only one day at a time. He got the point and got through it — all 300 days of it — one day at a time!
>
> The Rev. Chuck Greenwood
> Captain (Chaplain), U.S. Navy-Retired

Voluntarily spending time in Purgatoria in hopes of achieving something better in life is one thing. *Involuntarily* landing there is quite another matter.

The loss of a loved one can bring most anyone to the depths of despair, at least for a short time. Those who *never* recover have consigned themselves to Hades Gulch. Those who do, will spend some time in Purgatoria.

Perhaps the worst tenures in Purgatoria were endured by prisoners of war in Vietnam — men held captive under conditions so horrible that it's hard to imagine so many survived the ordeal and were able to get on with their lives.

First-rate military training played a major part in the ability of so many POWs to stand up under physical and mental torture lasting eight years and even longer.

Some lapsed into a hopelessness akin to Hades Gulch, for there were suicides, breakdowns and some long-term mental disorders. The remarkable resiliency of so many others, however, has been attributed to more than just "good training."

> Each man's values, from his own private sources, provided the strength enabling him to maintain his senses of purpose and dedication. Our values systems had in common the fact that they were based on rules, that they placed unity above self and that they precluded self-indulgence.
>
> Vice Admiral James B. Stockdale
> *A Vietnam Experience*

Navy Captain Robert Mitchell, a flight surgeon, conducted a long-term study of the men who spent years as prisoners in Vietnam. He examined many of the men shortly after their release and matched them with men of similar age, experience and physical characteristics who had *not* been held prisoner.

Fifteen years later, Capt. Mitchell and his colleagues were startled to learn that the ex-POWs were in generally better health than those who had not undergone the ordeal of captivity.

There were fewer heart attacks, attributed to being without red meat for a long period, and the increase in IQ scores was higher among the ex-POWs, probably due to mental exercises and creative activities that helped them endure captivity.

The ex-POWs also had no long-term psychiatric problems and were found to handle stress better than those who hadn't suffered at the hands of the North Vietnamese.

This suggests that, given the right training, values systems, personal courage, and deep and abiding faith, even so terrible a place as a North Vietnamese prison camp can leave a person stronger and more able to overcome life's challenges and move up the roadway.

Hades Gulch is a rut — the deepest rut of all. Purgatoria should *not* be a rut; rather, it should produce the kind of self-renewal and strength that enables you to move straight through the next city on the pathway, a huge rut in which reside many, many millions of people. It's called:

Malaisia (The State of Mediocrity)

Malaisia can be a *trap* for people experiencing the joy of breaking out of Purgatoria.

One day, the months or years of struggle and hard work pay off. Graduation at last!... Finally! The Gold Medal you've worked so hard to achieve!... Yes! You've starved yourself and suffered for three months to get your weight down to this level and you did it! Years of putting up with *stuff* and *finally* you got the job you've always wanted!

You made it! A grand and glorious leap from weeks or months or years in Purgatoria, all the way to this exhilarating *moment* in "Mecca."

But now what? For most people, when the celebrating stops and the joy of achievement wears off, it's a descent right back down to the City of Malaisia, capital of the State of Mediocrity.

The streets of Malaisia go around in seemingly endless circles and the signs that mark them are long-faded.

President Jimmy Carter inspired the name for this city when he warned in a 1979 speech that America's two greatest problems were energy and malaise. By energy, he referred to fuel supplies. By malaise, he alluded to a weakening of the American spirit and a kind of vague sense of ill-being that accompanies lack of action, moral decay and societal decline.

Malaisia, like Hades Gulch and Fat City, is a rut. It's simply a more comfortable rut than Hades Gulch and lacks Fat City's big bucks, expensive toys and trinkets.

There's pain in Malaisia. It's not the kind found in Hades Gulch, nor the temporary pain experienced in Purgatoria. It's an *endurable* pain that becomes acceptable. The stores in Malaisia sell a lot of sofas, hammocks, recliners, TV sets, aspirin and other pain-killing home remedies — all to enhance the endurability of the dull pain associated with "just getting by" in life.

A old dog lay on the front porch of a house, woefully letting out a low yowl now and then. A visitor inquired of its owner why the dog was laying there yowling. "He's laying on a nail," the owner explained. "Why doesn't he move to a more comfortable spot?" the visitor queried. "Well," answered the dog's master, "he probably figures it hurts more to move than it does to just lay on the nail and yowl."

Residency in Malaisia represents the "settle-for" style of living. Part of the endurable pain associated with living there is that, deep down, Malaisians know they can achieve more in their lives, but it's easier just to settle for what life hands them. After all, a mediocre life is *very acceptable* in Malaisia among so many mediocre people.

While there's a high rate of employment, there's also a huge amount of untapped potential in Malaisia.

People go back and forth from home to job, oblivious to opportunity and impervious to invitations to make more of themselves.

Life is much the same throughout the city, except that the ruts in the upscale part of town are more comfortable than the ruts in the low-income areas.

Television is the main source of entertainment in Malaisia and the more mindless the programming the better. After all, what could be more fitting, after a day of minimal effort, than spending an evening on a sofa reinforcing negative thinking or *avoiding* the need to think?

This doesn't mean everyone in Malaisia is lazy. Like some folks in Hades Gulch, there are people who hold down two or three jobs trying to keep up with bills or the Joneses. But there is little likelihood of becoming successful at any single pursuit, because Malaisians tend to lack focus.

The deepest belief among Malaisians is in the Free Lunch. The city, and the State of Mediocrity surrounding it, is a thriving market for every kind of get-rich-quick scheme and offer of something-for-nothing.

Unlike the people who live in Hades Gulch, there is a fair degree of hope among the residents of Malaisia. But the source of that hope lies more in *something coming along* than in *making something happen.*

Calvin: "I don't want to pay any dues in life. I want to be a one-in-a-million overnight success! I want the world handed to me on a silver platter!"
Hobbes, rolling his eyes: "Good luck."
Calvin, angrily: "Surely you concede I *deserve* it!"

Bill Watterson, cartoonist
Calvin and Hobbes

When stopping to ask directions, most Malaisians ask for the Path of Least Resistance. Sometimes, residents will work very hard at finding the *easy* way around a problem, exerting, in the process, more energy than would have been required if the problem were attacked head-on in the first place.

Procrastination reigns supreme in Malaisia.

> Visitor: "Your roof's leaking. Why don't you fix it?
> Host: "It's raining."
> Visitor: "Why don't you fix it when it's not raining?"
> Host: "Well, then it's not leaking."

Relationships among Malaisians are more superficial than deep and genuine. Often, they center on routines — bowling every Friday night with the same people, the bingo hall two or three nights a week with the same crowd, going to church every Sunday to sleep through the sermon and *appear to be* a Christian.

Many people spend most of their lives living in the City of Malaisia, hoping someone will give them a free ride up the roadway.

From a geographical perspective, the city's location in the middle of the road map suggests that it's *average*. But from a psychological perspective, there's no challenge to Malaisia's claim as capital of the State of Mediocrity.

> Mediocrity is a region bounded on the north by compromise, on the south by indecision, on the east by past thinking and on the west by a lack of vision.
>
> John L. Mason
> *An Enemy Called Average*

By today's standards, living in Malaisia and the surrounding State of Mediocrity too easily is regarded as *normal*. It is normal to spend evenings glued to the boob tube. It is *normal* to stay home on most election days. It is *normal* to take the path of least resistance in careers, in education, in relationships, in the practice of religion and in other aspects of life.

You are living somewhere in the State of Mediocrity if you are minimally to reasonably comfortable and would rather complain about life's shortfalls than go out and do something about them.

Do residents of Malaisia aspire for a better life? Of course! It's just a matter of having better luck, of some long-lost uncle leaving a wad in his will, of hitting the big jackpot Saturday night, etc.

Any one of those "strategies" would give you a free ride all the way up the road to:

Fat City (The State of Affluence)

Those who find their way out of Malaisia, and those who speed through it on the expressway that runs from Purgatoria straight through the middle of town, will find a fork in the road at the city's northern boundary.

One road leads to "Mecca" and the other goes to Fat City. To be undecided on which road to take is to remain in the City of Malaisia.

Most often, travelers on the roadway made their decisions on which city to head for long before reaching the fork in the road. The decision may have come on a sofa in Malaisia while fantasizing about life as it *should be.* Or it may have been the very focal point of tremendous effort and sacrifice back in Purgatoria.

Those motivated by fame and fortune and status probably never noticed the sign to "Mecca" as they sped on through Malaisia and the fork in the road, for their destination was never in question.

Occasionally, the *vision* is of "Mecca" but, suddenly immersed in fame and fortune, there's a sudden swerve to the glamor of Fat City.

The sign at the edge of town is fully gilded: "Welcome to Fat City, Capital of the State of Affluence."

People who live "in the fast lane" invariably are on the road to Fat City. Once there, they find a full range of material comforts and ego-massagers, befitting "Lifestyles of the Rich and Famous."

Main Street is loaded with BMWs, Jags, Corvettes and other cars reflecting "arrival." There are more exclusive clubs in Fat City than any other place.

Wine consumed in Hades Gulch may be from a brown paper bag. In Purgatoria, it may not be consumed at all, especially by those undergoing rigorous training. In Malaisia, the wine often is the best that money can buy on a coupon at the discount store. And Fat City? It's the most impressive label available, preferably served where there is both a red wine steward *and* a white wine steward.

People who brag about being "self-made" live in Fat City.

> The problem with self-made people is that they worship their creators.

There are a lot of titles in Fat City and great sensitivity to how they are used. Residents usually don't wait for someone to bestow the titles in conversation, but rather are quick to bestow the titles upon themselves.

Cocktail parties in Fat City offer abundant opportunities to engage in first-person-singular communication. Listening is simply waiting for the right moment to resume talking, or tuning out of conversation long enough to concoct another barrage of impressive patter:

I really am glad to meet you because as I was telling
your charming spouse just a moment ago, I enjoy
getting to know people who share my opinions on economic matters, especially since I became president of
the Society for the Advancement of Arbitrage and had
the opportunity to conduct a briefing at the White
House for which I received a presidential citation that
resulted in my picture being on the front-cover of Debt
Today magazine...and by the way, what did you say your
name was?

In and of itself, *wealth* is not the problem in Fat City. There are
wealthy people in "Mecca" as well, along with many people who are
simply rich in spirit. The difference is that a certain *level* of wealth is a
requirement to take up residency in Fat City.

There are two roads out of Fat City.

One leads back down the roadway. If the departure from Fat
City is due to a sudden loss of the material things on which residency
depended, it may be a fast plunge all the way down the road into
Hades Gulch.

The other road goes on to "Mecca." This road is open to those
who, without having to lose it all, come to believe there's much more to
life than the conventional happiness and material success that Fat
City has to offer.

And there are people lost in the fog somewhere between Fat
City and "Mecca." These are the people who are not sure *where* they
are from one day to the next.

Within my earthly temple there's a crowd.
There's one of us that's humble; one that's proud.
There's one that's broken-hearted for his sins,
And one who, unrepentant, sits and grins.
There's one who loves his neighbor as himself,
And one who cares for naught but fame and pelf.
From much corroding care would I be free
If once I could determine which is Me.

Edward Sandford Martin

Fat City is a rut. Although gold-plated, the rut can be even
deeper than Hades Gulch.

The biggest principle of life that's lost on people living in Fat
City is that happiness can't be bought. If you're living in Fat City, that
hasn't *fully* occurred to you, either. And why should it, so long as there
are the resources to continue a never-ending string of *things*?

Life can be happy in Fat City, at least in a "conventional" way. But carried to its extremes, life there can be especially tragic.

From the movies comes a compelling illustration. It was the extraordinary film by Orson Welles of the poverty-to-power climb of a newspaper magnate who, in a material way, really *did* end up having "everything."

> "For what shall it profit a man if he shall gain the whole world and lose his soul." See Citizen Kane for details.
>
> *New York Times* film review, May 2, 1941,
> Citing *The New Testament*

Don't be misled by the extreme cases, though. The fictional Mr. Kane and the real-life Howard Hughes notwithstanding, many Fat Citians *do* find life there pretty good — even *very* good and even for long periods.

For some in Fat City, though, inwardly driven in a quest for *more,* there is an inability to find contentment.

But for everyone who lives there, happiness is far more related to *satisfaction* than deep and spiritual self-fulfillment. Perhaps that's because too much wealth came too soon or that the focus on the material aspects of life has been so strong for so long that a kind of boredom sets in. The pursuit of happiness may require more and more novel, or even bizarre, experiences.

Relationships change more often in Fat City than in other cities along the roadway.

> There's a ritzy neighborhood in California where 5 out of 4 marriages end in divorce. How can that be? So many people got divorced 2, 3 or 4 times that, statistically, the average marriage never took place!

Although there's a relatively high divorce rate, Fat Citians pride themselves in being quite civilized about such matters. Prenuptial agreements, out-of-court settlements, joint custody and boarding schools for the kids are not unusual.

Lawyers do quite well in Fat City. Many of them, in fact, also live there.

Economic downturns are especially hard on Fat Citians, forcing many back down the road to Purgatoria or even all the way down to Hades Gulch.

Rarely are refugees from Fat City content to set up housekeeping in Malaisia. More likely than accepting a *settle-for* life in the State of Mediocrity, they choose Purgatoria for another run at fame and fortune. If it works, they're back in Fat City. If it doesn't, the new destination may be Hades Gulch in the State of Despair or yet another "go" at Purgatoria.

You might expect to find an ex-Fat Citian in a pin-striped suit standing on a street corner in Purgatoria holding a briefcase in one hand and, in the other, a sign reading: "Will Consult for Food."

The road south out of Fat City can be pretty crowded, especially in economic hard times and when the material aspects of life cease to provide satisfaction.

The other road out of Fat City goes in a different direction. It is the road to "Mecca." Choosing *that* road leaves behind the notion that money is the root of all happiness. It begs the difference between rich in pocket and rich in spirit. It leads toward a whole new perspective, rooted in the realization that even people *totally lacking* in material wealth can find a joy of living that's true and enduring.

> Some have too much, yet still do crave;
> I little have, and seek no more;
> They are but poor, though much they have,
> And I am rich with little store:
> They poor, I rich; they beg, I give;
> They lack, I have; they pine, I live.

> Edward Dyer

Traffic conditions on either road leading to "Mecca" are described in the title of an extraordinary book:

> *The Road Less Traveled:* A New Psychology of Love,
> Traditional Values and Spiritual Growth

> M. Scott Peck, MD

In this context, you'll find that less-traveled road leads to:

"Mecca" (The State of Grace)

If you think *truly* powerful people live in Fat City, think again. The trappings of power are everywhere, but much is missing.

Getting a Fat Citian to acknowledge something missing may not be easy. Loaded with material blessings, what could be missing?

In Fat City, what's most-often missing (besides humility) is *enough*. There is an endless quest for more. Sometimes, though, when the quest for more doesn't bring a hoped-for level of happiness, a Fat Citian may discover what so many in the State of Affluence find hard to pinpoint: That the "missing something" is an understanding of where power comes from and how it should be used and appreciated.

> Invariably, when asked the source of their knowledge and power, the truly powerful will reply: "It's not my power. What little power I have is but a minute expression of a far greater power. I am merely a conduit." I have said that this humility is joyful. That is because... the truly powerful experience a diminution in their sense of self.
>
> M. Scott Peck, MD
> *The Road Less Traveled*

"Mecca" is a city of joy. It's a place of spiritual fulfillment, with "spiritual" covering a wide range of meanings far beyond the narrow confines of a single brand of religion. It is not a "gated community" like Fat City, for in "Mecca" people may see *no* gates or, if they do, see them as beyond-life and, perhaps, pearly.

Like the other cities on the roadway, "Mecca" also is a capital city. Hades Gulch is the capital of the State of Despair, Purgatoria is the capital of the State of Anxiety, Malaisia is the capital of the State of Mediocrity and Fat City is the capital of the State of Affluence.

"Mecca" is the capital of the State of Grace.

To be in the State of Grace is to be in a state of joyful living, and to be in a state of joyful living is to be in a state of living beyond yourself. Citizenship in the city of "Mecca" cannot be bought, nor can it be earned. *Anyone* can live there, for citizenship is a gift *extended* to everyone but *accepted* by few.

Wherever you are now, you are there because you have granted yourself permission to be. If you are in a place of unhappiness, it is by your own choice. No one, no circumstance can make you unhappy without your permission.

Grace is a gift offered to the undeserving. It cannot be earned, only accepted. It is no more an entitlement than is happiness.

The gift of grace granting citizenship in the city of "Mecca" is a divine gift. If the God of your understanding is a loving God, the divine gift of grace is *unearned* and, most likely, *unmerited.* It is a gift offered to everyone, no strings attached.

Some accept this gift in part. Few accept it in its entirety, for it requires a selfless spirit and unravels the web of conventional wisdom.

Take excellence, for instance. The frenzy for excellence, spawned by a deluge of excellence books and other forms of unending exhortations, has created new heights of intolerance and fear throughout much of Corporate America.

There's no margin of error among the most avid disciples of excellence, and many a career has been ruined over interpretations of what constitutes excellence and what level of deviations should be professionally fatal. The same is true of excessive lust for winning.

> Americans love a winner and will not tolerate a loser.
>
> General George S. Patton Jr.

Excellence and winning are essential qualities in successful people. What distinguishes the Fat Citian from the citizen of "Mecca" is intolerance and an unforgiving spirit.

Intolerant and unforgiving people cannot live in the State of Grace, for they lack not only the ability to extend gifts of grace to others, but they lack the ability to forgive themselves for their shortcomings. Thus, they deny themselves the ability to accept a divine *gift* of grace.

Does this mean the people in "Mecca" are weak and unsuccessful? Not at all! Unlike the whiners often found in other places along the roadway, citizens of "Mecca" are able to deal with problems — their own and those of others — without having to "leave town."

> Actually, I'm grateful for all my problems. As each of them was overcome I became stronger and more able to meet those yet to come. I grew on my difficulties.
>
> J.C. Penney at age 95

An occasional stressful situation to one side, people who live under continual stress are not — and cannot be — residents of "Mecca." Tragically, more than half of all Americans suffer from hypertension by the time they reach their 50s.

If you are a citizen of "Mecca," you do not live a stressful life. You have a deep and abiding faith that helps you overcome the fears that cause stress. Your faith enables you to accept life's lack of guarantees and overcome life's problems with a spirit both good *and* strong.

In "Mecca," you are happy to live in a single neighborhood that extends beyond the city limits and embraces the entire State of Grace. There are no wealthy sections of town, nor any tracks where you may live on "the other side."

Your neighbors are *all* rich, in spirit if not in the material blessings of life; and, living where "status" is of no importance, you accept people for themselves rather than for what they represent.

Fat City is a city of *happiness,* but "Mecca" is a city of *joy.* There is a more-than-subtle difference between happiness and joy.

Happiness is a state of good fortune and contentment most-often stimulated by favorable circumstances or by other people. Some people are happier than others because they have created for themselves a greater *capacity* for happiness and because favorable circumstances bring out in them a greater sense of well-being.

Joy is a different matter, for it depends much less on *other* people and on circumstances. Joy wells up *within* people who radiate a zest for living and harbor a compulsion to share their joy with others, *no matter what.* Joyful people are unsinkable.

People living in the State of Grace — in "Mecca" — are joyful people. Their happiness is inward, deeply rooted and *contagious.* Look around you. Do you *know* such people? If so, get closer to them. If not, seek them out. "Catch" some of that contagious joy!

Down the roadway in Fat City, there are people who are, at various times, happy, contented and satisfied. But unlike the "Mecca" people, Fat Citians depend mainly on external factors, putting fulfillment at risk if the stimuli disappear and, often, replacing fulfillment with boredom if the same old stimuli *don't* disappear.

Here are a few ways to distinguish between people living in Fat City and in "Mecca."

In Fat City, people mostly...	In "Mecca," people mostly...
Focus on themselves	Focus on others
Show pride in their success	Are humble about success
Love things, use people	Love people, use things
Lead with authority	Lead by example
Give to get recognition	Give for the sheer joy of it
Are conscious of status	Are statured in conscience
Put trust in facts	Put trust in faith
Seek good connections	Seek good relationships
Have high self-image	Have high self-esteem
Take time out to relax	Take time out to live
See death after life	See life after death

"Mecca" as a destination is not a final resting place but is the ultimate base camp from which to pursue a joyful, enriching and totally fulfilling continuation of life's journey, richly blessed with a sense of ongoing renewal.

> We cannot dream of a Utopia in which all arrangements are ideal and everyone is flawless. That is a dream of death. Life is tumultuous—an endless losing and regaining of balance, a continuous struggle, never an assured victory.
>
> John W. Gardner

And now it's time to develop *your own answer* to the First Crucial Question: "Where are you now and where do you want to be?" Develop your answer in the context of *life overall,* not just a part of life that may be the burden or blessing of the moment. Consider *all aspects* of your life.

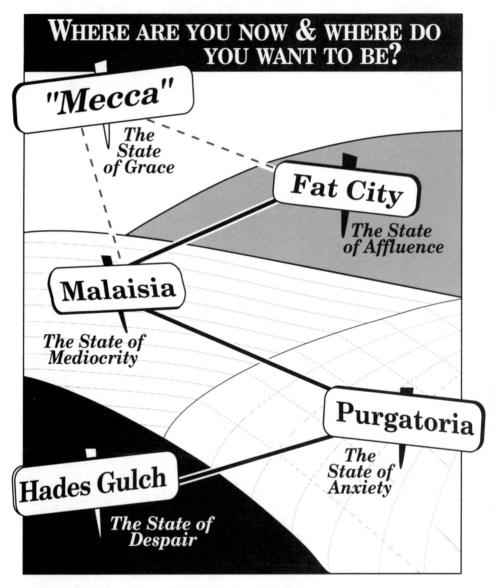

Activity: Draw a large dot in one of the cities, or along the roadway between cities, to describe "where you are now" *in life over-all.* Then draw a star in the place that identifies "where you want to be."

Activity: Now look back on your life, identifying the cities in which you "lived." This will help you reach your star, especially if there's a wide gap between your dot and your star. Put a check mark in the spaces that apply.

This is Where I've 'Lived' During My Lifetime

I've Lived In:	Much of the Time	Some of the Time	None of the Time
"Mecca"	_____	_____	_____
Fat City	_____	_____	_____
Malaisia	_____	_____	_____
Purgatoria	_____	_____	_____
Hades Gulch	_____	_____	_____

Activity: Finally, reflect on your dot and your star by listing, in priority order, three to five responses to two questions:

Why Did You Place the Dot Where You Did?

1. _____
2. _____
3. _____
4. _____
5. _____

What Would It Take to Reach Your Star?

1. _____
2. _____
3. _____
4. _____
5. _____

In seminars using the *Meccanize!*® process, feedback from participants shows an almost universal gap between where people are and where they want to be.

A session for senior-level managers attending a conference in Washington, D.C., for example, showed nearly 20 percent of the participants to be in Hades Gulch and none in "Mecca." As to where they *wanted* to be, all but one — a committed Fat Citian — put their stars squarely in "Mecca."

Overall, roughly a third of the seminar participants providing feedback reported citizenship in Malaisia or some nearby spot in the State of Mediocrity. Fat City is home to about 12 percent, another 12 percent are in Hades Gulch and, but for a fraction of 1 percent in or near "Mecca," the rest are in Purgatoria.

As to where people say they want to be, *no one* said they preferred Malaisia or points further down the roadway. Preference for "Mecca" is overwhelming, with 99 percent saying that's where they want to be and 1 percent saying, in effect, "just give me plenty of money and life will be great."

So now *you* have answered the first and easiest of the Five Crucial Questions: "Where are you now and where do you want to be?"

Get ready to tackle what, for most people, is the hardest question of all:

Chapter 7

The Second Crucial Question:

Whom Do You Choose To Be for the Journey?

- You Are Who You Were Programmed to Be
- Your Habits Reflect Your Programming
- You Are What You Consider Most Important
- 5 Choices Define What *Will* Be Most Important

Just who *are* you, anyway?

To what extent, if at all, have you thought about that ponderous question? How important is it to come up with a good answer? Is it a navel-contemplation exercise? Or is it fundamental to success?

Look back at your major pursuits in life. Think about times you asked yourself one or both elements of the First Crucial Question: "Where am I now? Where do I want to be?"

Perhaps you viewed those elements more in terms of "whom" than of "where." Maybe you put a career twist on your answers: "I'm an assistant now and I want to be a department head." Or maybe your state of mind was reflected in your answers: "I am an unhappy person now and I want to find joy in life."

Like many, you may have answered in monetary terms: "I'm flat broke now and I want to be financially free." Or maybe the First Crucial Question took the form of a relationship: "I'm single now and I want to be happily married."

If you were true to human nature, each time you answered the *first* question, you skipped on to the *third*. If so, you were saying: "Okay, I've decided where I am now and where I want to be. Now it's just a matter of figuring out how I'm going to get there."

Skipping the Second Crucial Question adds an unneeded burden to your journey through life. Not only does it make fulfillment of the how-do-I-get-there question more difficult, but it can reduce substantially the odds of success.

It's like planning a climbing expedition to the top of a very high and treacherous mountain, clearly identifying the starting point and the pinnacle to be reached — but with no consideration given to your ability to climb, the equipment and supplies that will be needed, or even the extent of your *commitment* to mountain-climbing.

Without redefining yourself as a mountain climber and doing what it takes to be a good one, the odds of success are zero to none.

Whom do you choose to be for the journey? That second question could well be the hardest of the five because it brings you face to face with the person you may find to be the most complex and puzzling of all — yourself. *Who are you?*

You Are Who You Were Programmed to Be

That may sound robotic, but it's true.

Some of your programming is genetic. You are born with certain physical features and attributes. The owner of the first nose pressed against the maternity ward window sets in motion a decades-long debate of whether you look more like your father or your mother.

Those who believe in the "good seed/bad seed" theory would add that much of your future personality and behavior is genetically determined as well.

Your programming is the sum of the familial, social, cultural and physical conditions in which you have made your journey through life from infancy up to this moment. By age 10, most of your *basic* values are programmed, including an underlying work ethic (or lack thereof), concepts of right and wrong, and sense of order.

If you grew up in a positive household surrounded by positive people, your programming will be largely positive. If your upbringing was in a negative environment, your programming most likely will be largely negative.

If you are the child of successful, *positive* people who helped program you to be successful, your odds for success are greater than if you grew up in a home full of *negative,* naysaying losers.

The worst of behavior, as well as the best, can be attributed to childhood programming. Most spouse abusers, for example, grew up in households where there was spouse abuse.

> It has often been reported that when abused children grow up, they become troubled adults, likely to pass the suffering on to their own children. This is another of America's secrets, perhaps our saddest.
>
> James Patterson & Peter Kim
> *The Day America Told the Truth*

Even if you were resilient, strong-willed and rebellious as a child, vowing to be the exact opposite of the people who raised you, chances are you internalized enough programming from your upbringing that, eventually, you'll reflect at least some of the negative values and behaviors.

Over the years, your programming undergoes much buffeting and changing, however. Significant emotional events can cause you to change your programming a little or a lot.

For example, if you grew up scoffing at danger, constantly taking risks and throwing caution to the winds, the sudden death of a close friend in a car crash could change your programming from reckless to cautious overnight — at least for a time.

Many a soldier with life-long programming as an atheist or agnostic has emerged from combat as a believer. And many a child of affluence has undergone substantial programming changes with the loss of the family fortune.

Your programming has much to do with every part of life's journey that takes you from where you are now to where you want to be. Your programming also will determine whether and how you reach your destination. The bad news is that success on the journey may be no greater than the quality of your programming. The good news is that you can *change* your programming and choose to be whomever you *want* to be.

> Your past cannot be changed, but you can change
> tomorrow by your actions today.
>
> David McNally
> *Even Eagles Need a Push*

Your Habits Reflect Your Programming

What are your habits? What behaviors have become so ingrained that you give no thought to doing otherwise? Which are good habits and which are bad habits?

Smoking is a habit. So is exercising and eating healthy food. Watching depressing TV soap operas can be a habit. So can nourishing your brain with tapes and books on how to live a more fulfilling life.

Are you habitually late or habitually punctual? Do you habitually toss papers on piles, then spend hours trying to find them; or, do you habitually file papers in ways that you can retrieve them immediately?

Consider the things you did yesterday without thinking. Were you on your feet at the first sound of the alarm, or did you groan through three or four gropes for the snooze button?

If you're married, did you share a warm and genuine affirmation of love before leaving for work, or did you simply bound out the door, late as usual, expressing nothing?

Your work habits will determine your degree of success at your job or in running your own business.

Do you habitually finish projects on time or are you always having to explain why they're late? Do you habitually compliment or criticize the people with whom you work — or do you habitually say nothing?

Winning is a habit and so is losing. Winners habitually hone their programming in positive, goal-oriented ways. Losers habitually reinforce their negative programming.

Bad habits *resist* change for the better. Good habits *seek* change for the better.

> ...Many people settle for — and actually practice — their limitations. They practice them so constantly and for so long a time that the limitations become habits.
>
> Norman Vincent Peale
> *How to Handle Tough Times*

Your programming influences the nature and the tenure of your habits. Your habits point toward a third element, the one that helps you answer the Second Crucial Question:

You Are What You Consider Most Important

What helps you decide to change some, much, or any of your programming? What compels you to break some habits and develop others?

Those decisions, consciously or otherwise, are driven by what you consider most important in life.

So, what in life is most important to you? What sits on top of all that programming and habitual behavior? What helps you decide whether and how to modify, discard or replace habits and programming?

You may have one pursuit in life that is so important that little else matters to you. Or you may have one or more relationships that you seek to balance with a particular pursuit. Or, like many people, you may have a dozen or more things constantly fighting for attention, with "most important" changing from day to day.

> What you consider most important defines whom you've chosen to be for all or part of life's journey.

If you were to make a list of all the things that are important in your life, you'd find that every item on your list would fit into one of three categories:

• **Material Wealth:** Money, houses, cars, jewelry, investments, and other tangible possessions. Call this *Having*.

• **Work and Other Activities:** Careers, jobs, hobbies, avocations, and all the things that consume time in the pursuit of income or self-satisfaction. Call this *Doing*.

• **Relationships:** Love, rapport, positive or negative interaction, and all manner of communication with other people, with a higher power and even with yourself. This is the essence of *Being*.

Your list probably will have more than one item in each category. But you also are likely to have one category that becomes dominant. Not only will one become dominant because of the *number* of items listed, but because of the extent to which the items represent important *needs* in your life.

This process of *self-definition* is at the core of your answer to the Second Crucial Question: Whom do you choose to be for the journey?

Perhaps the way you define yourself as of *where you are now* in life is exactly right for getting to *where you want to be*. More likely, though, getting to where you want to be will require changes in how you define yourself, and without making these changes, you will either be unable to reach your destination or your journey will be unnecessarily difficult.

Taking inventory of what's important may not be easy. Like most people, you may not have thought much about it — unless some important aspect of your life is threatened. But even then, the focus most likely would be on *what is threatened* rather than on the full menu of what you consider important and how you define yourself.

Your programming has a lot to do with what you consider important in each of the three categories.

If you were raised in a family rich in spirit but poor in material things, you probably put less importance on *Material Wealth* than if your upbringing were the other way around — poor in spirit and rich in material things.

If you have been surrounded by work-oriented achievers most of your life, climbing a corporate ladder may be what's *most important*. Accordingly, *Work and Other Activities* may take on greater importance than *Material Wealth* or *Relationships*.

If your programming has helped you become a deeply spiritual person, *Relationships,* especially with God, may be of greater importance than *Material Wealth* or *Work and Other Activities.*

The first step in discovering how you define yourself as of now is to make a list of what is most important to you in each of the three categories. The second step is to distinguish between items that are *needs* in your life and items that are *wants.*

Figuring out what is a need and what is a want may not be easy. Your programming largely will be responsible for how you perceive needs and wants, but your perceptions should fall somewhere between necessities for physical survival and a comedian's classic laugh-line:

> A need is any luxury your neighbor has that you
> don't have.

Here are definitions to distinguish between needs and wants:

• **Need:** Something of importance in your life that, if suddenly lost, would result in a major reduction in your overall happiness and sense of well-being.

• **Want:** Something of importance in your life that, if suddenly lost, while disappointing, would *not* result in a reduction in your overall happiness or sense of well-being.

The third step in determining how you define yourself now is deciding what is secure and what is at risk.

You brought *nothing* into the world and you will take nothing out. In that sense, nothing is secure. Like everyone, you have no guarantee that your life is totally secure from one day to the next.

So, you'll need two more definitions to understand what is meant by the terms in this context:

• **Secure:** Something that you are not concerned about losing because there are no significant threats to it.

• **At Risk:** Something that may be lost as the result of significant threats you have identified.

While few jobs are secure nowadays, consider yours secure if you *see* no significant threats to it. If your house is on your list, consider it at risk if you are behind in your payments, it sits in the path of a future highway, etc.

Now it's time to take inventory of what, as of now, is most important in your life.

Activity: On separate sheets of paper, list what is of greatest importance in your life as of now. Assign each item to one of the categories. Decide which are Needs and which are Wants. Write them below in priority order by category, being sure to list Needs ahead of Wants. Circle the **N** to identify Needs and the **W** to identify Wants. Then circle the **S** if the item is Secure and the **R** if it is At Risk.

What Has Been of Greatest Importance Up to Now

Needs vs. Wants			Secure vs. At Risk

Material Wealth (Having)

N	W	1. _____	S	R
N	W	2. _____	S	R
N	W	3. _____	S	R
N	W	4. _____	S	R
N	W	5. _____	S	R

Work / Activities (Doing)

N	W	1. _____	S	R
N	W	2. _____	S	R
N	W	3. _____	S	R
N	W	4. _____	S	R
N	W	5. _____	S	R

Relationships (Being)

N	W	1. _____	S	R
N	W	2. _____	S	R
N	W	3. _____	S	R
N	W	4. _____	S	R
N	W	5. _____	S	R

Activity: Now that you have prioritized your needs and wants in the three categories, determine which is of greatest importance in your life as of now — Material Wealth (Having), Work and Other Activities (Doing), or Relationships (Being). Assign percentages to each of the three (be sure they add up to 100). Then draw a pie chart in proportion to the percentages, labeling the slices *Having, Doing* and *Being.*

But first, use notepaper to "practice" on famous characters and others you know of:

> What would a pie chart on Ebeneezer Scrooge look like *before* he was visited by the ghosts of Christmas? As a well-known miser, how big would his Having slice be? He spent all his time *working* to accumulate wealth but took more pleasure in Having, so how big a slice would you assign to Doing? Is there *any* slice of Being?
>
> Try a pie chart on Albert Einstein whose life was his work and who cared little about Material Wealth.
>
> How about Mother Teresa, whose legendary Relation- ships with God and the needy drove her life's work?
>
> Draw charts for one or two others you know of, then do your chart below *as you have lived your life up to now.*

THIS PIE IS "I" NOW

MATERIAL WEALTH

_____%

WORK / ACTIVITIES

_____%

RELATIONSHIPS

_____%

You have defined yourself according to the importance you place as of now, on three slices of life — Material Wealth (Having), Work and Other Activities (Doing), and Relationships (Being).

To develop the *best* answer to the Second Crucial Question — Whom do you choose to be for the journey? — it's necessary to determine how you *should* define yourself in the future.

If your pie chart consists of an enormous slice of *Having* with lesser slices of Doing and Being, how successful will you be in moving from where you are now to where you want to be in the context explored in Part 1 — especially in light of the 10 trends?

For example, if Material Wealth is the most important slice of your life now, can you move up the road from Purgatoria to "Mecca" in times when, on average, there may be less wealth to be had?

Or what if the largest slice of your life up to now is in Doing? If you are defining yourself mainly by how far you climb the corporate ladder, could you reach your destination in life (Fat City? "Mecca"?) when the buildings supporting such ladders are collapsing, rungs are being chopped from the ladders and more people are scrambling for the fewer rungs that are left?

Or how about if you are in the rut called Malaisia, want to move up to "Mecca," and your pie chart is one big slice of Being? Will you *ever* reach your destination without increasing your slices of Doing and Having — at least a little? For example, will continuing to "*sacrifice everything* for our children, who often seem so ungrateful," *ever* allow you to climb out of your rut?

If, in answering the First Crucial Question, you are not *already* where you want to be, the pie chart you've drawn needs to be changed. To some extent, you will have to *redefine* yourself if you are to reach your destination.

Old Scrooge himself went through *big-time* redefinition after the ghosts created the sort of *significant emotional event* that enables people to transform themselves.

> He became a good friend, as good a master and as good a man as the good old city knew, or any other good old city, town, or borough, in the good old world.
>
> Charles Dickens
> *A Christmas Carol*

Scrooge probably lived most of his life as a Human-Having in Hades Gulch, trying to work his way to Fat City but destined never to get there, because (1) there never could be enough money in his counting house and (2) he never figured out how to get true *enjoyment* out of his wealth.

Scrooge's pie chart changed drastically on Christmas morning. The consummate Human-*Having* became a joyful Human-*Being*. And when the pie chart changed, so did the destination for his journey through life. He found an undreamed of place called "Mecca."

Is the pie chart showing how you define yourself now what it *should* be to get from where you are now to where you want to be? *Meccanize!*® includes a five-step process to help you redefine yourself.

Before starting that process, though, consider these points:

• A single dominant slice that all but squeezes out the other two will not enable you to reach either "Mecca" or Fat City.

Too much of anything is not good for you.

A person whose self-definition is 98 percent Having lacks the sort of emphasis on Relationships and Work or Other Activities that will make living in Fat City out of the question. Fat Citians need to be *doing* things to attain their conventional happiness. They also need *Relationships,* superficial though they may be, to satisfy their egos.

• Trying to balance the three slices equally won't get you there, either — unless your destination is Malaisia. To balance the three slices equally is to live a life of mediocrity.

If you do everything equally, you will do nothing well.

• There's no way to reach "Mecca" without a large slice of Being. Think about it: "Mecca" is joy of living. How many joyful people do you know who lack strong and abiding Relationships, especially their most personal ones? Probably none.

True joy is being married to your best friend.

"Mecca" is a *spiritual* fulfillment on life's journey. How many spiritually fulfilled people do you know who lack a strong connection to a higher power? Probably none.

Two cities have been formed by two loves: The earthly by love of self, even to the contempt of God; the heavenly by the love of God, even to the contempt of self.

Augustine
The City of God

"Mecca" is self-actualization. How many people do you know who truly are being all they can be in life who *haven't* built a win-win team of people with whom they can excel? Probably none.

Hitch one Belgian horse to a load and it can pull 8,000 pounds. Add a second Belgian horse and, together, they can pull 18,000 pounds. Train them to work well together and, between them, they can pull 25,000 pounds.

Here, then, are five sets of *choices* to help you decide how you *should* answer the Second Crucial Question: Whom do You Choose to Be for the Journey?

1. Do You Choose to Be a Victor or a Victim?

Much was said about "victimhood" in Part 1. We have, indeed, become a nation of victims, blaming others or circumstances for our own shortcomings and lack of success.

If you're like most people, you probably at least have *felt* like a victim at one time or another. And, like most, you no doubt have pointed a finger at other people when your own efforts fell short of the mark.

When you point a finger at someone else, three other fingers point back at you.

People who regard themselves as victims rather than victors are more likely to live in Malaisia or Hades Gulch than in Fat City or "Mecca." Victims also are more likely than victors to focus on Having rather than Doing or Being — even if Having is related more to food stamps and rent subsidies than country club dinner parties and luxury beach condos.

Broke people tend to be much more money-oriented and, in that sense, materialistic than rich people.

Money is a terrible master but an excellent servant.

P.T. Barnum

Whom have you chosen to *be* up to now? Mostly a victor or mostly a victim?

Activity: On the next page are five pairs of statements with rows of numbers in between. Read each pair carefully, then circle a number. If you believe the statement above the numbers fits you *completely,* circle the "5" or if it comes pretty close circle the "4." Similarly, if the statement below fits you *completely,* circle the "1" or if it comes pretty close circle the "2." Circle the "3" if both statements apply equally.

I have the power to shape my life and I take *full* responsibility for where I am in life today.

5   4   3   2   1

I'm at the mercy of forces beyond my control and feel powerless to change the circumstances of my life.

I readily accept responsibility when I am wrong and work hard at learning from my mistakes.

5   4   3   2   1

I'd rather avoid responsibility for mistakes; I'm good at coming up with ways to show they weren't mistakes at all.

I find joy in the success of those around me, even those who may not have my capabilities or work as hard as I do.

5   4   3   2   1

Others succeed by luck or "pull"; I resent people getting ahead of me, especially when they lack my qualifications.

No matter how bad things get, I know I have the power to endure and, eventually, to produce positive outcomes in life.

5   4   3   2   1

There's no use in beating my head against the wall; quite often, it's better just to give up and settle for what I've got.

My success is the result of help I have received from other people and/or from a power greater than myself.

5   4   3   2   1

I get things done in spite of other people; when I succeed, I deserve full credit for my success.

Add up the numbers you circled. If the total is 22 to 25, you're programmed as a Victor — congratulations! If the total is 18-21, you're *mostly* programmed as a Victor but should work on the areas you scored "4" or less. If your score was 13-17, you're too much of a Victim and have a lot of work to do. Pursue self-help books, tapes or programs and consider professional counseling. If you scored 12 or below, you are programmed as a Victim and need more help than you can get from books, tapes and seminars. Seek professional counseling!

Even when they use their victimhood to gain victories, victims ultimately fail. Their negative thinking undermines even the greatest of victories.

Examples abound of down-and-out people wrapped in their own victimhood who won huge gambling jackpots. It didn't take long for many of them to squander the money and return to what, for them, is normal — victimhood.

> In America, many victims of the system are actually volunteers who are cooperating in their own failure.
>
> Dr. Denis Waitley
> *Seeds of Greatness*

Examples also abound on the other side of the equation. There are countless people who, even in the worst of circumstances, *refused* to consider themselves as victims. They were determined to be victors and, backing belief with hard work, went on to achieve great things.

Victors are overcomers. A study of 300 world class leaders showed 75 percent had a physical disability, were abused as children, or grew up in poverty.

Consider Abraham Lincoln. He *failed at everything,* from school to storekeeper to his first four runs at political office — then went on to be what many consider America's greatest president.

If you have a streak of victimhood or are a total victim, you can *choose* to be a victor. But it will depend upon how you handle the second set of choices:

2. How Do You Choose to Think?

You *are* what you have chosen to *think* up to now and you *will be* what you choose to *think* in the future. To change your *life* for the better, change your *thinking* for the better.

Your thinking will determine your success or failure, underscored by the simple-yet-profound observation that people who succeed almost always *think* they will succeed, and those who don't succeed really, deep down, almost always *don't* think they will succeed.

How you think and *what* you think determine your level of happiness as well. If your destination for life's journey is Fat City, it is your thinking that will activate the conventional happiness that goes with the territory. And if your destination is "Mecca," your thinking will determine whether you can turn conventional happiness into *sheer joy.*

To be joyful, you first must be happy, recalling that joy is innate — within you and self-generating — and happiness is circumstantial, often depending on what other people do with you or for you.

Your mind is the processor of perceptions — the thinking machine — that places you along the roadway from Hades Gulch to Fat City or "Mecca."

> The mind is in its own place and in itself can make a heaven of hell or a hell of heaven.
>
> John Milton
> *Paradise Lost*

If you aren't already convinced that *Choosing How to Think* is the key to reaching your destination for life's journey, consider three blockbuster quotations from three very diverse sources. When considered together, these quotations make it obvious that you *can* choose how to think and the choices you make are directly related to where you are on the roadway.

The first quotation is from Joseph V. Bailey, president of the Minneapolis Institute of Mental Health. Bailey and his staff train substance-abuse counselors. In his book *The Serenity Principle,* Bailey lays the foundation:

1. **Thought creates our psychological experience and thinking is a voluntary function.**

You can choose to think or not to think. For better or worse, you can plunge deep into thought. At the other extreme, you also can choose to "vedge out" or, in the vernacular of the 1990s, "collapse in front of the boob tube and *rot.*"

As underscored in Part 1, television is the primary tool with which people *avoid* the need to think. There are other tools as well, such as Rap and other forms of "music" usually played at an ear-numbing volume that makes thinking, let alone meaningful conversation, impossible.

So if you *volunteer* to think, you're ready to consider the second of the three blockbuster quotes. It drives home the potential *consequences* of what you think and how you think.

The point has been made in the teachings of many religions and philosophies, but this version says it succinctly and well. It comes from ancient Buddhist scripture, as written in the Dhammapada:

2.   We become what we think... Suffering follows an evil thought.

By engaging in that voluntary function called thinking, you have determined who you are and, by continuing to *volunteer,* you are determining who you will become. If your thinking is evil or, in the modern context, "negative," you bring upon yourself some degree of suffering.

People are negative because, after volunteering to think, they think negative thoughts. Negative thinking brings unhappiness.

Cynical commentators in the news media excepted, negative thinkers rarely succeed in their career pursuits any more than they succeed in finding a joy of living. You'll find negative thinkers stuck in the rut of Malaisia, struggling with little result in Purgatoria, and sunk in the mental mire of Hades Gulch.

Positive people are the ones who *will* find happiness and even joy in life because, when they volunteer to think, they find ways to think positive thoughts. If they're living in Purgatoria, struggling to better themselves, it won't be for long. And when they do move up the roadway, they are unlikely to get bogged down in the mediocrity of Malaisia.

If you *still* haven't fully grasped the importance of continually volunteering to think positive thoughts, the third of these blockbuster quotes should bring a blinding flash of discovery.

It was a revelation that launched a movement called "Psychology of Mind," an approach to improving the human condition that is favored by a growing number of psychologists. It was a revelation that, shared by a friend, changed the life of Sydney Banks, a Canadian welder with no background in psychology, who founded the movement more than two decades ago:

3.   You're *not* unhappy. You just *think* you are.

Wow! It's so obvious and so true and so many people are so totally *oblivious* to it!

Unhappiness is unnecessary. It results from negative or "evil" thoughts that you voluntarily chose to let enter your mind. There is no reason on earth why you should *ever* be unhappy.

Like everyone else, you will have moments or even prolonged periods of sadness in your life, such as the loss of a loved one. But *unhappiness?* Why?

Unhappiness is strictly the result of your own thinking — *stinking* thinking, to be sure. You *become* what you think, and what you think dictates your attitudes and your actions. To be unaware of that simple truth is to be on an emotional treadmill.

> When we are unaware that our thoughts create reality, we become victims of our belief system and can only respond through our habits. This is a concept of sincere delusion.
>
> Joseph V. Bailey
> *The Serenity Principle*

Plus, *your* attitudes and actions can have a big impact on what *other* people think and *their* attitudes and actions toward you — just as you allow the attitudes and actions of other people to influence how and what you think. It's a cycle that, too often, is needlessly vicious.

If you think you're unhappy *because* of your marriage, you can choose to be happy in spite of your marriage. Your new-found happiness may even have a positive impact on your marriage partner and — who knows? — could even remove the conditions that you blamed for your unhappiness.

The same can be true of your job or even of a life-threatening illness, as demonstrated by the "terminally ill" person who literally *laughed* his way back to health.

> A merry heart doeth good like a medicine.
>
> Solomon
> *Proverbs 17:22*

Happy people tend to be incurable optimists. Unhappy people have chosen a pathway of pessimism, even cynicism.

You choose to think or not to think. You choose how to think and *what* to think. You *become* what you think. If you're unhappy, it's because you've *chosen* to think you're unhappy.

The most famous adjective associated with Thinking is the word "Positive." In his landmark book, *The Power of Positive Thinking,* Dr. Norman Vincent Peale offers techniques that, if accepted, would elevate even the most negative of thinkers from victim to victor.

These techniques include ways to believe in yourself, develop peace of mind, create your own happiness, generate an inflow of new thoughts and harness the power of prayer. To choose *positive* thinking is to choose what Dr. Peale calls "a victorious life."

Another adjective associated with Thinking is the word "Effective." Dr. Gerald Kushel, president of the Institute for Effective Thinking, offers three elements of "Uncommon Success."

> "Uncommon Success" means simultaneous success in three significant dimensions: (1) Successful performance on the job, (2) High level of personal satisfaction at work, (3) Success in personal and family life.
>
> Dr. Gerald Kushel
> *Effective Thinking for Uncommon Success*

Dr. Kushel says it's not unusual to find people who are successful in one or even two of the dimensions, but it is rare to find people who are successful in all three. In his research of 1,200 people regarded as successful in what they do, only *four percent* said they also were *happy* in what they do as well as being happy in their personal lives. That's only *48 of the 1,200!*

He identified four steps to an effective thinking process. The steps enable you to *Take Notice* when you're not moving toward uncommon success, *Pause* to reconsider your thoughts, *Identify* right thoughts to replace wrong ones and *Choose* to make the switch.

And here's a third adjective — *Possibility* Thinking, a philosophy developed by Dr. Robert Schuller. It offers a step-by-step process through which, with God's help, you can uplift yourself from failure to success, given that *anything* is possible.

> If you can dream it, you can do it.
>
> Dr. Robert H. Schuller
> *Success Is Never Ending, Failure Is Never Final*

To achieve a victorious life is to think *positively*. To achieve uncommon success is to think *effectively*. To reach "Mecca" also requires that you think of the great *possibilities* for your life, then give it your best day-to-day effort to be *productive* in your thinking.

Here are Five Principles of Productive Thinking to help you with the Second Set of Choices — Choosing How to Think:

1. **Be wary of your perceptions.**

Perceptions do not always equal reality. Sometimes they don't even come close.

Consider the viewpoints of people you respect when formulating your own perceptions. Face up to important realities, but use them as starting points for further progress — not barriers to future success. People insensitive to how they develop their perceptions tend to *react* rather than act thoughtfully and productively.

2. **Let your heart have faith, let your head have facts.**

Find a balance that works well for you and those around you. Blind facts are no better than blind faith when it comes to matters of this world. Learn when to be productively skeptical. But also learn *never* to be cynical.

3. **Control fear, anger and greed.**

None of them adds an ounce of self-fulfillment to life. To live in fear is to accept early death. To live in anger is to accept self-destruction. To live a life of greed is to deny yourself *any* hope for a joyful life in "Mecca."

4. **Love contentment but don't let it end your journey.**

To be *totally* content about everything *all* of the time is to live a life of mediocrity in Malaisia. True *joy* in life comes from a productive blend of contentment and *dis*-contentment, especially when the latter focuses on ways to help others find success and happiness .

5. **Let your productive thinking show!**

To others, you are what you *appear* to be. Make every day a great day for other people as well as yourself. Smile more. Laugh more. It's contagious. And it generates a cycle of thinking that becomes evermore productive.

These five principles should be of great help to you in choosing how to think, especially when blended with the principles of Positive Thinking and Effective Thinking.

Here is one other consideration before moving on to the third of the five sets of choices. Know where your thoughts, positive or negative, will lead you. The pattern is this:

> Your thoughts determine your attitudes
> Your attitudes determine your actions and deeds
> Your actions and deeds determine your habits
> Your habits determine your level of success in life

3. How Will You Sort Out Aspirations, Expectations and Entitlements?

You will become what you aspire to be if you expect it of yourself and do whatever work is necessary. To feel *entitled* to fulfillment of your Aspirations is to consign yourself to a life of unhappiness and frustration. People who see themselves as victims demand Entitlements as offsets to failure. People who see themselves as victors develop strong Aspirations as onsets to success.

To aspirate is to breathe. An aspiration is a breath of life and a *desire* for something better so strong that it breathes life into your efforts to achieve.

Big, positive aspirations not only are healthy, but are essential to a successful life's journey. These are the *dreams* which give a *reason* to reach for something better in life and the *hope* of getting it.

As underscored in Part 1, many in the 1990s have given up hope of achieving *The American Dream.* If you're one of them — if you have given up hope — consider this:

Your greatest barrier to fulfilling big, positive aspirations is *not* the economy or the glut of college graduates or the re-engineering of American corporations or any other external factor. It's how little you expect of yourself compared to how much you expect of other people.

Aspirations are realized through what you expect and *demand* of yourself. Aspirations are *killed* by what you expect other people to do for you.

Americans have institutionalized what they expect of other people. Such expectations have created a federal government that is much too big and a success rate in the institution of marriage that is much too small.

Reduced to a simple diagram, here's the problem:

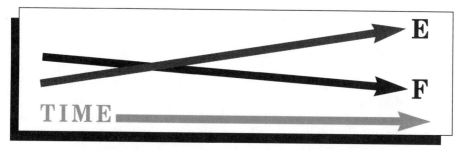

Over Time (T), people have come to Expect (E) far more of the institutions of society than the institutions are able to Fulfill (F).

The gap between Fulfillment and Expectations not only creates political turmoil but undermines the bedrock of American power — self-reliance and personal involvement in the care of others.

Think about it. Where do you or people you know turn when things go wrong? Too often, people turn toward the *wrong source:*

> When the going gets tough, the tough get going — on a campaign to demand that the government do something about it.

Where *should* you turn? When the performance bar of success is raised, should you aspire to get over the bar anyway by expecting *more* of yourself? Should you down-size your Aspirations so you *don't have to* expect more of yourself? Should you demand the government or other institutions lower the bar so it's easier to get over?

What *are* you *entitled* to, anyway? A good job? Free health care? Wealth without work? Or maybe it boils down to basic entitlements of the U.S. Constitution — Life, Liberty and the *Pursuit* of Happiness.

> Too many Americans have twisted the sensible right to *pursue* happiness into the delusion that we are entitled to a *guarantee* of happiness. If we don't get exactly what we want, we assume someone must be violating our rights.
>
> Susan Jacoby
> *Woman's Day*

To close the gap between what is expected of institutions and the ability of institutions to provide Fulfillment requires two steps:

1. *Work* harder and smarter at raising your Fulfillment level
2. *Expect* less of institutions and more of yourself.

Nowhere is this better illustrated than in what *should* be the most fulfilling of institutions, the institution of marriage.

What would the divorce rate in America be, and how many children would have to grow up in a hodgepodge of "exes", steps and halfs, if *both* partners worked harder and smarter on the marital relationship? What if both expected less *for* themselves from the *institution* of marriage and more *of* themselves as *partners* individually responsible for the marriage's success?

How many careers would be kept on track and how many small businesses would be saved with more emphasis on making things work and less on expecting other people to take responsibility?

When someone asked Jesus Christ whether to obey when ordered by Roman soliders to carry equipment one mile, the answer was as unpopular then as it is now. "No, you don't have to carry it *one* mile," Jesus said. "Carry it *two*."

But imagine what would happen if *everyone* went a second mile — as spouses, parents, employees, students, etc. The divorce rate won't drop to zero, productivity would go through the roof and alcohol abuse, drugs and crime would disappear, to mention a few.

If you expect too much of institutions and other people, you are unlikely to fulfill big, positive Aspirations.

> Blessed are they who expect nothing, for they are never disappointed.
>
> Alexander Pope

The *only* way to fulfill big, positive aspirations is to expect more of yourself. Where your own personal success is concerned, which of the following statements makes the most sense to you?

> If it's to be, it's up to a stronger economy.
> If it's to be, it's up to my staff.
> If it's to be, it's up to the Federal Government.
> If it's to be, it's up to my spouse.
> If it's to be, it's up to Lady Luck
> If it's to be, it's up to *me!*

Later on, in answering the Fourth Crucial Question (How Should You Chart Your Course?), you'll develop a vision for your future and set the goals necessary to achieve it.

For now, jot down what you consider to be big, positive Aspirations for your life. Include all major dimensions of your life, such as career or business pursuits, lifestyle, relationships with other people and spirituality. Draft them on scrap paper, then prioritize them here:

What You Aspire To

1. _____
2. _____
3. _____
4. _____
5. _____

What about expectations? What should you expect of yourself? Of others? Again, draft your list, then prioritize:

What You Expect of Yourself

1. _____
2. _____
3. _____
4. _____
5. _____

What You Expect of Other People & Institutions

1. _____
2. _____
3. _____
4. _____
5. _____

Review your lists.

Can you fulfill your Aspirations from what you expect of yourself and others? For example, do you aspire to be financially independent while expecting of yourself above-average performance in your present job? If your present job is your only significant source of income, and financial independence will require much more income, how will you fulfill your Aspirations through your present job?

Viewed from the other direction, to what extent are the Expectations of yourself up to the task of fulfilling your Aspirations? For example, if you aspire to be happily married (and to the same person forever), what Expectations of yourself assure you will do *more* than your share to make the relationship work well?

Are Expectations of yourself compatible with your Expectations of others? For example, do you expect of yourself great leadership qualities while expecting people you lead to do what they're told without question?

Finally, there's the risky business of Entitlements.

What You Feel Entitled To

1. _____
2. _____
3. _____
4. _____
5. _____

Think hard about what you have listed. Do you lean on Entitlements to fulfill your Aspirations? Entitlements should *never* be the determining factors in whether you succeed or fail on your journey through life.

Are there any "government entitlement programs" on your list? If so, are you undermining the fulfillment of your Aspirations? For example, does your Aspiration for a happy retirement depend *even a little bit* on Entitlement to monthly Social Security checks?

What *should* be on your list of Entitlements?

How about Entitlement to being treated with respect based on your treatment of others? How about being entitled to clean air and water based on your own willingness to be a responsible steward of the environment? How about being entitled to the responsibility for raising your children based on your performance as a responsible parent? How about being entitled to fair compensation for a good day's work?

In your journey through life, what is potentially productive and what is potentially unproductive in sorting out Aspirations, Expectations and Entitlements? Here are four considerations:

1. Big, positive Aspirations are healthy
2. All but the most basic Entitlements are unhealthy
3. High Expectations of yourself are healthy
4. Inordinate Expectations of others are unhealthy

So far, you've examined three sets of choices — whether to be a victim or victor, how to think and how to sort out Aspirations, Expectations and Entitlements. The fourth set of choices will determine the extent to which you will *ever* be able to fulfill your Aspirations:

4. Choosing How Far to Go

It's easy to have lofty aspirations and easy to do little or nothing with them. "Average" people have neither lofty aspirations nor the will to do whatever it takes to fulfill them. An extraordinary person not only has great aspirations but the will to *go all the way*.

When it comes to aspirations and the willingness to do whatever it takes, are you average? Above average? Extraordinary?

If you're average, studies show, you consider yourself *above average* in assessing your capabilities. But you also will be among the people who admit they are *not* performing to their full potential!

Remember those three important "W" words from Chapter 5: Want, Way, Work. If you Want more out of life, how badly do you want it? If you found a good Way to get it, are you willing to do the Work — no matter how hard it gets?

> I knew it wouldn't be easy to become a doctor, but it was something I wanted more than anything else in my life. I wanted to help people and I wanted the prestige and the income that comes with the profession. I also knew that the only way to become a doctor would be to graduate from medical school and that would take a lot of hard work. By the end of my second year in medical school, I was exhausted. Years of school, internship and residency still lay ahead. I've fallen in love with someone I have too little time to be with, and I've decided to quit medical school and settle for some other field where I can make use of what I've learned so far.

Do you want to be a winner — a *victor* in life? If so, never quit. Keep at it and at it and at it until you get what you Want.

That still leaves the question of changing aspirations — what you want to *win at*. When should you decide to try winning at something else? When is it okay to make a shift in your career pursuit or some other Aspiration in life? When is it *not* okay to give up trying? How far *should you go* in chasing your dream?

Only you can answer. But here are five guidelines to help:

1. Make sure what you Want out of life is carefully thought through and *written down*.

2. Understand that you may have to try more than one Way to get what you Want.

3. Set out to *succeed* at every Way you try.

4. Once you've chosen the *best* Way to get what you Want, be willing to do the Work by *learning to love it*.

5. If, after your *best effort* at doing the Work, you see no way you'll *ever* be able to learn to love it, try another Way or change what you Want.

When pursuing a Way to get what you Want, there are four conditions or "stages" of the effort:

ISAT. *I'll Succeed at This!* ISAT is the starting point. It's where the Work begins after the Want and the Way are chosen.

> If you're one of those people who would rather "go with the flow" than do whatever it takes to reach your destination, think of the fish. The successful ones overcome all obstacles to fulfill their destinies upstream. The only ones that "go with the flow" downstream are dead!

ITTA. *I Tried That Already.* How many times have you set out to succeed at something only to quit and try something else? By planning your Want and Way carefully, there should be few — *if any* — times when you give up on a major pursuit. The biggest reason many people quit is not to find a better Way but because they let other people talk them out of what they Want or the Way they chose to get it.

> The grass is always greener on the other side of the fence. That's because you're looking over the fence instead of handling all the crap it will take to make *your* grass greener than anyone else's!

IDTA. *I've Done That Already.* You reach this state when you let yourself believe nothing more can be accomplished, that you've achieved all the success you can achieve and, therefore, the best strategy is to quit and try something else. You're bored, telling yourself: "Been there, done that." While there are times it makes sense to declare IDTA, go back to ISAT and try something else, too often an IDTA decision is made on an excuse called burnout.

> There are two ways to change jobs — change employers or change yourself!

ILTE. *I Love This Experience!* What could be better to make sure the Way you chose will get you what you Want than learning to love the Work? Even in the *worst* of workplaces and private business situations, there are people who *love it* no matter how hard or how unpleasant the tasks and responsibilities.

> If work is what you're doing when you'd rather be doing something else, learn to love the work and watch how quickly "something else" begins to pale by comparison.

Here's a "road map" of the four conditions or stages of effort in pursuing a *Way* to get what you *Want*.

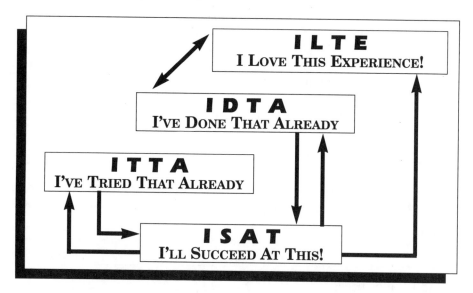

Starting at ISAT, you'll find the closest stage to be ITTA. If you find yourself going back and forth between ISAT and ITTA, you're not alone. Sadly, there are many people who, in the unfocused, instant-gratification, TV-oriented 1990s ride that shuttle often, never trying all that hard at anything and yet expecting success.

IDTA lies directly above ISAT. It is reached when you've gone as far as you can go in using a Way to get what you Want. You can keep plugging away at it until declaring burnout, or you can push on to ILTE — either confidant that what you love will eventually get you what you Want, or deciding to adjust what you Want to accommodate the Way you have come to love.

Loving the Experience is the highest level. If you love what you do, you will find ongoing excitement and are most likely to have found the Way to get what you Want.

Even so, there may come a time when the pursuit no longer is the Way to get what you Want. Then it's time to declare IDTA, go back to ISAT, and get going again.

In a state of ILTE, you may or may not achieve mastery of what you're doing. But by loving the experience, the *pursuit* of mastery should be ongoing and satisfying.

You may or may not have chosen to go *far enough* in what you've tried (ITTA), what you've done (IDTA), or what you learned to love (ILTE). Here's your chance to find out:

Activity: Take a hard look at the two most important things you tried to do but gave up on. Consider pursuits related to career, education, sports, hobbies, relationships, etc. Circle the number that indicates how hard you tried with "1" meaning you tried hardly at all and "5" meaning you went as far as *anyone* could have gone in trying to succeed at it. Describe why you quit. Then, if you circled a number less than "5," circle the word that indicates whether you could have succeeded if you had tried harder.

ITTA - I Tried That Already

1. What I tried:_____

_____

How far I went: (All the way!)   5   4   3   2   1   (Not very far)

Why I quit: _____

_____

Could I have succeeded?   Yes   No   Maybe

Am I glad I tried?   Yes   No   Maybe

2. What I tried:_____

_____

How far I went: (All the way!)   5   4   3   2   1   (Not very far)

Why I quit: _____

_____

Could I have succeeded?   Yes   No   Maybe

Am I glad I tried?   Yes   No   Maybe

Activity: Now take a hard look at the two most important pursuits in which you had much or at least some success, but you decided not to continue. How far did you *really* go in the pursuit? In considering why you decided not to continue, describe why in some detail? To what extent was it burnout? To what extent was it changed circumstances over which you had no control at all? If you could have controlled the circumstances, why didn't you?

IDTA - I've Done That Already

1. What I've done: _____

_____

How far I went: (All the way!)   5   4   3   2   1   (Not very far)

Why I quit: _____

_____

Could I have gone farther?   Yes   No   Maybe

Am I glad I did it?   Yes   No   Maybe

Did it lead to something better?   Yes   No   Maybe

2. What I've done: _____

_____

How far I went: (All the way!)   5   4   3   2   1   (Not very far)

Why I quit: _____

_____

Could I have gone farther?   Yes   No   Maybe

Am I glad I did it?   Yes   No   Maybe

Did it lead to something better?   Yes   No   Maybe

Activity: Finally, on the next page, look at two present pursuits in which you don't love the experience at all, or don't love it as much as you'd like to. Identify the payoffs for *learning* to love each pursuit. Identify the three most important circumstances it would take to love each pursuit, circling words to show whether the circumstances would be up to you or up to other people.

ILTE - I Love This Experience!

1. Pursuit: _____

_____

Payoff for learning to love it: _____

_____

What it would take for me to love it:		Which would be mainly up to:
• _____		Me Others
• _____		Me Others
• _____		Me Others

2. Pursuit: _____

_____

Payoff for learning to love it: _____

_____

What it would take for me to love it:		Which would be mainly up to:
• _____		Me Others
• _____		Me Others
• _____		Me Others

Review your self-examinations of what you've tried (ITTA), have done (IDTA) and could learn to love (ILTE). What can you discover about yourself? How *far* have you gone each time you set out to succeed at something (ISAT)? For the pursuits you've tried, how far *could* you have gone if you had tried harder and kept going?

Did you stop short of achieving your full potential? If so, why? How many times did you circle *Others* instead of *Me* in assessing what it would take to love a pursuit? Why? Could you take ownership of those items instead of ascribing them to others?

Now, you're ready to tackle the final set of choices.

5. *Choosing How to Define Yourself in the Future*

Before embarking on the Five Sets of Choices, you drew a pie chart showing how you define yourself as of this point in your life. You apportioned three slices in accordance with how much importance you put on Material Wealth *(Having* things), Work and Other Activities *(Doing* things) and Relationships (the essence of *Being* human).

Whom you choose to be for life's journey from this point on requires a new pie chart called *How I Will Define Myself in the Future.*

To draw that pie well requires careful reflection of what you have gained from this book so far, especially in three areas:

1. The nature of the times as presented in Part 1, especially how the *Continuous White Water* and *Ongoing Search for Stability* trends are likely to affect you.

2. Where you are now and where you want to be on the roadway connecting the Five Cities.

3. What you discovered about yourself in creating the first pie chart and the four Choices you've made so far.

But before putting pen to pie, *consider this:*

Activity: Here are three simplified maps of the Five Cities. Place a dot on each showing where you would be in life as of now when you consider *only* the slice of the pie noted at the top of each map.

WHERE I'D BE BASED SOLELY ON:

MATERIAL WEALTH	WORK / ACTIVITIES	RELATIONSHIPS
"Mecca"	"Mecca"	"Mecca"
FAT CITY	FAT CITY	FAT CITY
MALAISIA	MALAISIA	MALAISIA
PURGATORIA	PURGATORIA	PURGATORIA
HADES GULCH	HADES GULCH	HADES GULCH

Looked at in this way, what implications are there for your new pie chart? For example, if you are in Fat City where Material Wealth is concerned but Hades Gulch for Relationships, should you apportion less of a pie slice for Material Wealth and more for Relationships? If so, how much of a shift should you make?

No matter where you placed your three dots and what your original pie chart looks like, there are two traps to avoid when drawing your new pie chart:

Trap No. 1: Trying to *balance* the three slices. As emphasized earlier, to choose three *equal* slices is to choose a life of mediocrity. To make progress in any area, your slices will have to be at least somewhat *out of balance.*

Trap No. 2: Carving out a single slice so big that one or both of the other slices is crowded out or eliminated. All three slices must have importance if you are to reach "Mecca" or even Fat City.

To illustrate the two traps, consider that either extreme of all three slices can be destructive:

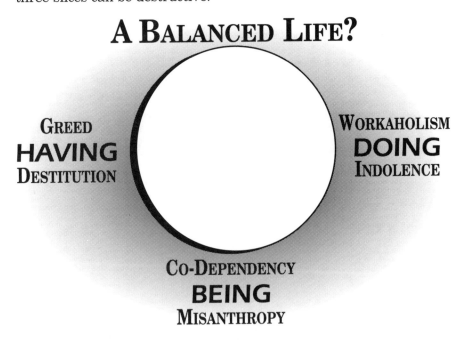

A BALANCED LIFE?

GREED
HAVING
DESTITUTION

WORKAHOLISM
DOING
INDOLENCE

CO-DEPENDENCY
BEING
MISANTHROPY

Finally, ask yourself: What does *success* really mean to me? What does *true happiness* really mean to me?

Ralph Waldo Emerson, the famous 19th century American essayist and poet, wrote what many consider to be the ultimate definition of success. You may agree with all of it, part of it, or none of it. How you relate to it, however, can make a big difference in how you draw your new pie chart.

Activity: Here is Emerson's definition broken into 10 parts and turned into an "Emerson Scale." Circle a number next to each part to indicate whether it fits you completely (5), doesn't fit you at all (1) or is somewhere in between (4, 3 or 2).

How I Stand on the 'Emerson Scale'

"To laugh often...	5	4	3	2	1
...and to have loved much...	5	4	3	2	1
...to win the respect of intelligent persons	5	4	3	2	1
...and the affection of children...	5	4	3	2	1
...to appreciate beauty...	5	4	3	2	1
...to find the best in others...	5	4	3	2	1
...to give of one's self...	5	4	3	2	1
...to leave the world a little better, whether by a healthy child, a garden patch or a redeemed social condition...	5	4	3	2	1
...to have played and laughed with enthusiasm and sung with exultation...	5	4	3	2	1
...to know even one life has breathed easier because I have lived."	5	4	3	2	1

Add up the numbers you circled, divide by 10, and circle the number closest to your score: 5   4   3   2   1

How did you do? If you agree with Emerson's definition and your score was low, what should you do about the size of the Relationships slice of your new pie? What new priorities should you set? If you put additional emphasis on the Doing and Having slices of life, can you do so in a way that reflects Emerson's perspective?

Activity: Reconsider what's important in your life by deciding relatively how much emphasis you should put on each of the three slices. On the next page, check a space beside each of the three slices to indicate more, less, or the same emphasis. Then, referring to the Needs and Wants you listed earlier, determine your tradeoffs.

How I Will Redeploy My Priorities

	More Emphasis	Less Emphasis	Same As Now
Material Wealth	_____	_____	_____
Work/Other Activities	_____	_____	_____
Relationships	_____	_____	_____

Here Are My Top 5 Tradeoffs

More Emphasis on: Less Emphasis on:

_____   _____

_____   _____

_____   _____

_____   _____

_____   _____

Activity: Now draw your new pie chart.

THIS PIE WILL BE "I"

MATERIAL WEALTH
_____%

WORK / ACTIVITIES
_____%

RELATIONSHIPS
_____%

Chapter 8

The Third Crucial Question:

What Will It Take to Reach Your Destination?

- The 5 Imperatives for a Successful Life

- Each Imperative Has 5 Personal Attributes

- Just What *Is* Success, Anyway?

- The MECCA Matrix Puts It All Together

- An Effective Tool to Assess Your Personal Power

So far, you have:
   • Examined Your Context for life's journey in Part 1, reviewing some history and examining 10 major trends and what opportunities or threats they may hold,
   • Answered the first and easiest of the Five Crucial Questions: "Where Are You Now and Where Do You Want to Be?" and,
   • Answered the second and, perhaps, most difficult of the five: "Whom Do You Choose to Be for the Journey?"
   Armed with *whom* you want to be and *where* you want to be, the time has come to equip yourself with what you'll need to get there.
   Review for a moment the "map" on Page 132. In or near what "city" did you place your dot? And where did you put your star?
   If you're like most people who answered the First Crucial Question — Where Are You Now and Where Do You Want to Be ?— your star is in "Mecca" and your dot is somewhere farther down the roadway.
   Or you may be among the few who, concentrating on the material aspects of life, decided you want to be in the comforts and conventional happiness of Fat City. Maybe you're already there.
   Your destination is important, but not as much as a gap

between where you are now and where you want to be. A gap means you need to answer the Third Crucial Question: What Will It Take to Reach Your Destination?

Recall that your "destination," in this context, is not an *end point* for your journey through life, but rather an attitudinal state in which your journey *continues*. As an end point, *death* is the destination of your journey through life on this earth. If you are a believer, that end point also will be the beginning of life *after* death.

Your "destination," then, is a new and better "place" — a new and better state of mind with which you can find greater personal fulfillment and even joy for the rest of your journey through life.

> Life is not a certain set of circumstances but a certain set of attitudes.

Closing the gap between where you are now and where you want to be requires:

The 5 Imperatives for a Successful Life

Here are the keys to achieving *anything,* including success itself — no matter how you define it. They are *The MECCA Factor.* Without harnessing the Five Imperatives, you will neither be successful nor reach your desired destination.

In the opening pages of this book, you reviewed the meanings of the word *Mecca.* The first meaning is the holy city in Saudi Arabia, the birthplace of the Prophet Muhammad and the destination of a pilgrimage usually taken by the Muslim faithful but once in a lifetime.

The second meaning embraces a variety of usages in the English language that are associated with success and happiness. These include "any place a person longs or desires to be," "achieving important life goals," and "reaching a longed-for state of happiness."

Based on the second meaning, "Mecca" may be your ultimate destination — a new place from which to continue your life's journey.

Now it's time to introduce a *third* meaning: MECCA, an acronym that stands for the Five Imperatives for a Successful Life. Acronyms are handy ways to make complex terms and concepts easier to understand. They also make things easier to remember.

MECCA the acronym embodies five powerful elements so essential to success and fulfillment of life's important pursuits that a serious shortfall in any of the five will virtually *guarantee* failure or, at the least, an inability to achieve your full potential.

Here are the *Five Imperatives.* Review them carefully. Consider why they are *sequential* — why you must master one before you can get full value from the one that follows.

M is for Motivation.

Without Motivation, you will get *nowhere*. If you're a highly motivated person, you will work hard to harness the power of the other four imperatives

Motivation mobilizes the *will* to succeed!

E is for Education.

Education is like the food and water supply for life's journey — nourishment for your brain. Unless you have a plentiful amount of Motivation, you will never be able to accumulate a plentiful amount of Education.

Education develops the *skill* to succeed!

C is for Concentration.

Being motivated to be educated is not enough. Motivation and Education must be *concentrated* on specific goals and pursuits if you are to be successful.

Concentration joins will and skill to a *way* to succeed!

C is for Communication.

All that Motivation, Education and Concentration are of no value unless you deploy them in the marketplace of effort and ideas. Life is a journey that cannot be taken successfully alone.

Communication puts will, skill, and way into *action!*

A is for Achievement.

When you harness your Motivation, Education and Concentration to the power of Communication, you will enjoy the sweet fruits of Achievement.

Achievement turns the first four Imperatives into *success!*

Do you see why the five Imperatives are *sequential?* If you are unmotivated, how could you do much of significance in your life? But even if you are *highly* motivated, you will go nowhere in life without Education and the other Imperatives.

A famous experiment demonstrates the outcome of stand-alone Motivation.

Processionary caterpillars are known for their strange habit of attaching themselves to one another, head to tail, and moving like trains along the forest floor, munching on leaves and pine needles.

John Henry Fabre placed a string of the caterpillars around the rim of a pot, forming them into a complete circle. They marched blindly, around and around a generous supply of their favorite food until, after several days, they simply died of starvation.

They were motivated, but didn't *know* enough to stop following blindly and go after some life-sustaining food.

Hunger is good — if it makes you work to satisfy it!

Proverbs 16:26

No matter how excited you get about a pursuit in life — no matter how much you might *hunger* for it, your Motivation will get you nowhere until you acquire the Education needed to attain it.

Without Motivation there is no Education. And without Education — be it from formal schooling or from experience known as "The School of Hard Knocks" — your Motivation, no matter how great, will have little value.

How many people do you know who seem only motivated to be educated? Perhaps they're the younger ones who seem to stay in school forever (at least until their parents run out of tuition money), endlessly going from one educational pursuit to another.

Or you may know of adults who, many years after graduation, are *still* going from one kind of job to another trying to find *something* that will hold their interest or bring them success.

Maybe — just maybe — such people roam endlessly from classroom to classroom and job to job because they lack sufficient Motivation. It is said that the world is full of educated derelicts. It is also said that Education can become a *life-delaying* end in itself.

People learn by probing and pursuing, not by sitting and soaking.

Education is the Imperative of the head. Motivation is the Imperative of the heart. Strong heart, strong head. Faint heart, dead head.

To harness the Five Imperatives for a Successful Life that spell MECCA, you not only must mobilize the forward-driving power of Motivation and the mind-expanding power of Education but, like focusing sunlight through a magnifying glass to create fire, you must *channel* those powers through the Third Imperative — the Imperative of Concentration.

Bring the *full* powers of Motivation and Education to bear on some *one main thing* and, whatever it is, you will succeed far beyond the person who divides attention among many things — the jack of all trades and master of none.

The main thing is to remember that the main thing is the main thing.

And yet, no matter how well you concentrate all that Motivation and Education, success will elude you without the Fourth Imperative in the sequence — Communication.

Communication is the key that unlocks the door of success.

Without Communication, the powers of Motivation, Education and Concentration will take you *nowhere.*

If you're typical, you spend 75 percent of your working life communicating with others. No matter how motivated and educated you are, and no matter how great your ability to concentrate your efforts, it is your Communication abilities that will determine how far you will go in your career, marriage, or pursuits of any kind.

You're not measured by what you *don't* know, but
how well you communicate what you *do* know.

President Ronald Reagan

Careers have been wrecked, marriages ended, lives taken, reputations ruined, wars started, friendships shattered, companies bankrupted, elections lost, and industrial disasters triggered, merely by the utterance of a few words.

The opposite is also true, whether it's the utterance of a few words on a TV commercial that propel a new product to undreamed-of heights of profitability, or the soft whispers of a marriage proposal joyfully accepted, or a simple but sincere apology that rekindles a friendship, or a much-welcome expression of pride by a parent to a child, or the three little words capable of lighting up almost anyone's life: *"I love you."*

What comes out of your mouth
will determine your future.

Francis P. Martin
Hung by the Tongue

Communication, more than any of the other Imperatives, is able to make up for your weaknesses or defeat your strengths. Of the five top reasons people are turned down for jobs, three have to do with Communication.

The Fifth Imperative — Achievement — is the payoff for developing and deploying the other four.

Achievement is the gateway to self-fulfillment and success. Achievement has one other powerful characteristic. It is among the greatest sources of Motivation.

The Five Imperatives, then, can be circular. The more you are motivated to learn and to concentrate and to communicate, the more you achieve; and the more you achieve, the more you are motivated to learn more, concentrate harder and communicate better.

> Give some troubled inner-city kids a taste of positive achievement and, inevitably, they are motivated toward even greater positive achievements.

To achieve is to be productive. To be productive is to win. The greatest achievements, though, aren't limited to cranking out more widgets than anyone in the company, or outselling your peers.

A great achievement could be as beautifully simple as touching a single life in a way that no one else could, perhaps by helping someone turn a setback in life into a victory, or by offering a simple bit of wisdom that leads to greater happiness or Self-Fulfillment.

The MECCA Imperatives offer an effective way to step back and look at how you have been doing in your life's journey so far and how you can accelerate your move up the roadway to your "destination."

What has held you back in your life's pursuits? Even if you are a great achiever, what has kept you from being an even *greater* achiever? Where are your greatest strengths? Where are your weak spots and shortfalls?

How puny or powerful is your Motivation to *go after* what you want? And what about the Imperatives necessary to *get* what you want — Education, Concentration and Communication?

How well do you *handle* Achievement? When you accomplish something substantial, does it *de*-motivate you onto a soft sofa somewhere in the City of Malaisia? Or does it further fire your drive toward a new and better place, perhaps toward "Mecca?"

> The greatest waste of our natural resources is the number of people who never achieve their potential. Get out of that slow lane. Shift into that fast lane. If you think you can't, you won't. If you think you can, there's a good chance you will. Even making the effort will make you feel like a new person. Reputations are made by searching for things that can't be done and doing them. Aim low: boring. Aim high: soaring.
>
> United Technologies Corporation

How would you rate yourself on each of the Five Imperatives ? Which one is your greatest source of strength? Which one is your greatest source of weakness?

If Motivation is your weakest among the imperatives, what is it that causes the shortfall? What *aspects* of Motivation would have to be strengthened if you are to become more motivated?

If Communication is your strongest factor, what *is* it that makes you so effective? Are there some aspects of Communication that you could improve, making it an even greater strength?

Each Imperative Has Five Personal Attributes

Look inside each of the Five Sequential Imperatives and you will find Five Personal Attributes that will help you determine what you must work on to overcome a weakness or develop a strength.

Begin your examination of the Attributes with an overview of what they are and why they're important:

The Motivation Imperative

> The world is full of willing people. Some are willing to work. The rest are willing to watch them.
>
> Robert Frost

Greatest and most important of the Five Personal Attributes of Motivation is the fundamental determinant of how well you will *ever* do in *anything.* Not only will this single Attribute control how much you will be motivated, but will affect every one of the Imperatives.

That single-most important Attribute is:

Self-Esteem. You will only *ever* be as good as you feel about yourself. If you suffer from low Self-Esteem, you bear a self-imposed burden that will make success harder to come by and life harder to endure.

Don't confuse Self-Esteem with ego. If you have a big ego and think you're God's gift to humankind, it could be your way of covering up low Self-Esteem. People with high Self-Esteem tend to be humble. People with big egos tend to be arrogant.

Self-Esteem is being your own best friend instead of your own worst enemy. It's a positive, natural feeling that you are of value to yourself and others.

There's much more to Motivation, though. Having high Self-Esteem doesn't make you highly motivated. While Self-Esteem is the Core Attribute of Motivation — the *Motivation of Motivation,* so to speak — there is an educational aspect of Motivation that is vital:

Purpose. No matter how high your Self-Esteem, you cannot be fully motivated until you have learned for yourself your Purpose in life.

Purpose is a moral or spiritual context for your life. It is having figured out what your *mission* in life really is and having sketched out a big, positive vision for the future.

The spiritual dimension of your life is implicit in your Purpose. If you have no belief in a power greater than yourself, finding and fulfilling a great Purpose for your life will be difficult at the least.

People with high Self-Esteem tend to be people who can define themselves through a sense of Purpose. Low Self-Esteem often makes a Purpose in life hard to find.

Motivation, however, *still* requires more. High Self-Esteem and a strong Purpose won't fully unleash the power of Motivation without:

A Plan. Less than five percent of adult Americans have any specific goals and only a tiny fraction of one percent have developed a well-crafted, *written* career and personal Plan. And yet, written goals and effective life planning are tied strongly to self-fulfillment and success.

A Plan is a process through which you identify what it will take for you to achieve success. It helps you identify what areas of Education will be important and where to concentrate your efforts.

It also gives you a basis for measuring progress and a way to keep focused on what's important.

While Self-Esteem is the Motivation of Motivation, and Purpose is the Education of Motivation, A Plan is the *Concentration* of Motivation. Does this mean there needs to be a *Communication* of Motivation? Absolutely! It's:

Enthusiasm. This Personal Attribute is the tip of an iceberg. Enthusiasm is how you communicate your Motivation to yourself and the rest of the world. It gives you the *inspirational fervor* that not only helps you achieve your goals, but carry out your Plan, fulfill your Purpose and raise even further your level of Self-Esteem.

Beneath the surface of Enthusiasm lie the powers of mental and physical energy. The more the Enthusiasm shines above the surface, the greater the mental and physical energy is stirred beneath the surface — *within you!*

The foundation of mental and physical energy is health and wellness. The body is the temple of the mind, the spirit and the soul. How well you take care of yourself physically, as well as mentally, affects your energy level and your level of Enthusiasm.

If you lack energy, you'll find it hard to muster much Enthusiasm. And your energy level will be controlled by how well you take care of yourself — including what and how much you eat, and the extent to which you keep yourself physically fit.

Enthusiastic people tend to thrive on good diet and exercise habits. You won't find much Enthusiasm among the couch potatoes who live in Malaisia!

But there's *still* more to Motivation. How do you *stay* motivated? What keeps you going, especially when the going gets rough?

It's the *Achievement* of *Motivation:*

Resilience. If you're going through "continuous white water" in your life, Resilience may be the most important of the Five Personal Attributes that comprise Motivation.

Unless you are resilient in the face of great change and upheaval, how can you possibly maintain a high level of Enthusiasm? How can you stick to A Plan? How can you stay fully committed to a Purpose and keep your Self-Esteem from plummeting into the pits?

The tough people who get going when the going gets tough are the *resilient* people. They're the ones who, like the unsinkable Molly Brown, turn *up* their energy levels and become *more* determined to *win no matter what!*

How resilient are you? How much does *it take* to dampen your Enthusiasm? Crush your spirit? Kill off your feelings of self-worth?

Resilience means persistence and determination. It means bouncing back from adversity. It means doing *whatever it takes* to keep stress from undermining your energy, and turmoil from dashing your hopes. It means *this too shall pass* and, no matter how hard it gets, your Aspirations *shall be fulfilled!*

Resilience not only helps you overcome obstacles and pull yourself back from life's inevitable defeats, but rids you of feelings of failure, no matter how big the setback. What may be failure to others becomes just one more *learning experience* for you.

Resilience forms the bridge from Motivation to:

The Education Imperative

Education is what remains after we have forgotten
all that we have been taught.

Lord Halifax

If you are among those who equate Education with schooling, take a closer look. What you could learn from the finest university in the entire realm of scholarship may be inconsequential compared to what you can learn from the School of Hard Knocks — your life's experiences.

The starting point for Education — *the Motivation of Education* — is:

Aptitude.   Here is either a springboard for learning or a major barrier to becoming successful.

Aptitude is your natural ability to learn and to do. It represents your talents and all those things you can become good at. Aptitude becomes a barrier, though, when your *attitude* toward your own capabilities is less than positive. As the motivational aspect of Education, your perception of Aptitude can be a major *de*-motivator.

How many times in your life did you quit a pursuit, or not bother even trying, because you decided you couldn't be any good at it? Have your life's pursuits been enhanced or diminished by how you scored on an aptitude test you took as a child? If people said you lack "the brains" to be successful in a certain career field, did you believe them? Do you *still* believe them?

You can do almost anything you set your mind to. Ability is an integral part of your belief system. With rare exception, you *can* do what you *believe* you can do, given Motivation to clear the hurdle of Aptitude.

It is your *perception* of your Aptitude — your belief in your own capabilities — that will set the limits of what you will learn in life and, ultimately, what you can achieve.

If the Motivation of Motivation is Self-Esteem, clearly the Core Attribute of Education — the *Education of Education* — is:

Self-Development.   This is your willingness to find opportunities to learn and to take full advantage of them.

You may think your peak years of Self-Development are those spent as a youth in the classroom. But to be all you can ever be, *every* year should be the peak year.

Your Self-Development should *accelerate* after graduation. You can cram your kit of capabilities with an abundance of career and personal experiences as well as an array of books, training courses, tapes, mentoring relationships and anything else you can get your hands on.

The key to *sustaining* Self-Development is staying teachable. As the years go by, most people apply the brakes to Education. They succumb to a "hardening of their mental arteries," leaving a narrower perception of their Aptitude. They redefine Self-Development as the minimum level necessary to get by. As a result, life can be less fulfilling, and while their "destinations" for life's journey may continue to be "Mecca" or Fat City, their most likely place of residence will be the rut called Malaisia.

If you are staying teachable, it means you have made a *habit* of ongoing Self-Development. You look continuously for opportunities to sharpen skills and broaden your storehouse of information, elements essential to accomplishing your Plan and fulfilling your Purpose.

Ongoing expansion and renewal of your Self-Development requires a Personal Attribute that is the *Concentration of Education:*

Creativity. Don't ever convince yourself — or let anyone else convince you — that you are not creative. *Everyone* is creative, for everyone is blessed with some amount of imagination and an ability to look at things from more than one perspective.

While so-called right-brained people may be more creative than technically oriented folks who use more of the left sides of their brains, some of the most creative solutions to problems have come from engineers and some of the most incisive analyses from artists.

By concentratinging your creative powers, you will never be at a loss for new ways to grow. Without Creativity, there can be no meaningful Education, and Motivation will be reduced to the plight of the caterpillars, going round and round, getting nowhere.

Creativity is making the new. It's also arranging the old in new ways. Its roots run deep into the Personal Attribute that is the *Communication of Education:*

Interest. Unending curiosity does much more than provide a platform for Creativity.

Within yourself, the breadth and depth of your Interest brings light into your life and helps you become more complete as a person. Beyond yourself, Interest communicates much about you to other people. You become a *person of interest* to others when your curiosity becomes genuine Interest in them and what *they* are interested in.

How do you *direct* your Interest? Do you dwell on those things you find interesting, or do you extend your curiosity and focus on what *other people* find interesting?

Have you compressed your range of Interest into a narrow comfort zone or are you constantly looking for new areas in which to learn and grow? Is the depth of your Interest shallow or deep, especially in areas important to fulfilling your Purpose and reaching your destination?

Just as the Communication of Motivation is Enthusiasm driven by energy, so it is that the Communication of Education is Interest. Boredom is a cause of fatigue. Intense Interest is a source of great energy.

And what about the *Achievement of Education?* It's an Attribute too often misunderstood:

Knowledge. Knowledge is power. Right? Wrong! Knowledge is *potential* power. It all depends on what kind of Knowledge you accumulate, how well you can retrieve it and what you can do with it.

Your Knowledge will have little power if it consists mainly of trivia — the so-called "nickel knowledge." It will have *little* power if it is obsolete. And it will have *no* power if it is vast but lacks relevance to the achievement of your goals in life.

Knowledge may lack power but still have Interest and, therefore, a certain amount of value. Such is the *background information* you keep stored in your mind. The most important Knowledge is that which is specific and essential to your success. Such is your *know-how* — the Knowledge with which you accomplish what's important.

Certain areas of Knowledge are of *great* importance and can give you enormous power. Knowledge of people and of language, for example, will determine how well you can harness Concentration and Communication, the Imperatives that now stand between you and Achievement.

Your brain's capacity to store Knowledge is virtually unlimited if you *choose* to tap all of your brainpower. But to make good use of what you know, you have to cross another bridge — the one leading to:

The Concentration Imperative

> Juggling apples, oranges, pie plates and flaming shish-kebabs makes a great circus act but is no way to live. Determine what's important, be sure you know all you need to know and concentrate your efforts.

Motivation without much Education is wasted motion. Education without much Motivation is motion wasted. Motivation with Education is ready to be channeled into a worthwhile pursuit.

Concentration begins with deciding on what to concentrate. That calls for the motivational aspect of Concentration, which is an essential Personal Attribute called:

Judgment. When should you say "yes" and when should you say "no?" Which of two or three or four courses of action would be best for you — or for your family, or for the business plan you're developing?

Judgment is the process through which you discern options and make choices. It's your decision-making process. Making good decisions requires a strong blend of wisdom and common sense.

Everything you need for good Judgment can be found within the Attributes of Motivation and Education. If you have high Self-Esteem, you are more likely to make good judgments than if you think poorly of yourself.

You also will tend to make good decisions if you are strong in the Attributes that follow, from having a clear Purpose to achieving an at-hand supply of practical, usable Knowledge.

Life is a melange of day-to-day decisions, minor judgment calls and major choices. Inevitably, a significant decision in one area of your life will have an effect on decisions to be made in other areas.

Having good *outcomes* from the motivational aspect of Concentration — Judgment, or deciding what to concentrate on — calls you to strengthen the educational component of Concentration, the Attribute known as:

Organization. How well-organized are you?

Using your Creativity, have you worked out some simple ways to keep track of things? Do you take advantage of the many good aids and systems that can keep you from being overwhelmed? Have you worked out simple routines that avoid time-consuming problems?

Perhaps you're one of the many people who should take a good time management course, but haven't, *because you don't have time.*

Think back to the Education Imperative for a moment. Learning how to be well-organized should be an essential part of your Self-Development. If Organization is a shortfall and you have decided not to take action, you are weak in the preceding Attribute — Judgment.

Learning how to be organized is one thing. Doing it consistently, along with handling well many other tasks and responsibilities, requires commitment to what is this Imperative's Core Attribute — the *Concentration of Concentration:*

Self-Discipline. Resilient people can keep going but people with a great deal of Self-Discipline go on to *win.*

Self-Discipline means *controlling* your life and not letting the exigencies of life control you. It's the power within you to defeat the greatest obstacle on the roadway to a better place — procrastination.

In your journey through life, you'll pay one of two prices — the price of Self-Discipline or the price of regret. If you lack Self-Discipline and are inclined to stay that way, eventually it will dawn on you that whatever pain may come with Self-Discipline will be *nothing* compared to the pain from the outcomes of an undisciplined life.

You can set out to improve Organization in your life with a time-management system. You will be better organized, however, only when you make the system work well for you through Self-Discipline.

Meet someone with *the best possible* Judgment, *tremendous* Organization and *total* Self-Discipline and little else, and you're likely to meet a person so totally logical as to be more of a crashing bore than someone destined to win big in life.

Success takes logic but in proper proportion. It's been said that if everything were *totally* logical, *men* would ride horses side-saddle!

So the Concentration Imperative requires an element of Communication, offering signals and messages within you and to other people that keep everything in:

Perspective. Without Perspective, you will never be able to take up residence in "Mecca," for there can be no self-actualization, "spiritual" fulfillment or joy of living.

Perspective is keeping a healthy amount of balance in your life, especially when your life must be somewhat out of balance to achieve what is most important.

It is said that people lacking in Perspective have a *deviated spectrum.* Without doubt, the worst deviations in your spectrum would include taking yourself too seriously and denying yourself the joys of a good sense of humor.

Lack of Perspective weakens all five Imperatives and every one of the Personal Attributes. For example, if you determine a godly Purpose for your life, do you cast it in the shadow of an angry God who will punish you for your transgressions? Or in the light of a loving God who will shed His grace on you?

Similarly, do you seek Knowledge with a reverence for rote, or a reverence for reason?

Without Perspective, the Concentration Imperative can turn you into a workaholic rather than a peak performer. Perspective is the buffer between the Concentration of Concentration — Self-Discipline — and the *Achievement of Concentration,* a key Attribute called:

Focus. This is your ability to concentrate on *doing* things so that, in Perspective, you gain a sense of accomplishment that a good job was done rather than a sense of relief that an onerous job is finally over.

Focus enables you to deploy Motivation, Education and Concentration *fully.* It also lets you overcome distractions and, at times, become productively single-minded.

Rooted in Self-Discipline, a strong sense of Focus will help you avoid letting that which is seemingly urgent block out that which is knowingly important. And by having additional roots in Perspective, you are protected from the fate of military pilots who become *so* focused that, instead of bombing or strafing the target, they fly into it.

The bridge to the Fourth Imperative is built of the Five Attributes of Concentration. The bridge deck itself, however, is made of the Perspective that helps you to shift Focus from yourself to others.

If you are bound for "Mecca," the only way to get there is through other people. Your access is by way of:

The Communication Imperative

The vacuum created by a failure to communicate will quickly be filled with rumor, misrepresentation, drivel and poison.

C. Northcote Parkinson's Final Law

180

Communication (no "s") is not the same as communication<u>s</u>. If you are like most people, you live in an almost constant cross-fire of communications. You are bombarded with *thousands* of messages every day. And you *send* many communications during every waking hour — through what you say, what you write, what you do, and what you reflect through facial expressions and body language.

All those communications may or may not result in Communication, which is a state of mutual understanding between you and one or more other people.

What is the *Motivation of Communication?* It's the Personal Attribute that *initiates* communication with other people:

Association. If you find it hard to be in contact with people — *to associate* — you will also find it hard to succeed in life and experience the true joy of living.

Life is a journey that can't be taken successfully alone. You can accomplish very little without other people playing a variety of major or minor roles in your life.

There are two aspects of Association:

1. As Judgment relates to Concentration (deciding what to concentrate on), so it is that Association relates to Communication (deciding who to associate with). You *become* what you think and, by extension, what you think determines who you associate with. As Proverbs 13:20 tells us, "He who walks with wise men becomes wise, but the companion of fools will suffer harm."

2. Establishing *new* associations with people is a skill you can develop with practice and good training. An important part of that skill is learning to be likable and approachable — to be a magnet that attracts other people, leading *them* to want to associate with *you.*

Your Association skills are high when you are good at striking up conversations in person or on the phone, making a good first impression on people, and finding it easy to make acquaintances.

There's much to learn if you are to be good at associating with people. The *Education of Communication,* the Attribute which poses the biggest learning challenge, is:

Interaction. Meeting and getting to know people is one thing. *Dealing* with them *productively* is something else!

How well you interact depends on your care and concern for others as well as your skills as a communicator.

To interact with others skillfully, productively and *consistently well* is not easy! The single most important aspect of Interaction is *understanding* yourself and other people.

Knowing how *you* think and why *you* think that way isn't enough. You also must gain a good understanding of how *other people* think and why *they* think that way. And there are specific habits and skills to develop:

Become a good listener. Master the art of conversation. Learn how to present your views persuasively. Be a good negotiator. Control your temper. Focus on win-win outcomes. Know when to push forward with Interaction and when to back off. Understand when and how to be accessible to others. Be sensitive to people's feelings.

Underlying all of those things, you'll find the need to speak and write the language effectively, be a good reader, store and retrieve information efficiently and consistently use the best communications *media* to send the best *messages* to the right people.

Interaction begins with Association. When practiced well, Interaction will result in what should be your *Concentration of Communication:*

Relationships. Without Association you will have no Interaction. Without Interaction you will have no Relationships. Without Relationships you will have no career success or joy of living.

How important are Relationships?

An intensive study to find out why a small town in Eastern Pennsylvania had fewer fatal heart attacks than a neighboring community traced the sole reason to cohesive, supportive Relationships through families and friends.

The death rate in the town was as much as 40 percent lower than the other town in the 1930s, '40s and '50s. But when new people arrived in greater numbers in the 1960s, Relationships weakened and the death rate from heart attacks rose to the level of the neighboring town.

How strong and positive are the Relationships in *your* life? If you're married, how strong are your Relationships with each other? Are you a member of a family that's harmoniously functional or stressfully *dys*functional?

How many true friends do you have and how strong and important are those Relationships? Do you have one or more career mentors — people ahead of you professionally who advise you and help you advance?

Your family Relationships form the foundation of your other Relationships. If you grew up in a cohesive family in which people interacted in warm and caring ways, you'll find it easier to develop and maintain good Relationships of all kinds. And what could help you find your "Mecca" more than a mutually supportive and loving spouse?

Be *very good* at Association and Interaction. Develop strong and enduring Relationships. That, coupled with the Imperatives and the other Personal Attributes, will help you radiate the Core Attribute of Communication — the *Communication of Communication:*

Self-Confidence. Neither you nor anyone was *born* with total Self-Confidence. You were, however, born with the first two of many fears that will become *barriers* to your Self-Confidence — the fear of loud noises and the fear of falling.

Self-Confidence is developed through skills to be learned. All five of the Imperatives are important to becoming self-confident. So are all the other Personal Attributes, especially the three *core* attributes you've examined so far — Self-Esteem, Self-Development and Self-Discipline.

You do not have to become fearless to gain Self-Confidence, only courageous. To be *fully fearless* is to be a fool. Courage is not the *absence* of fear but the *mastery* of fear. To be courageous is to overcome your fears, including those that always will be with you.

Fear of failure does more to undermine Self-Confidence than any other fear. Earlier, you identified things you tried already and did already but no longer do. Why did you quit? Did *fear of failure* undercut the confidence in yourself that could have helped you succeed?

Self-Confidence is what you communicate to yourself and the rest of world. It not only helps you overcome your fears, but underscores belief in yourself. And by radiating belief in yourself, other people are likely to believe in you.

When you're in search of a job or seeking a promotion, the decisionmakers are likely to consider your level of Self-Confidence. If they sense you have no confidence in yourself, they'll probably choose someone who does.

Thus equipped with Self-Confidence, you can gain the *Achievement of Communication:*

Recognition. A wall full of plaques is the *least* important part of Recognition. So is getting your name in the newspaper or even the Guiness Book of Records.

After-the-fact Recognition for what you've done is not nearly as important as before-the-fact Recognition of what you *will* be able to do in the future.

As the Achievement of Communication, Recognition comes in two forms:

1. Your ability to recognize your own capabilities and the opportunities that lie before you, and

2. Recognition by others that you do, indeed, have greater capabilities and are *worthy* of opportunities.

While people usually disdain those who blow their own horns, you shouldn't hide from the Recognition you truly deserve. In fact, you may deny yourself some opportunities if you continually deny others the pleasure of celebrating your accomplishments.

There also is a habit that, when used properly, can result in *additional* Recognition for you. It's the simple matter of being very good at extending Recognition to other people. If you recognize them, they will recognize you, and so will the people who see how much you are helping others accomplish.

Be good at marketing yourself, for no one can do it better than you can. More people being aware of who you are and what you can do, may make the difference between achieving your goals and having to settle for less in life.

Of the Imperatives for success in *anything,* Communication is the last one that now stands between you and the payoff. Recognition puts you on the bridge to:

The Achievement Imperative

> The highest reward for man's toil is not what he gets for it, but what he becomes by it.

> John Ruskin

It is a fundamental pattern of life that productive people win and unproductive people lose. That was true since God created humankind and it remains true today, no matter how many government programs try to change it.

Productivity produces Achievement. The secrets of being supremely productive are found in the Imperatives of Motivation, Education, Concentration and Communication.

The *rewards* of Achievement go far beyond money and ever-greater Recognition. They reach into your soul.

Like the other four Imperatives, Achievement involves five important Attributes. The motivational Attribute, the one that unlocks the door to Achievement, is:

Opportunity. The link between Recognition (the Achievement of Communication) and Opportunity (the Motivation of Achievement) should be very clear.

What should also be apparent is that Recognition alone won't *guarantee* that you can make the most of Opportunity.

A good example of this is the British Royal Family. Despite being *born* into a fabulous amount of Recognition, the inability of the young royals to maintain productive Relationships could bring the end of the monarchy as an institution taken seriously in the United Kingdom and elsewhere in the world.

Opportunity is your chance to achieve *more* in your life. Having it and making the most of it requires the best of your full range of

Personal Attributes, especially your motivational Attributes of Self-Esteem, Aptitude, Judgment and Association.

Given strengths in those Attributes, along with a high level of Self-Confidence and being able to recognize the right time and circumstances, you should be willing to accept Opportunity's *risks*. But you also must break the bonds of conformity and be a *visionary!*

There's little Opportunity to be found in doing the same things everyone else has done. There's *great* Opportunity in finding new things that can be done, or developing new ways to solve old problems, or repackaging old things in exciting new ways.

Opportunity is the motivational element of Achievement. The *Education of Achievement* is:

Expertise. If you are a person with *relevant* Expertise you will never be at the mercy of a person in an argument. Know what you're talking about, keep it current and have the experience to back it up!

The link between Opportunity and Expertise includes a great need to base your Expertise on every Opportunity to get information from the best sources. Experts built the "unsinkable" Titanic by listening to each other instead of those who expressed concerns. Amateurs built the Ark because Noah listened to God instead of those who were laughing at him.

If you constantly pursue Opportunity in all that you do, you will keep your Expertise from becoming irrelevant. You will also spot potential problems and help avert difficulties, perhaps even tragedies.

How would you like to be the leading expert on how to manufacture 8-track tape decks for automobiles? Or build drive-in theaters? Or sell corsets to young ladies in finishing schools?

If you couple Expertise in the *technology* of what you do with Expertise in *relating well to people,* you will gain credibility wherever you go. *You* will be the one people turn to for advice and direction.

The closest you'll ever come to being indispensible is when you know more about something of great importance than anyone else and are willing to share what you know in a thoroughly satisfying way.

Applying your Expertise, the educational aspect of Achievement, becomes the *Concentration of Achievement:*

Influence. While Knowledge is defined as only *potential* power, Influence can be viewed as your power *potential*. The greater your Concentration on *effectively* applying Influence, the greater the power you will achieve.

Influence may or may not involve leadership. Not everyone can or should become a leader. And yet there are many cases where success — or even survival — depends as much on the Influence of a sage behind the scenes as it does the leader on center-stage.

The *principles* of good leadership, however, apply to exerting Influence, whether you're a leader or not. These include setting a good example, and all that is embodied in the Attributes of Communication— especially Interaction and Self-Confidence.

You will be less likely to achieve great Influence if you have trouble interacting with others. And who would accept your Expertise if you lack Self-Confidence when offering it?

Up to now, the Imperatives and their related Attributes have represented who you are *becoming.* Influence defines for you, and other people, who you *have become.* The definition becomes much clearer in the *Communication of Achievement,* which is your:

Character.   The four Communication-related Attributes of the first four Imperatives — Enthusiasm, Interest, Perspective and Self-Confidence — all reflect your personality, or who you *appear* to be.

Other Attributes, such as Interaction, Relationships, Expertise and Influence, reflect your reputation, or who people *think* you are.

It is Character that represents to yourself and others who you *really* are. Your values are implicit in your Character. If you are of *good* Character, it means you have learned the *practical* as well as the moral value of doing what is right.

Many truisms are beacons to good Character, among them:
> Virtue is to the soul what health is to the body.
> Your word is your worth and your worth is your word.
> If you don't stand for something you'll fall for anything.
> Every great failure in life is a Character failure.
> There never was a person of good Character whose first thought was "what's in it for me."

If Influence gives you power, Character will be the test of how well you *handle* power. As Abraham Lincoln put it: "Nearly all men can stand adversity, but if you want to test a man's Character, give him power."

Your Character is also put to the test in major setbacks. Another great truism: "Character is what you have left when you've lost everything else you have to lose."

Your Character lights up the distinctive person you have become. It is the manifestation of Self-Esteem and the other Core Attributes, especially Self-Discipline.

It's no coincidence that Influence (the Concentration of Achievement) is followed by Character (the Communication of Achievement).

Character spawns charisma, the quality that determines whether people want to follow or be influenced by you. The stronger and more positive your Character in the eyes of others, the greater the Influence you will have.

Character is also the doorstep of the most important Attribute of all. It's the Core Attribute of Achievement — the *Achievement of Achievement:*

Self-Fulfillment. This last of the 25 Attributes is the one that may reflect your location among the five "cities" on the roadway. To have *consummate* Self-Fulfillment is to experience joy of living. And to bask in an ongoing joy of living is to have taken up residency in the place known as "Mecca."

Self-Fulfillment is also the outcome of how much (or how little) you have gained from the Core Attributes of the first four Imperatives for a Successful Life:

> Self-Esteem — The Motivation of Motivation
> Self-Development — The Education of Education
> Self-Discipline — The Concentration of Concentration
> Self-Confidence — The Communication of Communication

Your level of Self-Esteem controls your level of Motivation. Your ability to become more motivated will be determined by how well you gather strength from *all* of the Attributes and, as a result, increase your Self-Fulfillment.

Self-Fulfillment, now and in the future, also represents your *destiny* as reflected by where you are now and where you want to be among the five "cities."

Reflect for a moment on the 25 Attributes, especially the relationship of Character to Self-Fulfillment. See if you can find new and deeper meaning in a beautifully wise old saying, to which a bit of emphasis has been added:

> Sow a thought, reap an act;
> Sow an act, reap a habit;
> Sow a habit, reap a Character;
> Sow a Character, reap a destiny!

Life is like electricity. It can neither be collected nor stored. If you *thought* electricity could be stored in a battery, go back and review basic physics. When a battery is "charged," electricity is *not* put into the battery; rather, the battery's chemical properties are changed so that it can *manufacture* electricity when called upon.

And so it is with life. You can *store* certain properties in your brain and your biceps and other parts of your body. And, through the grace of God and proper maintenance, you can *extend* life for a long time. But you can't *collect life* and you *can't store life!*

Life is for you to *live!* To live a *self-fulfilling* life you must constantly recharge yourself, rejuvenating and extending the capacity of your Attributes and the qualities they represent.

Just What __Is__ Success, Anyway?

What *is* success? What does it mean to you?

Do you believe it to be Rollses and Rollexes and residences on the Riviera? Do you believe it to be titles and trophies and time on television? If you do, it's your choice. You took the fork in the road that leads to Fat City.

But if you took the *other* fork, or if you're living in Fat City now and have discovered a major void in your life, you may already have figured out that *true* success means something *beyond* amassing wealth or bounding up a career ladder.

There can be no inner sense that you are successful without a high sense of Self-Fulfillment.

Self-Fulfillment is your internal *measure* of success and it's an *ongoing* sense with peaks and valleys. In the valleys, it's the voice within you that whispers: "You *can* do it. You *will* do it. You *are* doing it. You *feel good* about yourself." At the peaks, it's the voice within you that cries out: "Yes! you *did* it and it feels *great!*" And "Yes! you can reach *higher* and do *better* and it will feel even *greater!*"

Success is being all you can be, no matter where you are now in life and no matter where you see yourself being in the future.

> If an individual is called to be a street sweeper, he or she should sweep streets even as Michelangelo painted or Beethoven composed music or Shakespeare wrote poetry. He should sweep streets so well that all the hosts of heaven and earth will pause and say, "Here lived a great street sweeper who did his job well."
>
> Martin Luther King Jr.

Success as measured by Self-Fulfillment means you can find joy in life even if your ambitions and attributes don't take you very far in what you have and what you do.

Is a single mom who survives by scrubbing floors and who finds joy in nurturing a child toward a better life more successful than a CEO who makes a seven-figure bonus by downsizing a company and finds satisfaction in a 20 percent increase in earnings per share?

Perhaps the *best* definition of success is one that underscores success as a *continuum* rather than an outcome. It gives greater latitude for success than any definition pegged to net worth or lofty status:

> Success is the progressive realization of a worthy ideal.
>
> Earl Nightingale

You can find far more Self-Fulfillment by plugging into *this* definition of success than you can find by viewing success as simply achieving a goal.

If you view winning as the *only* thing in sports or in life, you consign yourself to Purgatoria or worse — unless, of course, you *always* win. But if you always win, where is the challenge?

Self-Fulfillment enriches your life when it is *playing the game,* not just winning, that counts the most. Your "progressive realization" is in playing better and better, whatever the setbacks on your way toward your "worthy ideal."

The MECCA Matrix Puts It All Together

You have been offered the Five Imperatives for a Successful Life. There are Five Personal Attributes underlying each of the Five Imperatives. Added together, the Five Imperatives and the 25 Personal Attributes constitute your Personal Power for the 1990s and beyond. When assembled, they form:

THE **MECCA** MATRIX

	MOTIVATION	EDUCATION	CONCENTRATION	COMMUNICATION	ACHIEVEMENT
MOTIVATION You Need...	1 Self-Esteem	6 Aptitude	11 Judgment	16 Association	21 Opportunity
EDUCATION You Learn ...	2 Purpose	7 Self-Development	12 Organization	17 Interaction	22 Expertise
CONCENTRATION You Develop...	3 A Plan	8 Creativity	13 Self-Discipline	18 Relationships	23 Influence
COMMUNICATION You Show ...	4 Enthusiasm	9 Interest	14 Perspective	19 Self-Confidence	24 Character
ACHIEVEMENT You Can Attain...	5 Resilience	10 Knowledge	15 Focus	20 Recognition	25 Self-Fulfillment
COMMITMENT				SUCCESS	

Success comes through Commitment to the first four Imperatives, but only *after* you attain Self-Fulfillment in the progressive realization of your worthy ideal.

Study the matrix carefully. See how the Imperatives and the Attributes fit together.

Understand that while the Imperatives are sequential (without Motivation, *nothing* happens, etc.), the Attributes may come into play in a far less logical order. For example, Character may be the driving force when deciding your Purpose, and your Self-Esteem may go up or down depending on Relationships.

Certain logical sequences *do* occur, however. The motivational Attributes, for instance, can account for many teenagers turning to drugs. Low Self-Esteem leads them to feel that, educationally, they're not good for much (Aptitude), resulting in bad choices (Judgment), getting in with the wrong crowd (Association), and losing out on chances to achieve things in life (Opportunity).

And how many people do you know of who ran off the road to success by being very strong in only four of the five Concentration Attributes? Tremendous *Judgment.* Awesome *Organization.* Tough-as-nails *Self-Discipline.* Total *Focus.* In spite of all that, why did they experience failure? Probably because they neglected *Perspective.*

Look again at the matrix. You won't find an Attribute called *leadership.* So much has been made of leadership over the years it becomes hard to remember that the greatest leaders were first good *followers.* As important as leaders are, there is a far *bigger* need for good followers. And good followers have leadership *potential.*

You'll find the *makings* of a leader in the matrix. Leaders optimize all five Imperatives and have great strength in all of the Attributes, reflected especially in those associated with Achievement.

A good leader knows an *Opportunity,* and when and how to exploit it. A good leader has *Expertise* in leadership as well as the field in which leadership is applied. A good leader exerts *Influence,* without which there can be no leadership. And a good leader is a person of sound *Character* who sets a good example.

Good leaders also enjoy *Self-Fulfillment,* especially from helping *other people* succeed.

An Effective Tool to Assess Your Personal Power

Here's an opportunity to measure your Personal Power:

Activity: On the following five pages are pairs of statements to help you gauge yourself according to the 25 Attributes in the matrix. If the statement above the row of numbers fits you *completely,* circle the "5," or if it comes pretty close circle the "4." If the statement below the numbers is a perfect fit, circle the "1" or if it comes pretty close, circle the "2." Circle the "3" if both statements apply from time to time. On each page, score the Imperative by adding the circled numbers, dividing by five and writing the result in the space at the top of the page. Pay close attention to how you score each Core Attribute.

The Motivation Imperative   Overall Score: _____

• Self-Esteem •

I possess an inner peace and joy for living. I feel very good about myself all or nearly all of the time.

5   4   3   2   1

My life is filled with self-doubt and unhappiness. I rarely, if ever, feel good about myself.

Purpose

I have a clear, even "spiritual" understanding, of my Purpose in life, including what I want out of life.

5   4   3   2   1

There is no clear-cut Purpose to my life. I simply live from one day to the next.

A Plan

In line with my Purpose, I have developed a good Plan with specific goals and action steps.

5   4   3   2   1

My aims in life change from day to day. I have no well-developed Plan to guide me in the months and years ahead.

Enthusiasm

I'm very excited about what I pursue and I find it easy to muster the energy to get things done.

5   4   3   2   1

I find little to be excited about and have a hard time mustering Enthusiasm and energy to get things done.

Resilience

When the going gets tough, I'm one of those tough people who gets going. *Nothing* will keep me from succeeding!

5   4   3   2   1

I find myself devastated by major setbacks in my life and even little things "get to me" much of the time.

The Education Imperative

Overall Score: _____

Aptitude

There is virtually nothing I can't do if I put my mind to it and decide to make it happen.

5   4   3   2   1

My lack of talent and ability puts severe limitations on what I can learn and do.

• Self-Development •

I am doing everything I can to develop my capabilities, expand my skills and learn in areas important to my goals.

5   4   3   2   1

I am already sufficiently self-developed and don't see the need to do any more.

Creativity

I am an "idea person" with a vivid imagination who loves to create things and/or find new ways to solve problems.

5   4   3   2   1

I stick to the tried-and-true. Rarely, if ever, do I originate ideas or come up with new solutions to problems.

Interest

My curiosity is endless and I maintain a variety of interests, some of them unrelated to fulfilling my goals.

5   4   3   2   1

I have few interests, and what few I have are limited to what is necessary to get by.

Knowledge

I possess a rich storehouse of Knowledge, most of it in the form of know-how needed to succeed in life.

5   4   3   2   1

I know all I need to know and there's little else I would be interested in knowing.

The Concentration Imperative Overall Score: _____

Judgment
I'm an excellent decision-maker. I am very good at "calling the shots right" and deciding what is and isn't important.

5   4   3   2   1

I am a poor decision-maker. I find it hard to make up my mind, and/ or frequently make bad judgments.

Organization
I'm a highly organized person. I manage my time very effectively, allocating sufficient time to handle what is most important.

5   4   3   2   1

Day-to-day living is mostly chaos and confusion. I *never* can seem to get organized.

• Self-Discipline •
I have the kind of strong willpower that enables me to break bad habits and stick to things until they're done.

5   4   3   2   1

I have little self-control. I can't break habits on my own and find it hard to adhere to schedules and work regimens.

Perspective
My great strengths include being able to look at things in a broad context and keeping important matters in balance.

5   4   3   2   1

It's very hard for me to get a handle on the "big picture." I often lose sight of what's most important.

Focus
Once I decide on the right thing to do, almost nothing distracts me. I get the job done.

5   4   3   2   1

My attention span is very short. I tend to drift from one thing to the next.

The Communication Imperative   Overall Score: _____

Association

I find it easy to meet people. Making new contacts and getting into new groups is one of my strong points.

5   4   3   2   1

It's hard for me to meet people. I'm not comfortable in dealing with others and would rather keep to myself.

Interaction

I am highly skilled in interpersonal communication. I am a good listener and do well in establishing rapport.

5   4   3   2   1

My interpersonal communication skills are weak. I need much improvement in such areas as listening and establishing rapport.

Relationships

I have many friends and associates I can trust and enjoy building good — especially loving — Relationships with people.

5   4   3   2   1

I have few friends and/or family members I am close to. I find it very hard to build good—especially loving—Relationships.

• Self-Confidence •

I have total faith in my capabilities and believe I can succeed in whatever I choose to do.

5   4   3   2   1

I have strong doubts about my capabilities. It is very hard for me to muster Self-Confidence because of doubts about myself.

Recognition

I am well-recognized for what I do and who I am and it is of equal or even greater pleasure for me to give Recognition to others.

5   4   3   2   1

I feel left by the wayside many times. I find it hard to call attention to myself and/or compliment and praise other people.

The Achievement Imperative   Overall Score: _____

Opportunity
Many opportunities are and have been open to me. I recognize them and make the most of them.

5   4   3   2   1

Doors seem mostly closed to me. I rarely get the breaks I deserve and even if I did, I'm unlikely to take full advantage of them.

Expertise
I have turned Knowledge and experience into Expertise that is valued by others and helps me be successful.

5   4   3   2   1

There's not a lot that I'm good at. I know a little about some things, but there are few if any things of importance I excel at.

Influence
People continually turn to me for advice, guidance or leadership in areas important to my goals or helping them reach theirs.

5   4   3   2   1

For the most part, nobody pays much attention to me. Rarely if ever do people look to me for advice, guidance or leadership.

Character
I have a clear, organized and articulated set of values, live by them consistently and am *recognized* for living by them.

5   4   3   2   1

My values are unclear and I often find them shifting to fit the situation at hand.

• Self-Fulfillment •
I experience great satisfaction, even *joy* in the results of my efforts. I feel successful in the best sense of the word.

5   4   3   2   1

There's little satisfaction and joy in my life and what I do usually leads to mediocrity, boredom or failure.

Review your assessment, starting with your overall scores on the Five Imperatives. A score of 4.0 to 5.0 identifies one of your strengths, 2.5-3.9 is a development need, and 1.0-2.4 is a weakness.

In the context of life's journey, a strength means a *Clear Road* ahead. A development need is a *Steep Hill* calling for extra effort. A weakness is a *Roadblock* that requires a major change to move on.

Consider carefully the implications of high or low scores on the Imperatives. If, for example, Motivation is one of your strengths — a Clear Road — making it up a Steep Hill or getting around a Roadblock among the other Imperatives will be less challenging for you than if Motivation is a Roadblock.

Next, look at how you scored the Five Attributes under each Imperative. Are you faced with an Imperative that's a Steep Hill because of a single Roadblock? Are there two or three Steep Hills among the Attributes that, when strengthened, would turn your Imperative into a Clear Road?

The Fourth Crucial Question offers you an opportunity to set Personal Goals through which you can turn every one of those Steep Hills and Roadblocks into Clear Roads.

And in Part 3, Your Curriculum, you'll find 353 ways to do it, including scores of books and other materials to help you.

The Five Imperatives and the 25 Personal Attributes in the MECCA Matrix comprise your *Personal Power* for a fulfilling, successful and even *joyful* journey through life.

You've answered the first three Crucial Questions:
1. Where Am I Now and Where Do I Want to Be?
2. Whom Do I Choose to Be for the Journey?
3. What Will It Take to Reach My Destination?

Now it's time to tackle the Fourth Crucial Question and respond to a challenging invitation:

Please join the elite few people,
comprising less than one percent of
the adult population of the United States,
who have any *sort of well-thought-out*
and written *Personal Plan.*

Chapter 9

The Fourth Crucial Question:

How Should You Chart Your Course?

- Begin With the 3 Key Words: Want, Way, Work
- Chart Your Course in 5 Steps:
    1. *Write a Personal Mission Statement*
    2. *Create a Vision for Your Future*
    3. *Determine Your Key Objectives*
    4. *Divide Key Objectives Into Personal Goals*
    5. *Break Goals Down Into MECCA-Do-It's*
- Put Your Personal Plan Into Action

You have reached another fork in the road. You can follow the great majority of people, the ones with *no specific goals* in life. Or, you can be among the relatively few who not only know where they're going, but have put together a well-crafted and *written* plan to help them get there.

You can *chart* your course or you can keep going by *dead reckoning.* You can achieve success *deliberately,* or you can *hope* for success by stumbling across it.

People don't plan to fail, they fail to plan.

How much deliberate planning have you done so far in life?

If you're a *typical* American adult, you learned relatively little about planning since pulling a pot of hot soup from a stove top to discover a link between actions and outcomes. Who *taught* you how to plan? Have you ever taken a course on planning? What, besides ill-fated New Year's Resolutions, have you committed to paper?

You may have gone through phases of life and learned *nothing* about how to plan strategically, tactically, thoughtfully and thoroughly. Or, you may have had some very *good* lessons and experiences during those phases of life up to now. Check them out:

- **Early Childhood.**

Planning was done for you—by one or both parents and by your teachers. In school, most everything was determined by requirements based on what *other people* thought you might need or be good at.

- **The Teen Years.**

If you were a typical teenager, conflict and upheaval probably made good planning a near-impossibility.

You may have had *huge dreams* of great success — and little or no thought on *how* they would be attained. You probably clashed with parents, teachers and peers over what you wanted to be when you grew up, whether and how to buy a car, the clothes you wore, the people you associated with, your hair style, a nose ring...whatever.

Planning among you and your peers was so haphazard that having any two or three teens show up at the right time and right place was a near miracle. You probably timed homework and other activities around the TV schedule. And you may have learned how to maximize pleasure while minimizing work.

- **The College Years.**

At last — a dose of *reality!* Or was it? You got caught up in course options, living arrangements, Greek letters, sports, dating, protest marches, anguish over changing your major, parents at a distance with advice that sounded antediluvian, some good professors and some who couldn't make a living in the areas they were teaching if their lives depended on it, and, near the end, *fear of not finding a job.*

Perhaps you took a study-habits course, got an "A" and, with a big exam looming, *still* stayed up all night on a desperate exam-cramming coffee binge.

Was a course in planning even *offered?* If it were, did it teach you how to plan your *life?* Or, was it a business course that taught you how to develop a production schedule for a mythical company?

- **The Career Years.**

If you went to work for a well-run organization, you finally may have learned something about planning.

Your employer probably had a *mission statement* to help you understand your job in a larger context. And you may have attended briefings and received booklets explaining a strategic vision, guiding principles, key objectives and goals for each department.

If you became a manager, you probably found yourself *responsible* for a piece of the organization's plan. If you became a good manager, perhaps it was because, first, you became a good planner.

And, if you became an effective manager, or employee at any level, you also found the need to become a good *manager of your time.*

If that were true, you are certain to be running at least the career part of your life through some sort of time management device to help you plan where to be, when to be there, and with what materials in hand.

While some bits and pieces of on-the-job planning may have crept into the rest of your life, the odds are that you *still* haven't done much to harness the power of effective career and personal planning.

• Marriage and Family.

If you're married, consider whether your *wedding* was your greatest single planning effort up to now. Dates had to be set, places nailed down, bridesmaids color-coordinated, menus selected, rings and gifts chosen, and everyone had to show up at the right place at the right time in the right attire.

If you had a huge wedding, the planning may have rivaled the Normandy Invasion, and the nervous family of the bride undoubtedly hired a bridal consultant complete with clipboard, 2-way radio, police whistle and a degree in behavioral psychology.

Through your wedding vows, you accepted a divine *plan* to love, honor, cherish, and care for one another until the very end. And *that,* in all probability, was your single biggest exposure and commitment to a relationship in which *the odds are against you.*

More than half the marriages in the United States end in divorce. Why? Often, it's because of poor or virtually non-existent planning. What planning *does* take place may be so focused on creating an impressive marriage *ceremony* that little attention is paid to planning an enduring *marriage.*

If you're a *typical* married person in the Career Years, there are two careers with attendant work pressures to endure, along with an array of other challenges, especially when children come along.

When you fell in love, you probably didn't think of falling into a good his-and-her career and personal planning process. Without such a process, your odds of staying together get worse. *With* one, they get much better. That's especially true if, together, you learn the MECCA Imperatives and *help each other* strengthen Personal Power, then develop realistic, well-coordinated career and personal plans.

And if you're *not yet* married, share the whole process with your partner-to-be *before* you tie the knot. Answer the Five Crucial Questions *together.* Develop your plans *together.*

The process will help you reconcile differences *together.* And if your differences are irreconcilable, the process will help you identify them and part friends *before* vows are exchanged.

> ...for better or for worse, richer or poorer, in sickness and in health until *death* (not irreconcilable differences) do us part.

Begin With the 3 Key Words: Want, Way, Work

In Chapter 5, you learned the Three Vital Questions that provide an *internal* context for your journey through life. The *external* context, you'll recall, was covered in Part 1 through the 10 trends and other characteristics of the world around you.

If you've cut back on what you *Want,* is it because you can't find the right *Way* to get it? Is it that you are unwilling, or believe you are unable, to *Work* harder, smarter, or a combination of the two? Are you overwhelmed by Continuous White Water?

If you've found a good *Way* to get what you *Want,* should you dream bigger dreams? As what you *Want* is attained, should you back off on *Work* to enjoy some of the things you have dreamed of?

If you aren't getting what you *Want,* should you *Work* harder and smarter, or find another *Way* to get what you *Want?*

Begin charting your course and developing your plan by identifying what it is you *Want* out of life. Assume you *could* find a *Way* to obtain all the time, money and security you would need. In other words, step back from the daily struggles to survive, or to get by, or to thrive, and *dream big!* What would be most important to you? Why would each of these Aspirations be so desirable?

Refer to your new priorities and pie chart in Chapter 7.

Activity: List in order of importance your five greatest Aspirations for an abundant and fulfilling life — your view of life in "Mecca," for instance. Assume you had all the time, money and security needed. Then describe why you would find each of them so desirable.

What I *Want* — If I Had a *Way* to Get It

1. _____

   Why? _____

2. _____

   Why? _____

3. _____

   Why? _____

4. _____

   Why? _____

5. _____

   Why? _____

Now ask yourself how much of what you *Want* could be achieved through the primary *Way* (or ways) you're currently engaged in to get from *where you are now* to *where you want to be*.

Activity: In the blank next to each number, write a key word or two as a reminder of the five big Aspirations you just identified. Then, for each, check one of the three choices to test your current *Way* along with the *Work* associated with it. If you check "maybe" or "yes," note by when you could reasonably expect it to happen. Then describe the *Work* you would have to do.

Will My Current *Way* Get Me What I *Want?*

1. _____ : No _____ | Maybe _____ Yes _____

by _____ if I would_____

_____

2. _____ : No _____ | Maybe _____ Yes _____

by _____ if I would_____

_____

3. _____ : No _____ | Maybe _____ Yes _____

by _____ if I would_____

_____

4. _____ : No _____ | Maybe _____ Yes _____

by _____ if I would_____

_____

5. _____ : No _____ | Maybe _____ Yes _____

by _____ if I would_____

_____

How did you do? If your current *Way* could or should get you what you *Want,* are you willing to do the *Work* you identified? If your current *Way* won't enable you to get what you *Want,* should you (1) abandon some or all of your dreams, or (2) find a better *Way* to get what you *Want?*

Those and other decisions can be made wisely as you complete your answer to the Fourth Crucial Question.

Chart Your Course in 5 Steps

Here are the five steps to chart your course for the balance of your life. They should be taken with a keen eye on your answers to the first three Crucial Questions, your assessment on the MECCA Imperatives and their associated Personal Attributes, and how you responded to the Want-Way-Work activities on the preceding pages.

- *Step 1:* **Write a Personal Mission Statement.**

This is the essential starting point if you are to *fulfill* your answer to the First Crucial Question, *Where Are You Now and Where Do You Want to Be?* It also *summarizes* your answer to the Second Crucial Question, *Whom Do You Choose to Be for the Journey?*

Your Mission also will draw upon elements of the MECCA Matrix, starting with the first three Personal Attributes of the Motivation Imperative.

The Core Attribute of Motivation, Self-Esteem, gives you the license to *determine* your mission. The educational Attribute of Motivation, Purpose, is *defined* in your mission. And your mission becomes the *basis* for the Concentration Attribute, which is A Plan.

- *Step 2:* **Create a Vision for Your Future.**

By painting a vivid word picture of the life you *Want* and are willing to *Work* for, you anchor the First Crucial Question — *where you want to be.* And you extend from the present to the future the Second Crucial Question — *whom you choose to be.*

Your Vision for the Future commits you to the deployment of *all* Five Imperatives and the Personal Attributes that comprise them. And, the bigger the Vision, the greater your commitment must be if you are to fulfill it.

Your Vision should be *evolutionary*, not set in concrete. As the *universe* of your career and personal plan, it should continue to expand and be charted, never leaving you at the dead-end of having done everything with nothing left to do.

- *Step 3:* **Determine Your Key Objectives.**

What are the *major pursuits* in your life that, when accomplished, will enable you to *realize* your Vision?

Key Objectives are your highest priorities. They may involve career pursuits, educational achievements, marriage and family, a new hobby — any great pursuit in line with your Mission and Vision.

The more clearly you identify your Key Objectives, the easier it will be to set priorities. How many Key Objectives can you pursue at the same time? Which one is of greatest importance? Which ones should be put on hold until others are accomplished?

Prioritizing Key Objectives protects you from the frustration and near-certain failure that comes with going in too many directions at the same time. It's telling yourself: "I can do this or I can do that. And I can do *both* this and that *well* if *first* I do this and *then* I do that."

• *Step 4:* **Divide Key Objectives Into Personal Goals.**

Breaking a major pursuit into manageable pieces is essential to *any* planning, be it in business, in sports, in a church, or in *life*.

Life *is* like a journey, but it's also like assembling a puzzle. You stare at a daunting pile of 500 pieces and decide that your Key Objective is to put the whole thing together. But unless you organize the effort into specific steps, you're consigning yourself to long evenings of frustration. You may even throw the whole thing in the trash rather than stick with the effort until you *win*.

So break your Key Objective into Personal Goals. You may decide to find all of the border pieces and assemble them first. Then you may separate the remaining pieces into those likely to depict sky, land, people, buildings, whatever.

Like Key Objectives, you should prioritize your goals. Which goal is most important? Which ones should be put on hold until which other ones are achieved?

• *Step 5:* **Break Goals Down Into MECCA *Do-It!s.***

You'll find that breaking Key Objectives into Personal Goals doesn't go far enough in developing an effective career and personal plan. You may need to divide some or all of your goals into even *smaller* pieces if you are to make the most of your planning process.

In doing this, methodology is more important than terminology. You can call them projects or tasks or sub-goals or jobs or activities or whatever you want. The term recommended in the *Meccanize!®* process is *MECCA Do-It!* To achieve each Personal Goal, you must identify and prioritize a series of smaller steps.

Success rides on these *day-to-day efforts* to achieve your goal.

If you *don't* achieve a goal, most likely it is because of your unwillingness to *do whatever it takes* to get the goal's day-to-day components accomplished. But you *will* get them accomplished if you put the *full power* of the Five Imperatives behind *every one* of them and, through Motivation, Education, Concentration, Communication and Achievement, go out there and *Do-It!*

To continue the example, your Key Objective is to assemble the puzzle. If your first Personal Goal is to assemble the border, you'll achieve the goal faster and easier if you identify and prioritize the components. For example:

1. Find all the edge pieces, 2. Pick out the four corner pieces, 3. Place the corner pieces in their most likely positions, 4. Sort edge

pieces by color and pattern in relation to the corners, 5. Assemble the sides starting with the most-obvious, then: *Do-It!, Do-It!, Do-It!, Do-It!*

The five planning steps *answer* the Fourth Crucial Question, How Should You Chart Your Course? They give you a Personal Planning Process that looks like this:

PERSONAL PLANNING PROCESS

WHERE YOU WANT TO BE

Vision for the Future

Key Objectives

Personal Goals

MECCA Do-It!s

Personal Mission

WHERE YOU ARE NOW

Now take a much closer look at each of the five steps and, proceeding one step at a time, develop your plan.

1. Write a Personal Mission Statement

Words That Give Direction to Your Journey Through Life
In Keeping With Whom You've Chosen to Be

You'd have a hard time finding a company, non-profit organization or government agency that *didn't* have a mission statement. It may be long or short, simple or incomprehensible, written down or in the founder's head, well-communicated or kept under lock and key — but it's there somewhere.

Trying to run an organization without a mission statement is like trying to drive a car without a steering wheel. The best organizations tend to have the best mission statements — short, powerful and widely understood both inside and outside the organization.

Organizations need direction. And so do you. A well-managed

organization identifies and communicates direction through a well-developed mission statement. And so should you.

As a child, direction was set *for* you (or *should* have been!). As an adult, you may have found a new direction or may continue according to the direction given to you as a child. Or, you may be among the many who *lack* direction, wandering from one pursuit to another, unable to figure out what they should *make* of their lives.

One of the best rationales for developing a Personal Mission Statement can be found in a book that has helped hundreds of thousands of people become more successful:

> People can't live with change if there's not a changeless core inside them. The key to the ability to change is a changeless sense of who you are, what you are about and what you value... With a mission statement, we can flow with changes.
>
> Steven R. Covey
> *The 7 Habits of Highly Effective People*

Covey goes on to say that a mission statement is like your personal constitution. His urging that you develop a personal mission comes as part of a habit he identifies as *beginning with the end in mind*. Note where *Personal Mission* is located on the Personal Planning Process diagram. It's at the *beginning*.

A Personal Mission Statement, then, is words that give direction at the *beginning* of your personal planning process. In developing a good mission statement, you must not confuse its purpose with the other four steps in the planning process.

Here's an example of how to distinguish among the five steps. Let's pretend you're a team in the National Football League:

Team Mission	Win football games
Vision for the Future	Win the Super Bowl by _____
Key Objective now	Get in this season's playoffs
Goal to work on now	Win today's game
DO-IT! to work on now	Score a touchdown on this drive

The mission identifies what the team is all about. It reminds everyone of what is important and needs to be done on an ongoing basis. The mission need never change.

The vision is what the team realistically could accomplish by a specific time in the future, given maximum attention to the mission.

The other three elements represent the well-organized, step-by-step process to achieve the Vision by fulfilling the Mission *well*.

Coming up with an effective Personal Mission Statement may not be easy, especially if you haven't given much thought to what your life is, or should be, all about.

In the *Meccanize!*® workshops, participants develop a good *draft* of their mission and are urged to give it much additional thought before finalizing it.

If you're starting from scratch in this process, don't expect to come up with your mission in life in a few minutes or even hours. Take your time, get it right, feel good about it and commit to fulfilling it.

Your mission should be firmly linked to the five Personal Attributes of the Motivation Imperative as well as the five Core Attributes of the MECCA Matrix (page 189). Consider how they tie in:

- **Self-Esteem.** Your Mission will be greatly influenced by how you feel about yourself and your own potential.

- **Purpose.** Your Mission is the *embodiment* of your Purpose in life. It should reflect why you believe you were placed on this earth.

- *A Plan.* You can't develop an effective career and personal Plan without determining your Mission.

- **Enthusiasm.** You should be *excited* about fulfilling your Mission, and the mere fact of having *identified* a clear Mission for your life should raise your overall Enthusiasm level considerably.

- **Resilience.** Your best defense against the changes and setbacks that are inevitable in life is the *"changeless core within you"* that comes from commitment to a good Personal Mission. The better the mission and the stronger your commitment to it, the more Resilience you will have.

Influenced at the outset by Self-Esteem (the Motivation of Motivation), the other four Core Attributes have important roles to play in your Mission as well:

- **Self-Development.** This is the educational aspect of fulfilling your mission. What you set out to *learn* should be *driven* by your Personal Mission.

- **Self-Discipline.** Your mission probably won't be *easy*. Your level of Self-Discipline will be your primary strength in sticking with your mission and plan, then attaining your Vision for the Future.

- **Self-Confidence.** The higher your Self-Esteem, Self-Development and Self-Discipline, the greater your level of Self-Confidence. When you *know* you can fulfill your Mission, you will fulfill it.

• **Self-Fulfillment.** Each day that you are fulfilling your Mission in life you are *raising* your over-all level of Self-Fulfillment. The same is true of carrying out your Personal Plan and working toward, and eventually achieving, your Vision for the Future.

What are the characteristics of a good Personal Mission Statement? For the most part, they are the same characteristics found in a good organizational mission: relevant, succinct, realistic and, perhaps, containing emotion.

As employees may be *smitten* by an especially good company mission statement, so it is that you can *smite yourself* with a good Personal Mission.

Here are five qualities you should incorporate:

S *Short.* Twenty words at most, 15 or less if you can. The shorter it is, the easier it will be to remember.

M *Meaningful.* No empty words. You know when you're on track and when you stray from your Mission.

I *Inspirational.* You should be invigorated by your Personal Mission; maybe even raise a few goose bumps.

T *Timeless.* You may change it someday, but it should be written as though it will go on forever.

E *Empowering.* Your mission should leave you plenty of room to grow and give you license to grow.

Here are five *drafts* of Personal Missions. How would you rate them? How would you characterize the people who wrote them, based on the Imperatives and Attributes of the MECCA Matrix? Could you improve upon them?

Instill love, independence and compassion in family and friends so that their lives will also be enriched as they strive for their own missions and goals.

Assist others in becoming all they are willing to become.

Lead a life I love by loving myself and others as the human beings they are, achieving fulfillment by encouraging others to realize all the joy that life can provide.

Just enjoy life.

Run the family businesses in a way that assures maximum profits and, as a result, the largest possible inheritances for all those entitled to share in the estate.

You may have found one or more of them outrageous, amusing, hollow, uplifting, not good or not bad. What's important, though, is to see where five people *started* their efforts and what you might learn as a result.

Here are five mission statements that, after one or more drafts and a lot of reflection, emerged in *final* form. By no means should you consider them "model" statements. They simply illustrate some careful selection of words and emphasis on the priorities identified in the Second Crucial Question:

Emphasis on Having
Attain great wealth in order to enjoy life to its fullest.

Emphasis on Having & Doing
Build my professional practice so I can enjoy a lifestyle commensurate with a seven-figure income.

Emphasis on Doing
Experience the happiness that comes with being the best in all that I do.

Emphasis on Doing & Being
Experience joy and achievement by helping others become successful.

Emphasis on Being
Live a life of love, beauty, joy and laughter with family, friends and community.

What can you learn from these mission statements? Do they offer some ideas for you? Are you ready to develop your own Personal Mission Statement? Could you develop one that embraces all three slices of life — Relationships (Being), Work and Other Activities (Doing), and Material Wealth (Having)?

Activity: Using a separate sheet of paper, develop a first draft of your Personal Mission in life. When you have checked it against the SMITE Scale and other factors, edited it into a final draft and write it below:

_____

_____

_____

_____

2. Create a Vision for Your Future

A description of life as you want it to be by a future date,
based upon ongoing fulfillment of your Personal Mission.

For your Personal Mission to be of value, it must *lead* somewhere. Of what value is a mission unless you see worthwhile results from pursuing it?

Pity those who might identify their mission in life with a single word — *Work.* Unless the work results in something fulfilling or at least meaningful, life's journey is made somewhere down the roadway, probably in or near Hades Gulch.

By developing a written statement of your Vision for the Future, you add *value* and specific *meaning* to your Personal Mission.

Another term for vision is *dream-building.* Use the full power of such Personal Attributes as Creativity, Interest, Judgment, Perspective and Opportunity to paint a vivid picture of life as you *want* it to be, as it *can* be, and as you're willing to *make* it be.

Distinguish between big, realistic dreams and pure fantasies. If you're a person of modest means and average ambition whose mission is simply to enjoy life, your Vision for the Future should not depict "Lifestyles of the Rich and Famous." Owning a nice car might fit your vision, but owning a twin-jet private aircraft? Pure fantasy.

On the other hand, if you're *driven* by a willingness to do *whatever it takes* to fulfill your vision, the bigger the dreams the better.

As with the SMITE qualities of a good mission, here are five qualities of a good vision. Create a vision that is GRAND:

G *Growth-oriented.* A vision for your life as it is today is no vision. If you're not growing, you're dying. Envision growth. See *more* in life. *Stretch* yourself!

R *Realistic.* Envision the achievable and, in stretching yourself, what is *conceivable.* Be guided by belief in yourself, not by what others say you can't do.

A *Assessable.* You should be able to measure progress toward the realization of your vision. To be rich isn't enough. Rich in what? *How* rich?

N *Noble.* If "Mecca" is where you want to be, your Vision for the Future should reflect the excellence and high ideals that are associated with residency there.

D Date-Specific. While your Mission is timeless, your vision should have a date attached to it, preferably long-term (two years or more into the future).

Your vision should be in *harmony* with your Mission. If your Mission is simply to make money and have fun, your Vision for the Future should paint a vivid picture of *how much* wealth you will have accumulated and *what kinds* of fun you will be having by a date two or more years hence.

If your Mission is to experience a joy of living by serving God and humankind, your Vision is *out of synch* if it depicts wild romps across the beaches of the world.

Here are examples of Vision statements based on the Have-Do-Be criteria. Note that unlike your Personal Mission, there is no need to keep your Vision for the Future short and, therefore, easy to memorize.

Emphasis on Having
By (date), I will be living in a million-dollar-plus home in an elegant, gated community. My home will have white columns in front and a large, screened pool on expansive grounds adjoining a private lake. I will have developed an income that will enable me to buy an island in the St. Lawrence River as a summer retreat and, for winter, I will have a 60-foot Hatteras motoryacht with twin diesel engines, full electronics and custom furnishings, professionally maintained at a private yacht club in the Florida Keys.

Emphasis on Doing
By July 1, (year), I will have completed work on my masters degree and will have become the manager of my department. I will have joined at least two more non-profit boards of directors and will have reduced my golf handicap by at least half. I will have purchased and restored a 1965-67 Ford Mustang convertible and will have all the equipment needed to start a woodcrafting hobby in a shop I will have built in my garage.

Emphasis on Being
By mid-(year), I will have met and married the right person, settled into a comfortable home near our families and have at least two children, hopefully a boy and a girl. I will have made great progress on the spiritual dimension of my life, including the completion of a major Bible study course and will have become a teacher in the primary department of a Sunday School. I also will have made at least one overseas missionary trip, preferably to Africa, and, if possible, with my new spouse. Surrounded by many new friends, my spouse and I will have become very focused on helping others meet their needs.

Your Vision for the Future is more likely to incorporate elements of Having, Doing *and* Being, not just a single dimension. Here's another example, this one bringing together all three slices:

Emphasis on Having, Doing & Being

By the beginning of (year), I will have earned a masters degree degree and an executive position with a major company. The income from my new position, combined with my prior savings, will enable me to settle down and start a family. I will find the right person to become my partner in life, possibly by expanding my activities at church and as a community volunteer. By the time we are ready to marry, I will have the resources for an extended honeymoon as well as a substantial down payment on a home in a nice neighborhood where we can raise children.

If you have trouble coming up with a good Vision for the Future, you're not alone. Many people in these times find it hard to envision a bright future, achieving great things, or life with the joys of being in "Mecca." An old adage (somewhat modified) expresses the importance of having both a mission *and* a vision:

A Mission without a Vision is drudgery;
A Vision without a Mission is sheer fantasy;
A Mission with a Vision is the road to victory.

Activity: Review your Personal Mission. Then, using a separate sheet of paper, develop a first draft of your Vision for the Future. Check it against the GRAND Scale and other factors on the preceding pages, then edit it into a final draft and write it here:

_____

_____

_____

_____

_____

_____

_____

_____

Developing a Shared Mission & Vision

Harmony between your Personal Mission and your Vision for the Future is important. Harmony also is important between you and a planning partner.

Disharmony in the missions and visions of two people in a marriage is a major reason marriages fail. Chances are, the partners never identified *before* the marriage their own missions and visions; then, having made some adjustments to accommodate each others' needs and interests, developed *shared* mission and vision statements.

If you are already married, perhaps for the second or third time, would it be helpful for you and your spouse to go through this process together?

You may be deeply in love today, but your relationship may become one more divorce statistic if you are unable to synchronize your *life plans* starting with a *shared* mission and a *shared* vision.

It's quite possible for two people with greatly different missions in life to stay married to each other, perhaps even *happily* married. For example, one partner may be devoted to acquiring wealth and the other, because of the wealth, may be able to fulfill a mission of helping others. Or, there could be harmony between a homebody who loves to be alone and a person who loves to make a living from traveling all over the world.

Despite accommodation or even harmony between two very different missions, serious problems in a marriage may arise if visions are out of synch.

His Vision
By (date), I will be enjoying life as a socially active New Yorker, living in a luxury penthouse overlooking Central Park South...

Her Vision
By (date), I will be enjoying life as a cattle rancher in the Australian Outback totally isolated from the chaos of New York...

Unless, of course:

Our Shared Vision for the Future
By (date), we will lead exciting lives of contrasts, enjoying six months each year in a luxury New York penthouse apartment during the theater season and the other six months totally "away from it all" as cattle ranchers in the Australian Outback...

Share this process with your planning partner, if you have one. Map out your Personal Mission and Vision statements, then develop a compatible Shared Mission and a Shared Vision for the Future.

2

MECCA Factor

3. Determine Your Key Objectives

*Major Life Pursuits in Support of Your Personal Mission,
Usually Requiring Months or Years of Effort*

So far, you have charted your course by developing a Personal Mission statement that gives direction to your journey through life in keeping with whom you've chosen to be. And, you have anchored your long-term outlook with a Vision for the Future that describes life as you *want it to be* in keeping with your Personal Mission.

As illustrated by the Personal Planning Process on page 204, fulfilling your vision requires determining and prioritizing major life pursuits, called Key Objectives.

Distinguish carefully among your mission, vision and Key Objectives. For example, if you are young and totally focused on a career as a concert pianist, experiencing the joy of sharing your gift of music with others is *not* a Key Objective. Nor is becoming the *world's greatest* concert pianist. Rather, the foundation of your Personal Plan might look something like this:

Personal Mission
Experience fully the joy of music by sharing with others my gifts as a concert pianist.

Vision for the Future
By 2015, I will be recognized as the world's greatest living-concert pianist, having...(describe crowning achievements)

Key Objectives
1. Graduate with highest honors from Julliard by (date).
2. Marry someone who shares my love of music and will be supportive of my career by (date).
3. Play my first major Carnegie Hall recital by (date).

Many Key Objectives would be needed to fulfill such a big, long-term Vision. But it's far better to identify *nearer-term* objectives and *achieve* them than hang dates on a years-long string of milestones certain to change.

You can change the date on a Vision statement to later or sooner at anytime. Having painted a clear picture of what you want in the long-term, what's most important is focusing on the next one to several years.

The example of the concert pianist is one-dimensional. Music is this person's whole life, even to the nature of a future marriage partner.

213

Your life's pursuits, however, may be much more diverse. If so, you may identify Key Objectives that are loosely related or not related at all to each other. While you may have Key Objectives not covered specifically by your Mission or your Vision, none should be *in conflict* with your Mission and Vision.

Some Key Objectives may have specific target dates and some may be of an ongoing nature, although their subordinate Personal Goals, as explained in a moment, will have target dates. Example:

Personal Mission
Enjoy a life of professional success and good relationships with family and friends.

Vision for the Future
By (date), I will have at least doubled the size of my professional practice. I will be proud of my role as a loving spouse and parent, and will have helped our sons and daughters get college educations. With the children grown and gone, I will concentrate more on golf, tennis and other recreational pursuits with family and friends. I also will have developed and will be implementing a comprehensive financial plan that will help assure me a secure retirement.

Key Objectives
(For a calendar year)
1. Increase net income from my practice by at least 20 percent.
2. Help achieve the next major bonus level in our network marketing business by June 1.
3. Become accredited in my profession by Nov. 15.
4. Strengthen my personal power (MECCA Matrix attributes)

In this example, the target date for the first Key Objective is the end of the year, the time frame for *all* of the Key Objectives.

Setting Key Objectives annually is a good way to plan, even rolling out a fresh set on New Year's Day in place of those traditional resolutions that tend to be widely touted and quickly forgotten.

The second Key Objective is an example of one due for completion during the year. This is a couple building a network marketing business together. The *other* spouse is taking the lead and has the Key Objective to *achieve* the next bonus level. This spouse's role is to *help* achieve it. When achievement is at hand, they'll sit down together and decide on a *new* Key Objective to continue building their business.

The third Key Objective (become accredited) is an example of a one-time effort. Once achieved, there will be no need to repeat it in the Personal Plan.

The last Key Objective (strengthen my personal power) could go on forever. It is a very *broad* Key Objective that, based on the Five MECCA Imperatives and the 25 Personal Attributes of the matrix, can cover virtually any kind of self-improvement goals.

Self-improvement should be of prime importance to everyone, so you should include this simple, four-word Key Objective in your plan: *Strengthen My Personal Power.* Let the Imperatives and the Attributes, along with your self-assessment, guide you. Then draw upon the ideas found in Part 3.

How Many Key Objectives Should You Have?

If you come up with more than four or five — six at the very most — you're having one or more of these problems:

• Mixing up Key Objectives and Personal Goals.

Let's say that in addition to (1) Make a big career move, (2) Get your daughter married off in grand style, (3) Finish your doctoral thesis and (4) Strengthen your personal power, you also set as your Key Objectives for the coming year or so (5) Quit smoking, (6) Reduce weight to a monthly average of 20 pounds less than it is today and (7) Develop and stick to a vigorous exercise regimen.

That's *seven* Key Objectives — or is it? The last three are related to your health and would fit nicely under a Key Objective called *Improve My Health.* That would leave you with *five* rather than seven Key Objectives.

If you wanted to cut your Key Objectives to *four,* you could put the three health-related items under *Strengthen My Personal Power,* since they relate to the Motivation and Concentration Imperatives along with such Personal Attributes as Self-Esteem, Enthusiasm (the umbrella covering energy, health and wellness) and Self-Discipline.

To go even further, if you wanted to cut your Key Objectives down to only *three,* you also could make the completion of your doctoral thesis a Personal Goal under *Strengthen My Personal Power* since it relates well to the Education Imperative.

• Trying to go in too many directions at once.

Let's say your Key Objectives for the new year are (1) Break the all-time sales record where I work, (2) Earn an associate degree from a community college, (3) Double the net income from my sideline business, (4) Help my son become an Eagle Scout, (5) Strengthen my personal power (you'll need *plenty* of that!) and (6) Go on a once-in-a-lifetime African safari.

Unless you're super-human, or already have a couple of those Key Objectives nearly achieved, you're trying to go in too many directions at once.

Use the process to set priorities and allow time to assure that you can *achieve* each Key Objective. Which ones *must* be done this year? Should the safari wait until next year? If you're going to have to work a lot of nights and weekends to break the sales record, which is the more important use of the time that remains — getting the associate degree or helping your son earn the rank of Eagle Scout?

- **Trying to plan too much, too far ahead.**
If you are a 23-year-old newlywed with dreams of an idyllic professional and family life within the next 25 years, avoid the temptation to develop such Key Objectives as: (1) Find a better job in a bigger company by the end of the year, (2) Earn a masters degree in biochemistry within five years of joining the bigger company, (3) Have three children by age 35, etc.

The first objective is the only one that, for the coming year, can be divided into Personal Goals and pursued effectively.

How could you *plan* for the masters degree that far ahead? By the time you'd be ready to even *start* on the program, you might find biochemistry irrelevant to your career. And how could you *possibly* divide three children into Personal Goals 12 years in advance?

Use your Vision for the Future to paint as vivid a picture as possible of future family life and professional achievements, then set Key Objectives that will point in that direction. As you update your plan, adjust both the Vision and the Key Objectives to stay on course and keep *moving forward*.

- **Additional guidelines for Key Objectives:**
> List them *in order of importance* without regard for when they are to be achieved. Key Objective No. 1 should be your single most important pursuit.

> Aim high to stretch your abilities but not so high that you become overwhelmed. Be sure you are *willing and able* to accomplish what you set out to do.

> Make each Key Objective a single subject. Be wary of the word "and," for a Key Objective with an "and" in it probably contains more than one major pursuit.

> Set realistic deadlines. Prioritize. Back off deadlines for Key Objectives of least importance so you can *tighten* deadlines for those of greater importance.

> Make sure each Key Objective has the strongest, most appropriate action verb. *Earn* a masters degree... *Become* a deacon... *Enjoy* a three-month world cruise... *Exceed* last year's net income record...

> State your Key Objectives in *positive* terms; e.g., set out to "Improve your outlook on life," not "Stop having a rotten attitude."

> Make Key Objectives *measurable*. There must be a clear sense of when and with what degree of success the Key Objective was accomplished. Either achievement is implicit in the language of the Key Objective itself, or the Key Objective is achieved when every one of its goals are accomplished.

> Use clear language. The clearer, more precise the language, the easier it will be to stay on course and carry out your plan.

> Assemble objectives and goals logically. List Key Objectives in order of importance. List goals under each objective chronologically.

Activity: Review your mission and vision as well as other decisions you've made so far. Then, following the guidelines, draft your Key Objectives on a separate sheet of paper. *Try to end up with no more than four,* including "Strengthen my Personal Power." Edit them carefully, then put them in order of importance and write them here:

1. _____

_____

2. _____

_____

3. _____

_____

4. _____

_____

5. _____

_____

6. _____

_____

4. Divide Key Objectives Into Personal Goals

Specific activities which, when accomplished, will result in achievement of your Key Objectives.

Key Objectives can be overwhelming. What may *seem* so desirable and attainable when you draft your Personal Plan can become a major source of discouragement if you try to achieve it in its entirety all at once. Too easily comes the feeling *"it can't be done,"* so you quit.

Divide each Key Objective into Personal Goals. Not only will you make Key Objectives achievable, but you create a step-by-step process to chart progress. You also reinforce Motivation each time you achieve a Personal Goal.

How do you eat an elephant? One bite at a time.

Let's say you have a Key Objective to start a part-time business that, within a year, will produce $2,000 a month in net income.

You don't want to grab the first "opportunity" that comes along, but you *do* want to move methodically and quickly, making the best decision in the shortest time.

Keeping in mind that your Personal Goals later will be further divided into bite-size MECCA *Do-It!s,* here's how you might organize your Key Objective.

Key Objective

By May 1, launch a part-time business with high long-term income potential that will produce at least $2,000 in monthly net income by the end of its first year.

Personal Goals

1. Create a foundation for future success in the business by determining why I want to have the business. By Jan. 10.
2. Decide the maximum amount of time and money I would be able to invest in the business. By Feb. 1.
3. Develop a list of business opportunities that could meet my criteria.   By March 21
4. Select the best business opportunity based on a thorough examination of the options.   By April 15.
5. Launch the business. By May 1.

You have set the basic criteria for your business venture by *clearly wording* the Key Objective. You're looking for something that is part-time, has good long-term income potential and should produce at least $2,000 a month in net income by the end of its first year.

Your Key Objective? *Launch* the business by May 1. You divide the effort into five manageable Personal Goals.

Your first Goal is a starting point too-often overlooked when planning. You're asking yourself, loud and clear, a very *powerful* question: *"Why would I want to do this?"* Lack of a strong reason is an underlying cause of failure in many career or life pursuits.

Remember the three most important words in planning? *Want, Way, Work.* In this example, your *reason* to put time, money and effort into something *has* to be based on something you *Want.* Your Key Objective? Find the best *Way* to get it.

Will you be willing to do the *Work* involved in making your part-time business a success? If you succeed in finding a viable *Way* and you have a powerful reason based on what you *Want,* the answer most likely is *yes!*

Your second Personal Goal brings you face-to-face with additional criteria for your Key Objective. You want $2,000 a month by the end of the first year. But what are the *outer limits* of the time and money you could invest?

If you're nearly flat broke and have bad credit, it's obvious that buying a $250,000 franchise is not an option. And if you're already working 70 hours a week, "part-time" should be closer to 10 to 12 hours a week than 25 to 30.

You could have combined the third and fourth Goals but, wisely, you remembered to divide your Key Objective into *manageable* pieces.

Developing a good list of opportunities fitting your criteria (Goal No. 3) is no easy task. Nor is making a final selection based on having thoroughly investigated the two or three choices that appear to be the best (Goal No. 4).

So, you have developed five Goals in chronological order and will focus on them one at a time, doing your best to meet or beat the deadlines you have set for yourself.

The fifth Goal is due for completion on the same day as your Key Objective. When the last of the Personal Goals is accomplished, you have achieved your Key Objective.

In this example, your Key Objective is to *launch* a part-time business. Since you won't know its nature until you check out the opportunities and make a decision, your Key Objective can't reach further than getting started.

Your second Key Objective already has been identified: *Build* your new business to a net income of $2,000 a month by the end of the year.

You won't be able to divide the second Objective into Goals until you know the nature of your new business. When you do, you'll develop a well-thought-out set of Personal Goals to take you from $0 monthly on Day 1 to $2,000 by the end of the year.

Activity: Practice the process by choosing one of the Key Objectives you wrote on page 217. Use a separate sheet of paper to draft up to five Personal Goals to achieve it. When you're satisfied, write the Key Objective and the goals that support it on the next page. Be sure to put the goals in order of their due dates (By ____). The due date on the last Personal Goal should be the same as the due date on the Key Objective, unless the objective will continue into later years. In that case, you would add goals later until your objective is reached.

Key Objective # ____ : _____

_____ By _____

Personal Goals

1. _____

_____ By_____

2. _____

_____ By_____

3. _____

_____ By_____

4. _____

_____ By_____

5. _____

_____ By_____

5. Break Goals Down Into MECCA *Do-It!s*

Specific day-to-day tasks that will result in achievement of your Personal Goals.

You determined what you *Want* out of life by answering the first two Crucial Questions and developing your Personal Mission and Vision for the Future. You outlined the *Way* to get what you *Want* by identifying major life pursuits called Key Objectives. And, you learned how to make Key Objectives manageable by breaking them down into Personal Goals.

With the *Want* and the *Way* identified, all that remains is the make-or-break tough part — the *Work*. No matter what or how much you *Want* and no matter how good the *Way* to get it, you *will not succeed* without doing the *Work*.

Like everyone, you don't plan to fail. And, having come this far in the *Meccanize!*® process, you're not failing to plan because you know what you *Want* and you have determined the best *Way* to get it.

The important first step in doing the *Work* is to complete your Personal Plan by reducing each Personal Goal to small, bite-size pieces called MECCA *Do-It!s*.

It is those small, day-to-day tasks that will determine whether you achieve your Personal Goals and Key Objectives and, ultimately, *whether* you fulfill your Personal Mission and Vision for the Future.

The more you break your Plan into small, manageable pieces, the less likely it is that you will become overwhelmed, discouraged and give up on the pursuit.

> Nothing is particularly hard if you divide it
> into small jobs.
>
> Henry Ford

Suppose, for example, what you *Want* more than anything else in life is warm, loving companionship. The *Way* to have it, you decide, is to get married. The problem is that you know of no one you would want to marry, and all your life you've been very shy around the opposite sex.

Key Objective No. 1 in your Personal Plan is: *Get Married.* And with shyness your biggest obstacle, you make overcoming it Personal Goal No.1. You map out additional goals — No.2: Develop a prioritized list of specific qualities to look for in a spouse, No.3: Figure out how and where to meet people with those qualities, No. 4, No. 5, etc.

But no matter how well you map out the other Goals, your chances of achieving the Key Objective are slim to none unless you accomplish Goal No. 1 which, on the face of it, is a formidable task.

So you break the Goal into bite-size pieces. For example, *find a good book* on how to do it...and then read the book...and then *make a list* of what three or four ways might work best for you...and then *try* each of those ways...and then *decide* which one to focus on...and then...

Those small steps are your MECCA *Do-It!s*. They will determine whether you will achieve your Personal Goals and, ultimately, your Key Objective.

If you are *still* single 10 years later, is it because your Key Objective was "bad" or that you started with the "wrong" Personal Goal? No, it's because you never *got* the book...or you got the book but never *read* the book...or you read the book but never *made the list*...or...

Failure to attend to the *little* things can undermine even the greatest of plans.

> A little neglect may breed mischief: For want of a nail
> the shoe was lost, for want of a shoe the horse was lost;
> and for want of a horse the rider was lost.
>
> Benjamin Franklin
> Maxims, *Poor Richard's Almanac*

You can achieve *anything that's possible* if you plan it in small, do-able pieces; then, apply to each piece your full powers of Motivation, Education, Concentration, Communication and Achievement, *just go out there and DO-IT!*

MECCA *Do-It!s* can turn your Plan into an effective *Personal Planning Process.* As words on paper, your Plan is of no value. But your Personal Plan will be of *tremendous* value when you continually improve it, consistently act upon it and constantly accomplish those little *Do-It!s.*

Let's use self-improvement efforts as an example of how to organize a Key Objective into Personal Goals and MECCA *Do-It!s.* The time frame is a calendar year. (Personal attributes from the MECCA Matrix related to each Goal are in parentheses.)

Key Objective # ____ : Strengthen My Personal Power.

    Goal # 1: (Organization): Implement a system that will help me make much better use of time. By May 15.

        Do-It! # 1: List at least 10 payoffs for making better use of my time. By Jan. 21.

        Do-It! # 2: Find the best seminar, course or other program to increase my time-management skills. By Feb. 1.

        Do-It! # 3: Complete the program. By April 1.

        Do-It! # 4: Implement the process in a way that will work best for me. By May 1.

        Do-It! # 5: Get feedback from peers to confirm I am managing time better. By May 15.

    Goal # 2: (Knowledge): Expand my access to information that is important to my career. By Sept. 15.

        Do-It! # 1: Join the professional association. By Feb. 1.

        Do-It! # 2: Attend the association's trade fair. On March 26.

        Do-It! # 3: Buy a computer modem. By Aug. 15.

        Do-It! # 4: Select the best on-line network and subscribe to it. By Sept. 15.

    Goal # 3: (Self-Esteem): Reduce weight to a monthly daily average of no more than 150 pounds. By June 30.

        Do-It! # 1: Average 160 or less. By Jan. 31.

        Do-It! # 2: Average 158 or less. By Feb. 28.

        Do-It! # 3: Average 156 or less. By March 31.

        Do-It! # 4: Average 154 or less. By April 30.

        Do-It! # 5: Average 152 or less. By May 31.

        Do-It! # 6: Average 150 or less. By June 30.

    (Keep it off with 6 more Do-It!s to be at 150 or less)

Note the due dates. Always list *Do-It!s* in chronological order. Under each Personal Goal, try to achieve one *Do-It!* before tackling the next. Achieve each goal *one step at a time.*

Activity: Choose one of the Personal Goals you wrote on page 220. Use separate paper to break it into MECCA *Do-It!s.* When you're satisfied, write them below as an example. Be sure the due date on the last *Do-It!* is the same as the due date on the Personal Goal.

Goal # _____ : _____

_____ By_____

MECCA Do-It!s

1. _____

_____ By_____

2. _____

_____ By_____

3. _____

_____ By_____

4. _____

_____ By_____

5. _____

_____ By_____

If you are a very organized, highly detail-oriented person, you may feel the urge to break a *Do-It!* into even *smaller* pieces. If so, simply call them Tasks and organize them in due-date order. And if that's *still* not enough detail for you, break the Task into a series of Sub-Tasks.

Put Your Personal Plan Into Action

If you are involved in *organizational* planning, you know the only thing worse than having a plan that gathers dust on a bookshelf is having no plan at all.

Whether its an organization's plan or your Personal Plan, the *process* of developing it should be of great value. But if nothing is done with the plan after the ink is dry, the value quickly declines to zero.

Here are five steps to put your Personal Plan into action:

• Finish Writing Your Plan.
You've developed a Personal Mission, Vision for the Future and Key Objectives. Plus, you learned how to break each Key Objective into Personal Goals and each Goal into bite-size, one-step-at-a-time MECCA *Do-It!s*. Now finish drafting your Plan.

• Decide on a Format.
The *Meccanize!*® Planning Packet contains special inserts to personal-size planners. It's available to help you *(see ordering instructions in the back)*. Or, devise your own paper or computer format.

• Coordinate Systems & Eliminate Duplication.
Your Personal Plan will be broader and longer-term than the daily, weekly and monthly goal-setting tools found in most other systems. Keep the elements of your plan together. Use your calendar or day-planner to remind you of your Personal Plan's due dates.

• Stick With the Process!
You gain the most from your Personal Plan when you make the *process* a habit. Harness such Personal Attributes as Enthusiasm, Resilience, Creativity, Self-Discipline and Focus. Reward yourself when you achieve objectives, goals, etc. Reset them when you don't.

• Update Your Plan Regularly.
Review your Mission, Vision and Key Objectives at least annually. Continually update everything else. When a barrier is insurmountable, re-do that part of the plan. Reset priorities to accommodate opportunities. Keep the process dynamic and *be flexible!*

It is a bad plan that admits no modification.

Publilius Syrus
Maxim 469

Activity: Complete your Personal Plan. Put it into action. Focus the full force of the MECCA Imperatives on your Personal Mission and Vision for the Future, and each Key Objective and Personal Goal. Then *Do-It! Do-It! Do-It!*

Chapter 10

The Fifth Crucial Question:

When Will You Know You've Arrived?

- You Have Become Whom You've Chosen to Become
- Your Personal Power Is in High Gear
- You Have Charted Your Course Well
- You Have Followed Through on a Good Plan
- You Have Engaged Ongoing Support

Knowing you've "arrived" is easy when the journey is to visit a loving relative. You know you've reached your destination because of the hugs and kisses, perhaps even tears of joy.

You may have a strong sense of "arrival" in your career when you're handed the proverbial keys to the executive washroom, or get to drive a company car with leather seats.

But knowing when you've arrived on *this* journey may not be so easy. For one thing, a destination such as "Mecca" involves a deep and "spiritual" sense of well-being rather than a physical sense of reaching a spot on a map or the psychological sense of accomplishing a series of Key Objectives and Personal Goals.

"Mecca," after all, is the capital city of the State of Grace. Living there *surrounds you* with the greatest of all gifts, the gift of divine assistance *offered free* to those who are willing to accept it.

"Arrival" means an *enduring* sense of destination — a better place from which you can *continue* life's journey. It means a new and positive *outlook* on life. It means a new set of attitudes that take you far beyond brief periods of joy and fulfillment ("Mecca" moments).

It means you have developed powerful new positive attitudes that carry you all the way to joy of living and a new zest for life. And, it means life's inevitable periods in Purgatoria and even Hades Gulch will be short-lived, enabling you to return quickly to your "home" at the top of the roadway.

If "Mecca" *is* your destination of choice, arrival need not wait until all or most elements of your Personal Plan are accomplished. Joy of living should come from *pursuing* worthwhile dreams as much, if not more, than from achieving them.

Avoid a trap that many fall into. Don't use fulfillment of your Key Objectives or even realization of your Vision for the Future as a license to stop growing. Develop even *grander* dreams and set even *bigger* Key Objectives to make your dreams come true. Keep going, keep growing!

> When all is said and done, there's nothing left to say or do — except to become completely bored.

Like the others, the Fifth Crucial Question has five components. Each is related to one of the questions:

You know you've arrived (Question #1) when you've:
> Become whom you've chosen to become (Question #2).
> Shifted Personal Power into high gear (Question #3).
> Charted your course well (Question #4).
> Developed and are following a good plan (Question #4).
> Engaged ongoing support (Question #5).

You Have Become Whom You've Chosen to Become

The Second Crucial Question (Whom Do You Choose to Be for the Journey?) is the toughest of the five. It helps you develop an *internal context* for life's journey. It gives you a firmer basis for success, now and in the future.

Your brief review of history, your examination of important trends in Part 1, and your answer to the First Crucial Question (Where Are You Now and Where Do You Want to Be?) gave you a basis for how you should *define* yourself. This self-definition points to how you can *live* your life instead of just working your way past one milestone after another.

> First I was dying to finish high school and start college.
> Then I was dying to finish college and start working.
> Then I was dying to marry and have children.
> Then I was dying for my children to grow up.
> Then I was dying to retire.
> And now I am dying and suddenly realize I forgot to live.

Here is a checklist to help you determine whether you have answered the Second Crucial Question. If you can check all five in the affirmative, you have become whom you have chosen to become:

_____ Revisiting the Victim/Victor assessment (page 146), there's no doubt I'm now programmed as a Victor.

_____ I have incorporated the Five Principles of Productive Thinking into my life (pages 151-152) and have come to believe that my personal happiness depends totally on how I choose to think.

_____ My choices of Aspirations, Expectations and Entitlements (pages 155-156) not only are realistic, but are heavily weighted *toward* positive and achievable Aspirations and *away from* a pervasive thirst for Entitlements.

_____ After carefully charting and analyzing my track record on how far I chose to go in the past (pages 160-161), I am now able to *love the experience* as well as strive for mastery in my major pursuits.

_____ I have charted my priorities among Material Wealth, Work and Other Activities, and Relationships (page 166), and I am living my life in harmony with those priorities.

Your Personal Power Is in High Gear

The Five Sequential Imperatives of MECCA can help you along every foot of your journey. Use the MECCA acronym to test your capabilities in making a career decision, to strengthen a relationship, to achieve your Key Objectives and other elements of your Personal Plan, as well as to help you in other important aspects of life.

Your Personal Power is in high gear when you have eliminated every Roadblock and every Steep Hill that you identified on your self-assessment (pages 191-195). High gear is having every one of those Personal Attributes on the MECCA Matrix (page 189) identified as a Clear Road for the continuation of your journey

Reinforcing *all* your Personal Attributes should be an ongoing, life-long process.

There are some Attributes in which you have inherent strengths. For example, you may be an outgoing person to whom Association comes naturally and never has been a problem. It is a Clear Road and always will be.

On the other hand, you are very likely to have some Attributes subject to back-sliding. These are Attributes that *never were* your great strengths that, nonetheless, you've turned into Clear Roads.

Example: Let's say you've been disorganized most of your life but now, thanks to a new system, you now see Organization as a Clear Road. Without ongoing reinforcement, how long will it be until bad habits start creeping back and you become disorganized again?

Keeping your Personal Power in high gear is important. Identify attributes that could slip back into becoming impediments to your progress.

Circle all the Personal Attributes you'll want to pay ongoing special attention to:

Motivation

Self-Esteem   Purpose   A Plan   Enthusiasm   Resilience

Education

Aptitude   Self-Development   Creativity   Interest   Knowledge

Concentration

Judgment   Organization   Self-Discipline   Perspective   Focus

Communication

Association   Interaction   Relationships   Self-Confidence   Recognition

Achievement

Opportunity   Expertise   Influence   Character   Self-Fulfillment

You Have Charted Your Course Well

Your Personal Planning Process (page 204) is the key to turning good intentions into terrific outcomes. The five elements of the process enable you to translate your answers to the first three Crucial Questions into clear direction and specific actions.

One more piece of evidence that you've *arrived* (or are well on your way) is when you can check off each of those first three Crucial Questions as having been answered:

1. Where Are You Now and Where Do You Want to Be?

_____ Referring to where I put the dot and the star on the map (page 132), I have crafted my statements of Personal Mission and Vision for the Future in ways that point clearly toward my star.

_____ I have arrived and where I want to be and am living my life in a way that will help me remain there.

2. Whom Do You Choose to Be for the Journey

_____ Throughout the development of my Personal Plan, I have been guided by the five sets of choices (pages 145-166) and nothing that I have planned is in conflict with those choices.

3. What Will It Take to Reach Your Destination

_____ The Five MECCA Imperatives serve me well as a constant reminder of what I need in order to succeed in any pursuit.

_____ Through effective goal-setting and ongoing reinforcement, all 25 of my Personal Attributes now have become Clear Paths.

You Have Followed Through on a Good Plan

The *Meccanize!*® process includes a day-to-day means to organize your Personal Plan and track your progress. You can develop your own format or you can obtain the *Meccanize!*® Planning Packet at your book store or through the ordering process in the back of book.

Here is a checklist that, when completed, confirms you are following up on a good Plan:

_____ My Personal Plan has been organized into a good format and is kept up to date.

_____ I printed my Personal Mission and Key Objectives on a wallet card (included in the *Meccanize!*® Planning Packet), carry it with me, and refer to it regularly to help me stay focused.

_____ If my Personal Plan includes *shared* statements of Mission and Vision, I am working closely with my planning partner for mutual support.

_____ My Key Objectives are clearly identified, with each divided into Personal Goals that I am accomplishing persistently and consistently.

_____ I am making good use of the MECCA *Do-It!* process, breaking each Personal Goal, where practical, into manageable pieces and keeping each *Do-It!* before me until completed.

_____ I work on elements of my personal Plan day-by-day, review the over-all plan regularly and do a major update at least annually.

_____ Once each month, or at least quarterly, I assess where I am on the roadway, posting a new dot to note a change.

You Have Engaged Ongoing Support

Life is a journey you cannot successfully make alone. Similarly, a personal planning process is an activity that, at best, would be *very difficult* to undertake alone.

Whether it's the advice of a trusted friend or the active participation of your spouse, putting one or more additional minds to work on your behalf vastly improves your chances of success in your pursuits as well as your willingness to stick with the planning process and make the most of it.

Getting advice is easy.

> Nothing is given so profusely as advice.
>
> Rochefoucauld

Getting *sound* advice is another matter.

> Never trust the advice of a person in difficulties.
>
> Aesop

The key to getting *sound* advice is turning to successful people. Just as you wouldn't seek a medical opinion from someone who flunked out of medical school, so it is you shouldn't rely on financial advice from someone who is broke, career advice from someone who couldn't hold a job, or marital advice from someone who couldn't make a marriage work.

Even *professional* advisors should be considered with caution. How successful are they *personally* in the fields in which they are advising?

> Where is there a successful stockbroker to turn to for advice? Any stockbroker who is truly successful will have accumulated so much wealth that he or she won't have to be a stockbroker! Even the *best* of them are defeated now and again by darts thrown at the stock listings!

Successful people are the best advisors. Seek the advice of those who have *done it*. Get second and third opinions when there's any doubt at all. Like everyone, you should have a list of people you can turn to for good advice in various areas of your life.

But for *ongoing* support of a comprehensive planning process, consider the personal *involvement* of:

A Planning Partner

Your spouse or a trusted relative, friend or business associate actively supporting your planning process.

The best planning partnerships are between people united in marriage and who have a deep and abiding love-based interest in each other's success.

Partnerships also can be very productive outside a marriage, even if the partnership — by design or by circumstance — isn't long-term. What's important is commitment to the planning process and that *both* partners gain from it, even if the support given is one-way.

You have established a productive planning partnership when you can check all of the following:

_____ You are comfortable sharing ideas and feelings in an atmosphere of mutual respect and positive reinforcement.

_____ Mutual support between the partners is based on use of a common planning process, avoiding the distractions of having to understand and adapt to different systems.

_____ You hold each other accountable for achieving results from your planning process in a climate of confidentiality and constructive activity. Accountability includes mutually agreeing to clear deadlines for achieving Key Objectives, Personal Goals and MECCA *Do-It!s* with praise and celebration for achievements and positive reinforcement for shortfalls.

_____ When support is intended to be a two-way street, you give and receive support in generally equal portions but with each partner providing more than a fair share of help when the other has great need.

_____ You devote the time necessary to making the partnership productive, typically dedicating larger amounts of time to assure development of sound Personal Plans — then setting aside shorter periods regularly to fine-tune and track progress.

_____ You help each other find and take full advantage of opportunities and experiences that will result in achieving Key Objectives and Personal Goals.

Partnership with one individual can be extended to a team of people. In the *Meccanize!*® process, this is called:

The MECCA Empowerment Team

A mutually supportive partnership of people genuinely interested in each others' success and willing to help each other develop and carry out their Personal Plans.

You may have close friends who, having similar interests and needs, quite easily could become a MECCA Empowerment Team (MET). Or, if you are married, you may know another couple who also could benefit from this process.

Businesses and other organizations use teams to develop and carry out organizational plans. The three main advantages of individuals doing likewise are:

1. Positive peer pressure that comes when a *group* of people hold each other accountable for results.

2. A greater diversity of opinions and advisers available to support the planning process.

3. Stronger positive reinforcement when elements of a Plan are achieved and celebrated.

Here are five guidelines for setting up a MECCA Empowerment Team and operating it successfully:

1. Keep it small, keep it confidential.

Consider four as the minimum for a good team. Fewer than four denies diversity of viewpoints. Consider 12 to be the maximum. More than 12 spreads individual support too thin and may result in *too many* different viewpoints.

If others like what you're doing and want to join, consider going over 12 until the new people get started, then split into two teams. While the two teams would operate separately, they could get together from time to time — especially when there are successes to be celebrated.

Agree at the outset that what is shared through the process is strictly confidential. What is said in meetings should stay in meetings.

2. Organize it.

Decide who should lead the initial meeting of the team, then develop a clear mission statement. Use the definition of a MECCA Empowerment Team as your guide.

Decide how often to meet, when, where and who should be responsible for leading meetings. Consider rotating locations and leadership, giving everyone a turn.

3. Bring planners and other materials to meetings.

Initially, you probably will be helping each other develop plans. Later, the MET's activities will focus on tracking, updating, advising, encouraging, and celebrating success.

Everyone should bring their written plans, day-planners, meeting notes and other helpful materials. Use this book as your primary reference, not only as a guide to the *Meccanize!*® process, but to help spawn ideas and overcome individual problems.

4. Establish a meeting format and stick to it.

Consider these guidelines:

> Members, including the discussion leader, should sit on chairs arranged in a circle or, when possible, at a round table. Everyone should have "equal" seating. Planning partners should sit next to each other.

> Besides the discussion leader, someone other than the discussion leader's planning partner should be designated as the meeting's recorder. The recorder's main duty is to keep track of individual and team commitments, reporting them for followup discussion at the next meeting.

> Establish MET traditions such as opening and closing prayers, "high-fives" at adjournment, special recognition for the person who accomplishes the greatest number of MECCA *Do-It!s,* a humorous "penalty" for arriving late, forgetting a planner, etc.

> Be consistent with the meeting format. Have each individual or pair of planning partners report progress made and problems encountered since the previous meeting. Achievement of Objectives, Goals and MECCA *Do-It!s* should be reported, along with current location on the roadway. At each meeting, consider sitting in the same order and having a different person start the reports.

> Agree to a time limit on reports and strictly observe it. The discussion leader should keep track of time, letting the person speaking know when a minute or two remains and when time is up.

> Include in the meeting format a process called SAGA (Special Accountability for Goals and Attributes). Each person identifies the most important Goal to be achieved by the next meeting as well as the most important Personal Attribute on the MECCA Matrix to be worked on. Results achieved on SAGA items can be included in the opening round of reports. New commitments for the next meeting should be made just before adjournment.

> Between the opening round of reports and the closing round of SAGA commitments, allow time for such activities as extra support for a person with special needs, discussion of a specific topic, an audiocassette or videotape, verbal book reviews or, simply, open discussion.

5. Reinvigorate, rejuvenate, renew.

A MECCA Empowerment Team should be a dedicated group of people who not only work hard to help each other, but enjoy the process *and* each other's company. Although a MET can go on productively and enjoyably for years, there probably will be times when new life needs to be pumped into the team.

Vary the format, help others form a team, get together with other teams, bring in speakers, do whatever is necessary to help people *grow, grow, grow!*

Onward!

Having...

• Completed your context for life's journey by determining what it is you *Want,* deciding upon (or beginning a search for) the best *Way* to get it, and committing to whatever *Work* is involved in order to become successful;

• Started with the right questions and at least *begun* the process of answering:
> Where Are You Now and Where Do You Want to Be?
> Whom Do You Choose to Be for the Journey?
> What Will It Take to Reach Your Destination?
> How Should You Chart Your Course?
> When Will You Know You've Arrived?

...you now should be ready to take full advantage of a large and diverse array of resources to help you deal with the trends and realities of life in these times, as presented in Part 1, and the questions, choices and planning process, as presented in Part 2.

Part 3

Your Curriculum

What to Learn & Where to Learn It

- 365 Ways to Strengthen Your Personal Power

- Keep Growing & Going

You live fullest when you keep learning.
You live strongest when you keep growing.
You live longest when you keep striving.

Chapter 11

365 Ways to Strengthen Your Personal Power

- Interpret Your Self-Assessment Scores
- Find the *Best* Ways to Strengthen Your Personal Power
- Choose from a Wide Variety of Learning Resources

In this chapter you'll find 365 ideas, strategies and resources for self-improvement, organized according to the MECCA Matrix.

Pick the ways that best suit your needs. Add to your Personal Plan those requiring significant effort. Simply apply those that don't.

You rated yourself in Part 2 on the Five Imperatives for a Successful Life, the acronym for which is MECCA: Motivation, Education, Concentration, Communication and Achievement. Your score for each Imperative was based on how you rated five important Personal Attributes. Collectively, the Imperatives and the Attributes constitute your *Personal Power.*

Now it's time to *strengthen* your Personal Power by finding the best ways to capitalize on your strengths, overcome your weaknesses, and attend to any development needs you discovered about yourself in the assessment.

For each Imperative and Personal Attribute, translate each score from pages 191-195 into one of the three conditions for your life's journey. Put a check mark in the space next to *Clear Road* to identify one of your strengths; *Steep Hill* for a development need on which you should work harder, or *Roadblock* for a weakness that could stand in the way of your success.

Consider each Imperative or Attribute a Clear Road if you scored it "5," a Steep Hill if scored "3," or a Roadblock if scored "1." Choose between Clear Road and Steep Hill for each item you scored "4." Similarly, choose between Steep Hill and Roadblock for anything you scored "2."

In making judgment calls on an Imperative, be guided by how you scored its Core Attribute — Self-Esteem, Self-Development, Self-Discipline, Self-Confidence, or Self-Fulfillment.

Circle the numbers of any ideas or resources that would help you. Draft your action steps based on what's presented here. Also jot down the best ideas and resources *you* can come up with.

> **Note:** Books cited in this chapter are available in most book stores or public libraries. Unless otherwise specified, tapes are available from CareerTrack at 1-800-334-1018, or Nightingale-Conant at 1-800-525-9000, or major book stores. Films cited are available at most video rental stores.

The Motivation Imperative

____ **Clear Road**   ____ **Steep Hill**   ____ **Roadblock**

1. Your fears undermine your Motivation. What are you afraid of? Make a list of the fears that stand between you and success. Prioritize them. For each, determine the best ways to overcome them.

2. Motivation comes in two main forms — *intrinsic,* the drive within you, and *extrinsic,* what someone else does to get you going. Which type motivates you more? Reduce the need for other people to motivate you. Build up the fires of motivation within yourself.

3. Become fully aware of how many times you *initiate* action, rather than constantly responding when *other people* initiate action. If necessary, keep a side-by-side log in which you jot down in the left column important activities you initiated and, in the right column, important activities initiated by others. Consider initiatives at home, on the job, in organizations you belong to, etc. Bottom line: work on becoming a *self-starter!*

4. Examine your reading, listening and viewing habits. Feeding yourself a constant diet of negative news is a major *de*-motivator. Read Positive Mental Attitude (PMA) books instead of a daily diet of newspapers and magazines filled with "ain't-it-awful" stories. Turn off the talk shows and turn on the motivational tapes.

5. Take a motivational course. Check local colleges, training centers and traveling seminar schedules to see what's available. Check with the training or human resources department where you work.

6. **Book:** *If It's Going to Be, It's Up to Me,* Dr. Robert H. Schuller, HarperCollins

7. **Audiocassette Seminar:** *The Psychology of Human Motivation,* Dr. Denis Waitley, Nightingale-Conant.

8. **Book:** *The Courage to Live Your Dreams,* Les Brown, Avon.

• *Self-Esteem* •

____ Clear Road   ____ Steep Hill   ____ Roadblock

9. You will only be as good as you feel about yourself. With that in mind, how did you rate your Self-Esteem? If it's a Clear Road, what makes it so? If it's a Steep Hill or Roadblock, why? Write your answer in 50 words or less.

10. Make side-by-side, chronological lists of your successes and failures. Cross out all the failures that actually *contributed* to your growth and later success. Does that help you feel *better* about yourself?

11. Distinguish between high Self-Esteem and a big ego that can be a cover for *low* Self-Esteem. When do ego and pride interfere with how you feel about yourself? Get feedback from a close friend or family member.

12. Review your inventory on page 141 and your trade-offs on 166. Which items contribute to your Self-Esteem? Which ones are simply ego-related?

13. Help other people. Lending a hand to others is one of the *best* ways to feel better about yourself.

14. Be honest with yourself: Do you tend to build yourself up by putting other people down? Whenever you do so, you're reinforcing low Self-Esteem in order to fatten your ego. "Target" one or two people for deserved praise. *Be sincere!* Prove to yourself that simple acts of finding good in others helps you feel good about yourself.

15. If you have children, help raise *their* Self-Esteem and feel the positive effects it will have on you. If you have children ages 8 or under, order a book called *Why I'm Special* from CareerTrack. It contains an array of esteem-building games, puzzles, drawings to complete and other activities.

16. Dress for success. Be well-groomed. Take pride in your personal appearance. The more you look and act as though you feel good about yourself, the more you will.

17. Learn how to *accept* compliments graciously. Never cast them aside as undeserved. Learn to praise yourself and you'll find it easier to accept praise from others — and *feel good about it.*

18. If Self-Esteem is a Roadblock for you, seek professional help. Find a good counselor. Ask whether a support group would be advisable and, if so, which one.

19. **Book:** *The Psychology of High Self-Esteem,* Nathaniel Branden, Bantam.

20. **Book:** *Self-Love,* Robert H. Schuller, Jove.

21. **Book:** *Silver Boxes,* Florence Littauer, Word Publishing.

22. **Audio, Video or Video Seminar:** *Self-Esteem and Peak Performance*™, CareerTrack.

Purpose

____ Clear Road   ____ Steep Hill   ____ Roadblock

23. Make a list of famous people you greatly admire. From their biographies, identify what you believe to be the guiding purposes in their lives. What can you learn from it?

24. Do a "values audit." Make a list of the principles that you try to live by. Rate yourself on how you adhere to them. Revise the list to make clear the principles you will live by in the future.

25. Jot down some things you have done that will "leave the world a little better place." Consider people you have helped and causes you have supported. Are there things you have done that have made things worse? How can you learn from what you have identified?

26. How would you like to be remembered? Read some obituaries in your local newspaper. Then pretend you're a reporter writing *your* obituary the way you would *like* it to be written some day. Write the first few paragraphs and the headline you would like to see.

27. Take a hard look at the *spiritual* side of your life. Who is your higher power? In whom or in what do you believe? Can you find ways to strengthen your spirituality?

28. Turn to scripture. Attend worship services. Seek the counsel of clergy or other advisers in coming to grips with your beliefs.

29. Be selective when exploring "new-age" solutions to the age-old problem of finding Purpose and meaning in life. There are some enlightened teachers and philosophers as well as some hucksters and charlatans. Stay away from cults and charismatic people who seek your obedience as well as your money. You may have already found what you're looking for in your childhood religious teachings.

30. **Books:** *The Bible, The Koran, The Talmud* (and other religious books that give spiritual dimension to life).

31. **Book:** *Even Eagles Need a Push,* David McNally, Dell.

32. **Book:** *The Road Less Traveled,* M. Scott Peck, M.D., Simon & Schuster.

33. **Audiocassette Seminar:** *21 Days to Self-Discovery*™, CareerTrack.

34. **Film:** *The Terry Fox Story,* (cancer patient runs 3,000 miles across Canada), Ralph Thomas.

A Plan

____ Clear Road   ____ Steep Hill   ____ Roadblock

35. How goal-oriented have you been? If you've set goals, have you *ever* put them in writing? If so, what process did you use to help

you accomplish your goals? Your answers should underscore the need to develop A Plan.

36. Understand the difference between fantasies and dreams. Don't base your Plan on fantasies, for they waste your energies on wishful thinking directed toward the unattainable because you're unable or unwilling to do whatever it takes. *But...*you should develop big, positive dreams — things that you *are* willing and able to work for— to give direction to your Plan. Stretch your dreams to the limits, remembering that virtually *anything* is possible if you want it badly enough.

37. Avoid the trap of trying to go in too many directions at once. Prioritize what you want to accomplish. Put less-important pursuits on hold in order that you can focus on what is of greater importance.

38. Use the goal-setting process explained in the Fourth Crucial Question. It will help you break your goals into manageable pieces so you can overcome them rather than let them overwhelm you.

39. Find the best way to hold yourself accountable for achieving your Plan. At the outset, review your Plan with your spouse or others you can trust. Keep them advised of your progress. You are *more accountable* when you do what you've already told other people you will do than you are when your goals are known only to yourself.

40. Attach rewards to achievement. Give up or deny yourself something of importance until a goal has been accomplished.

41. **Book:** *The Magic of Believing,* Claude M. Bristol, Prentice Hall.

42. **Book:** *Who Stole the American Dream?* Burke Hedges, INTI Publishing.

43. **Audio or Video Seminar:** *Goals,* Zig Ziglar, Nightingale-Conant.

Enthusiasm

____ **Clear Road**   ____ **Steep Hill**   ____ **Roadblock**

44. Identify the four or five most enthusiastically committed people you've ever known. Find out how they got that way and how they keep it up. *Learn* from them.

45. Assess your general Enthusiasm level by getting feedback from your family, friends and associates, or from a good counselor. Are you usually upbeat or downcast? Are you an optimist whose glass is half full, or a pessimist whose glass is half empty?

46. Have yourself videotaped presenting an idea or trying to sell something you believe in. Watch yourself carefully. Does your Enthusiasm show? Try it again, this time overacting. You'll be surprised to see how much more enthusiastic you are while not appearing to overact at all.

47. Make two lists of things that are important to your success: one with what you are *most* enthusiastic about and the other with what you are *least* enthusiastic about. Take one or two items from your "least" list and see what happens when you commit yourself to being demonstrably enthusiastic about them.

48. Take time out to "sharpen your saw," unlike the struggling lumberjack who simply couldn't take time for the one thing that would have made the job easier. Unwind once in awhile. Get rejuvenated.

49. An important commitment to yourself is your physical well-being. Have regular physical exams and get good medical advice.

50. Keep physically fit through good diet and exercise. Reinforce yourself by joining a health club or by forming your own workout "team." Be sure to get a checkup before starting a new diet or exercise program.

51. Steer clear of programs that promise miracle results with little or no effort on your part. Fads don't last and can be harmful. Commit to a good *long-term* program and stay with it.

52. Chart your fitness regimen. Keep a log of exercise repetitions, distance run or walked, etc. Post results, good or bad, on your refrigerator or another place where they will serve as a reminder to *keep at it.* Ask others to support your program by giving you positive reinforcement.

53. If weight is a problem, be wary of miracle drugs, crash diets and the like. Besides being potentially dangerous, they may have only temporary results. Consider achieving and maintaining a healthy weight level as a life-long effort in which a healthy diet is the key. Keep a weight log. Get and heed sound advice.

54. Be a good sleep manager. Too little or too much can reduce the level of Enthusiasm needed for Achievement.

55. **Book:** *The Tough-Minded Optimist,* Norman Vincent Peale, Fawcett Crest.

56. **Book:** *The Go-Getter,* P.B. Kynes, Henry Holtz & Co.

57. **Book:** *The Sleep Management Plan,* Dale Hanson Bourke, Harper Collins.

58. **Book:** *Eat Better, Live Better,* Reader's Digest.

59. **Audiocassette Seminar,** *Life by Design,* Dr. Rick Brinkman, CareerTrack.

Resilience

_____ **Clear Road**   _____ **Steep Hill**   _____ **Roadblock**

60. Tackle your toughest problems and goals first. Get anything out of the way that might dampen the energy and Enthusiasm needed to fulfill your Plan.

61. Think of change as life's No. 1 inevitability and No. 1

Opportunity. Learn to identify and focus on the *positive* aspects of change rather than the negative.

62. When faced with sudden or major change, identify with "super-resilient" people like Thomas Edison who "never had any failures — only learning experiences."

63. Find constructive outlets for your frustrations, such as meditation, vigorous sports, or even the Japanese-style "soundproof room with punching bags." Master the art of *letting off steam* in ways that you won't hurt yourself or others by "blowing up."

64. Write down two or three instances in your life when you were experiencing a lot of stress. Who created the stress and kept adding to it? If you look hard enough, you'll find that *you* did. Identify specific lessons learned that will help you handle stress now and in the future.

65. Take a stress management course. Community colleges and company training deparments usually offer them, and there are many good traveling seminars. There are also books and cassette programs to teach you how to reduce stress.

66. If change is being imposed upon you by circumstances beyond your control, examine carefully the *terms* under which you accept or reject the change. Your attitude can almost always overcome the down-sides of change. It's a lot harder to control other people's *actions* than it is to control your own *reactions*.

67. Know your limitations when trying to control situations. Weigh carefully the extent to which it's even *possible* to control outcomes. If you can't control or influence outcomes, you can control your attitudes and efforts.

68. Not all stress is bad. Learn the difference between "bad stress" (distress) and "good stress" (eustress), then work at eliminating the former and harnessing the latter.

69. Put life's defeats and challenges in a *positive* perspective. Remember that Babe Ruth became the home-run king by striking out 1,330 times and that God saved Daniel *in* the lion's den not *from* the lion's den.

70. **Book:** *How to Stop Worrying and Start Living,* Dale Carnegie, Pocket Books.

71. **Book:** *One Step at a Time,* Bob Wieland, Zondervan.

72. **Book:** *Yes You Can Heather,* Daphne Gray, Zondervan.

73. **Book:** *Resiliency,* Tessa Albert Warschaw, Ph.D. & Dee Barlow, Ph. D.

74. **Books:** *Storms of Perfection* (Vols. 1, 2 & 3), Andy Andrews, Lightning Crown.

75. **Video Seminar:** *Mastering Change: Managing Your Future in an Age of Uncertainty*, Mark Sanborn, CareerTrack.

76. **Film:** *Memphis Belle,* Warner Brothers.

The Education Imperative

____ Clear Road   ____ Steep Hill   ____ Roadblock

77. What does Education mean to you? Do you see it as a formal process that ended with childhood or as the life-long vital imperative that it is? Your attitude toward Education will determine your altitude in life.

78. The Five Attributes of Motivation give you the will to learn and become better educated, but the essential first step in learning is learning how to learn. Examine the process by which you learn. Do you capitalize on each learning experience? Do you constantly try to "reinvent the wheel?" Have you developed sound learning habits?

79. **Book:** *New Passages,* Gail Sheehy, Random House.

80. **Book:** *Learning to Use What You Already Know,* Stephen A. Stumpf & Joel R. DeLuca, Berrett-Koehler

81. **Audiocassette Seminar:** *Breakthrough Learning Skills,* CareerTrack.

Aptitude

____ Clear Road   ____ Steep Hill   ____ Roadblock

82. Know and understand your Aptitude. If you've taken aptitude tests, review your scores. Be sure you haven't erected barriers to your own success because of scores on tests you took years ago.

83. Consider taking a new Aptitude test, especially if years have passed since your last one. Compare the results. You may be surprised at what you find.

84. Think back to childhood. What were you told by parents, teachers, peers and others that you couldn't do or wouldn't be any good at? Did you believe them then? Do you *still* believe them?

85. Test scores notwithstanding, what do you believe you're good at and not good at? List your strengths and weaknesses, then determine the extent to which Aptitude really applies. Have you falsely blamed your weaknesses on a shortcoming in Aptitude?

86. Match desires and needs to skills and abilities. Focus on areas for which you have both high desires and needs on the one hand, and skills and abilities on the other.

87. Distinguish between abilities and interests. Make sure you don't discount your potential because of your likes and dislikes. Remember: Success may depend on doing what is *necessary* as well as what you *like* to do.

88. Beware of strengthening negative beliefs about yourself. Most people impose limits on themselves, saying "I don't have the ability to do this" when, in fact, they're held back only because of

negative beliefs about themselves. If you think you can, *you're right!* And if you think you can't, *you're right!* Which way do you *tend* to think? Which way *should* you think?

89. Demonstrate to yourself the ability to overcome self-imposed limitations by doing or learning something you've always imagined to be beyond your capacity.

90. Constantly remind yourself that the Motivation Imperative *precedes* the Education Imperative, and lack of Motivation poses a far greater limitation upon you than Aptitude, lack of intelligence, talent or "natural ability."

91. **Book:** *Playing Hardball With Soft Skills*, Steven J. Bennett, Bantam.

92. **Assessment Instrument Package:** *Self-Directed Search Sample Pack,* Psychological Assessment Resources, Inc., 1-800-331-8378.

93. **Audiocassette Seminar:** *The Genius Within You,* Alexander Everett, Nightingale-Conant.

• *Self-Development* •

____ **Clear Road**   ____ **Steep Hill**   ____ **Roadblock**

94. Make a list of everything you've done in the past year *at your initiative* to improve yourself. Include courses taken, self-help books read and seminars attended. How long is your list? How relevant to your Plan are the items on the list? What *level of commitment* to your own Self-Development does the list reflect?

95. Examine your career-related Key Objectives and Personal Goals, then research the criteria for success in the areas represented. Support your Plan with *specific* Self-Development steps.

96. Check on employer-offered training opportunities that could help meet your development needs and help you achieve your goals.

97. Obtain continuing education catalogues from your local university, community college or school district. Circle all the courses that could possibly help you fulfill your Plan, whether job-related or not; then go back and set priorities.

98. Visit your library or a good book store. Look for titles that would be of greatest help to you.

99. Review evaluations of your work. Look for opportunities to improve. Seek additional feedback from your boss, from a mentor or other associates.

100. Make a list of Self-Development priorities for the coming year. Decide which would be of greatest benefit, make a schedule, integrate your priorities into your Plan and get going.

101. Develop networks of people, or individuals, who can share Education and training experiences with you. At work, look for ways to add new dimensions through job rotation, temporary assignments, etc.

102. Take courses with people you know. Inspire each other to learn and develop.

103. Join the professional association that is likely to be of greatest help in advancing your career. Attend meetings. Read the publications. Attend workshops and seminars. Seek out, and network with, members and association leaders who can help you grow professionally.

104. **Book:** *Straight A's Never Made Anybody Rich,* Wess Roberts, Harper Collins.

105. **Book:** *Worklife Transitions: The Adult Learning Connection,* Paul Barton, McGraw-Hill.

106. **Audio Seminar:** *Reading Dynamics®,* Evelyn Wood, CareerTrack.

Creativity

___ **Clear Road**   ___ **Steep Hill**   ___ **Roadblock**

107. Uncouple from the idea that some people are creative, others aren't. *Everyone* is creative, especially you. Jot down three or four creative things you've done, just as a reminder.

108. In an age marked by the need for continuous improvement, get into the habit of looking at the conventional and asking "why?" Then, look for the unconventional and ask *"why not?"*

109. Make a list of circumstances that get in the way of your efforts to become more creative. Eliminate as many as you can — or find ways to work around them.

110. Have fun tinkering, but don't get obsessed by it. Identify the top priorities for change and apply your imagination. Learn how to strike a productive balance between deploying the tried-and-true and reinventing the wheel.

111. Enhance your Creativity through the many workshops, tapes, books and mind-bending games that are readily available.

112. When faced with a problem, start the creative process by finding creative ways to restate the problem. Good solutions may emerge when you find a better way to define the problem.

113. Buy a pack of index cards. Each day, write one fresh idea on each of three cards. That's 21 ideas a week, about 90 per month. Leave room at the top of the card to write in categories. Sort the cards at the end of each week. Pick out the best and most practical ideas to act upon.

114. Have *fun* being creative. Lighten up. The more serious the effort, the harder it is to fire the imagination. When you can, poke fun at the problem. Be irreverent. Pretend you're a stand-up comic doing a routine based on the problem. Then get serious and solve it.

115. Nurture Creativity by creating a *creative environment* that works for you. Do your best ideas come under pressure? While meditating in a hot shower? While jogging or walking?

116. Stop being judgmental. Every time you pass judgment on yourself or somebody else, you close a door to Creativity.

117. **Book:** *A Whack on the Side of the Head,* Roger von Oech, Warner Books. (Also pick up Von Oech's *Creative Whacks* card set available from Creative Think, Menlo Park, CA.)

118. **Book:** *The Creative Edge,* William C. Miller, Addison-Wesley.

119. **Book:** *Creativity in Business,* Michael Ray and Rochelle Myers, Doubleday.

120. **Audiocassette:** *Creative Imagination Exercise,* Carol Kinsey Goman, Crisp.

121. **Audiocassette:** *What a Great Idea!* Charles "Chic" Thompson, Harper Audio.

Interest

____ **Clear Road** ____ **Steep Hill** ____ **Roadblock**

122. List interests beyond your obligations to career and family. Evaluate how each enriches or diminishes your life. Focus on what's enriching. Rethink what diminishes.

123. Become an *avid reader.* Join a book club or literary circle. Subscribe to publications. Forage through the public library. Set annual, monthly, even weekly goals for the quantity — and quality — of what you read.

124. Keep track or make an honest estimate of how many hours a week you spend watching television. What sorts of programs are you watching? Do they expand your Interest horizon, or simply consume your time? Should you cut back on TV hours and add hours for books, lectures, trips to museums, new hobbies and other pursuits that could expand your Interest?

125. Think of *travel* as an opportunity to learn and become more "rounded." It need not mean a costly trek to Tibet. Fascinating things always are nearby. If you go to the same place and do the same things on your vacations year after year, try something new and different on your *next* vacation.

126. Take lessons. Music lessons, art lessons, dancing les-

sons, whatever. Take lessons with your spouse or a close friend to build *common* interests.

127. Think about *people* you find interesting. Isn't it true that you find them interesting because they are interested in interesting things? To what extent are you?

128. Have at least *one hobby.* Find something to unwind into — to help you *recharge your batteries.*

129. Declare war on boredom. People and things can't bore you, you *choose* to be bored by them. Jot down the four or five you find most boring. Pick one, then see what happens when you decide to over-do it and become *fascinated.*

130. Do occasional reality checks on your *level* of Interest and on your *range* of interests. Make sure you have a good balance between your variety and intensity of interests, and your ability to stay focused on your Plan.

131. **Book:** *Developing a 21st Century Mind,* Marsha Sinetar, Random House.

132. **Book:** *Inside America,* Louis Harris, Vintage.

133. **Book:** *New World of Travel,* Arthur Frommer, Prentice Hall.

134. **Book:** *Crafts & Hobbies,* Reader's Digest Books.

135. **Game:** *Trivial Pursuit,* Parker Brothers.

Knowledge

___ **Clear Road**   ___ **Steep Hill**   ___ **Roadblock**

136. Remind yourself that Knowledge is not power, but only *potential power.* Distinguish between your storehouse of information and your power base of Knowledge that is important *know-how.* Identify weak spots in know-how, especially in knowing how to *apply* what you already know.

137. The vast majority of what you know now will be *forgotten* later. How do you *retain* what you've learned? Find ways to file, record or keep ready for reference important things you've learned and will need to call upon again.

138. If you have a computer, tap into a database. Phenomenal amounts of Knowledge you could never store in your brain are readily available via modem.

139. Get to know your area's public and university library systems and the people who run them. Much information can be accessed by phone or Fax as well as modem.

140. Build a good library at home and use it. Organize your library in ways that make it easy to find books, tapes, discs and other important references. Be sure to include basic reference tools

such as an almanac, encyclopedia, unabridged dictionary, etc. If you have a CD-ROM drive in your computer, you can get an entire encyclopedia on a single disc and update it easily and inexpensively.

141. Take a memory course. There are many good ones offered on tape, at seminars or through local colleges.

142. Build Knowledge through *involvement*, not just through books and by rote. The more involvement, the more understanding. The more understanding, the more practical and useful will be the Knowledge you acquire.

143. **Book:** *You're Smarter Than You Think,* Linda P. Moore, Holt Rinehart.

144. **Book:** *Instant Recall: Tapping Your Hidden Memory Power,* Jeff Budworth, Bob Adams Inc.

145. **Book:** *Internet in Plain English,* Bryan Pfaffenberger, MIS: Press.

146. **Audiocassette:** *The Executive Memory Guide,* Hermine Hilton, Simon & Schuster.

The Concentration Imperative

____ **Clear Road**   ____ **Steep Hill**   ____ **Roadblock**

147. Review how the Imperatives and Attributes fit together. Motivation drives Education which, if you're highly motivated, can leave you awash in Knowledge. It is through Concentration that you give *value* to what you know and are willing to do.

148. Effective Concentration reduces wasted effort in your life. Rate yourself on how well or how poorly you pursue what is *truly important*. How have you done so far in making the most of what you have and in pursuing what you want?

149. Habits are made and broken within the Concentration Attributes. Make a list of your habits. Which ones help you succeed and should be reinforced? Which ones hold you back and should be eliminated?

150. **Book:** *The 7 Habits of Highly Effective People,* Steven R. Covey, Simon & Schuster.

151. **Book:** *Concentration! How to Focus for Success,* Sam Horn, Crisp Publications.

152. **Book:** *Doing It Now,* Edwin C. Bliss, Bantam Books.

Judgment

____ **Clear Road**   ____ **Steep Hill**   ____ **Roadblock**

153. Make a list of the most important decisions you've made over the past two or three years. Were the results good, bad or

somewhere in between? Critique your performance as a decision-maker. What lessons can you learn in order to produce better decisions in the future?

154. Consider *how* you make decisions. Do you follow formulas? Flip coins? Do you assemble data and weigh alternatives? Get advice from others? Identify ways to improve your Judgment and try them out.

155. Always weigh both *means* and *ends* when making a decision. Be careful when trying to use ends to justify means. Good decisions match the right means to the right ends. There's no *right way* to make a *wrong* decision!

156. Distinguish between Judgment and being judgmental. Are you *open-minded* when making decisions? Do you jump to conclusions, *then* decide?

157. Err on the side of the long-term. Decisions often are made with insufficient attention to what might happen down the road.

158. Explore decision-making models and processes. Find one that works well for you. Use it whenever it makes sense, but only as a guide. Never trust a formula to make a decision for you. Your *well-tested instincts* are at least as good as someone else's magic formula.

159. For each alternative, develop best and worst possible outcomes as well as the most likely outcome.

160. Do a *sanity check* before finalizing major decisions. Does your intended course of action make sense? Find a devil's advocate — someone who will provide an outsider's view of your alternatives as well as your decision-making process. Does your intended course of action *feel* right as well as look or sound right?

161. **Book:** *Choices,* Shad Helmstetter, Pocket.

162. **Book:** *Secrets of Executive Success,* Rodale.

163. **Book:** *Taking Charge,* Perry Smith, Avery.

164. **Job Aid:** *The Problem Solving Machine,* GOAL/QPC, 1-800-643-4316.

165. **Film:** *Command Decision,* Sam Wood.

Organization

____ **Clear Road**   ____ **Steep Hill**   ____ **Roadblock**

166. Be a *systems person.* Do much better than the average executive who wastes six weeks per year looking for things. Have a place for everything and keep everything in its place.

167. Select a good time-management system such as the Franklin Planner or Day-Timer. Take a course on how to use it,

tailor it to your specific needs and *make it an integral part of your life.* Don't waste your money on a top-flight system if you don't plan to use it well.

168. When handling paperwork, handle each paper once. Take the time to *complete* action on it rather than put it aside to start all over again with it later.

169. Organize your work so *you* manage *it,* rather than the other way around. Break large projects down into series of small tasks. Set priorities. When practical, get the hard items out of the way first, then tackle the easier ones when you may have less physical and mental energy.

170. **Book:** *Getting Organized: The Easy Way to Put Your Life in Order,* Stephanie Winston, Warner Books.

171. **Book:** *Organize Yourself!* Ronni Eisenberg, Collier Books.

172. **Book:** *Time Management Made Easy,* Peter A. Turla, Dutton.

173. **Book:** *A Manager's Book of Lists,* Sam Deep and Lyle Sussman, SDD Publishers.

174. **Audiocassette Seminar:** *Work Smarter,* Michael LeBoeuf, Nightingale-Conant.

175. **Audio or Video Seminar:** *Taking Control of Your Work Day™: Get Organized Once and for All,* Dick Lohr, CareerTrack.

176. **Audiocassette Seminar:** *Time Tactics of Very Successful People,* CareerTrack.

• *Self-Discipline* •

____ **Clear Road**   ____ **Steep Hill**   ____ **Roadblock**

177. Understand the relationship among the first three Core Attributes — Self-Esteem, Self-Development and Self-Discipline. The better you *feel* about yourself, the more you will want to *improve* yourself and the more you will be willing to *impose discipline* on yourself. If Self-Esteem is a *Roadblock,* look again at your scores on Self-Development and Self-Discipline.

178. The key to Self-Discipline is *self-control.* To what extent do you keep control of yourself in stressful situations? How often and to what extent do you lose your temper? If you fly off the handle frequently, get help. Remind yourself continually that staying composed under pressure is *vital* to your success.

179. Find *positive outlets* that will help you relieve pressure. Jog. Meditate. Engage in sports. An hour of racquet ball to relieve a bad day at work is far better than an hour of being grumpy with your family.

180. Divide your day into segments. During your time to work, concentrate your full attention on work. During your time to relax, forget work and *relax!*

181. Understand that the opposite of Self-Discipline is self-defeat. If *you* don't discipline yourself, *someone else will.*

182. Self-Discipline is the practice of *temporary* self-denial. How willing are you to say *no* to things that distract you from doing what is important? Self-denial means delayed gratification. To be more successful in your pursuits, make this vow: *I will do today what others won't so I can do tomorrow what others can't.*

183. *Believe* in your Plan. Be *driven* by it. Review it, update it and constantly renew your commitment to it.

184. Defeat habits and practices not in your best interest. Remember: you have the power *within you* to stop or start almost anything. Demonstrate to yourself and others that you can *over-come* habits the average person can't, and *achieve* what the average person won't.

185. Enter into agreements with other people, holding one another accountable for eliminating bad habits, establishing or reinforcing diet and exercise regimens, etc.

186. Use charts on the refrigerator, diary entries, notations in calendar books or any other kind of visible performance log to help reinforce your resolve.

187. **Book:** *Managing Yourself,* Alfred Goodloe et al., F. Watts.

188. **Book:** *Doing It Now,* Edwin Bliss, Bantam.

189. **Book:** *Do It! Let's Get Off Our Buts,* John-Roger and Peter McWilliams, Bantam/Prelude Press.

190. **Audiocassette Seminar:** *The Science of Self-Discipline,* Kerry Johnson, Nightingale-Conant.

191. **Audio, Video or Live Seminar:** *Self-Discipline and Emotional Control™,* Tom Miller, Ph.D, CareerTrack.

192. **Film:** *Ghandi,* Columbia Pictures.

Perspective

___ **Clear Road**   ___ **Steep Hill**   ___ **Roadblock**

193. Take time out to laugh — at yourself, at what you're doing, at life around you. Others will take you *more* seriously when they see you taking yourself *less* seriously, and vice versa.

194. Learn to enjoy comedy. The comics page of your newspaper, editorial cartoons, comedy films and TV sit-coms can help us laugh at ourselves and the troubles of the world around us.

195. Be wary of obsessions. Take a careful look at the *risks* as

well as the rewards of trying to do too much of anything. Always know the price as well as the payback of what you're seeking.

196. Concentrate on the philosophical and spiritual dimensions of your life. Spend more time counting your blessings than counting your money.

197. Avoid turning leisure activities into chores, especially if you are engaged in a high-pressure job. Your diversions should be activities that are enjoyable, not those which add to on-the-job stress.

198. Are you a perfectionist? If so, you're not leading a *constructive* lifestyle. Strive for *excellence*, but draw the line short of trying to be perfect in all that you do.

199. Ask these three questions before taking on new goals, tasks or responsibilities: (1) will this add value to my life and, if not, should I do this at all? (2) If it *will* add value, how can I accomplish it in order to achieve *maximum* value? (3) What price must I pay to achieve this, and how can I minimize it?

200. **Book:** *Success Trap,* Dr. Stan J. Katz and Aimee E. Liu, Ticknor & Fields.

201. **Book:** *Modern Madness: The Hidden Link Between Work and Emotional Conflict,* Douglas LaBier, Touchstone.

202. **Book:** *The Laughter Prescription,* Peter Dana, Ballantine.

203. **Audio, Video or Live Seminar:** *Stress Management for Professionals™: Staying Balanced Under Pressure,* Roger Mellott, CareerTrack.

204. **Film:** *Citizen Kane,* Orson Wells.

Focus

___ **Clear Road**   ___ **Steep Hill**   ___ **Roadblock**

205. Plan your work, then work your Plan. Each time you set out to do something, decide on a logical sequence for your actions. Set realistic deadlines and meet them consistently.

206. Examine the *environment* in which you're trying to Focus your efforts. Will it support or detract from your efforts to concentrate on what needs to be done?

207. Limit your accessibility. Set aside times for people to see you, for answering the telephone, etc. The fewer the distractions, the better the Focus on the task at hand.

208. Based on your over-all Plan and a good inventory of your capabilities, set *specific goals* and ways that they can be measured.

209. Prepare for setbacks. Reinforce your energy and Enthu-

siasm. When faced with roadblocks, ask yourself whether the problem is "I can't" or "I don't want to."

210. Banish procrastination by eliminating the word "later." For example, instead of saying "I'll do this later," say "I'll have this done by 9 a.m. tomorrow." Then *hold yourself accountable* to meet the deadline.

211. Be *passionate* about what you're doing. If you believe in what you're doing and are enthusiastic about it, you will accomplish it well, will *enjoy* getting it done and will feel it add value to your life.

212. **Book:** *Focusing,* Eugene T. Gendlin, Bantam.

213. **Book:** *Getting Unstuck,* Dr. Sidney B. Simon, Warner Books.

214. **Audiocassette:** *The Power of Focused Thinking,* Edward de Bono, Nightingale-Conant.

215. **Film:** *Awakenings,* Robin Williams.

The Communication Imperative

____ Clear Road   ____ Steep Hill   ____ Roadblock

216. How do you rate yourself as a communicator? Are you in the top 10 percent of the people you know? The top half? Be honest — and careful! About 25 percent of the people asked that question by researchers ever-so-modestly put themselves in the *top one percent!* Your biggest barrier to communicating effectively may be your own assumption that you're good at it.

217. Get feedback from people who are willing to be candid. Ask them what you could do to be more effective as a communicator. Pin them down to the one most important change you could make.

218. Life is a continuum of Communication, or *lack* of it. Strengths in Motivation, Education and Concentration will be to no avail without strength in Communication. Jot down what you believe to be your five greatest strengths and five greatest weaknesses as a communicator. Review and, as necessary, revise your lists *after* learning ideas and strategies for the Five Attributes of Communication.

219. **Book:** *How to Win Friends and Influence People,* Dale Carnegie, Pocket Books.

220. **Book:** *50 One Minute Tips to Better Communications,* Phillip Bozek, Crisp.

221. **Book:** *Skills With People,* Les Giblin.

222. **Video Seminar:** *Abraham Lincoln on Communication™: The Persuasive Power of the Well-Chosen Word,* Dr. B. Eugene Griessman, CareerTrack.

Association

____ **Clear Road**   ____ **Steep Hill**   ____ **Roadblock**

223. Stop depending on others to associate with *you*. Reach out to associate with *them*. Research shows nearly 70 percent of people are uncomfortable in making initial contact. So if you're waiting for others, it may be a long wait.

224. If you think you're shy, take a hard look at Square One, your level of Self-Esteem. The better you feel about yourself, the easier it will be to establish contact with others.

225. Think of yourself as *a product going to market*. You've focused your capabilities on achieving certain goals but how do you *appear* to the people who would "buy" your product?

226. List people and organizations whose support is most important to reaching your goals. Determine the best ways to establish or widen those contacts.

227. Connect with others through volunteer activities, professional associations, special projects and the like. *Practice* in settings where mistakes won't be costly.

228. Develop and *practice* a good self-introduction. Include a clear description of what you do. Before using it, make sure it is appropriate to the situation and to the people you want to meet.

229. Always wear a name tag high on the right side so it's easier to read when shaking hands. When you print your own name tag, make big, bold block letters that can be read from a distance.

230. Your personal appearance is important! How you *look* usually means more than what you *say* when you make a first impression. Get feedback and good advice on dress and grooming.

231. When meeting people, concentrate more on getting them to feel *they're impressing you* than in trying to get them to feel that you're impressing them. Association with others should set the stage for developing rapport and good Relationships.

232. Prepare for meetings. Bone up on subject matter likely to be discussed or suitable for conversation. Be well-versed and knowledgable, but never come off like a know-it-all.

233. If making contact with others is a Roadblock for you, get professional counseling or find help through a support group or a program that will raise your Self-Esteem and Self-Confidence.

234. **Book:** *Making Contact,* Virginia Satir, Celestial Arts.

235. **Book:** *Instant Rapport,* Michael Brooks, Warner Books.

236. **Book:** *Great Connections: Small Talk & Networking for Business People,* Anne Baber and Lynne Waymon, Impact.

237. **Book:** *Psycho-Geometrics,* Susan Dellinger, Ph.D, Prentice-Hall.

Interaction

____ **Clear Road**   ____ **Steep Hill**   ____ **Roadblock**

238. Assess your listening skills. A good communicator is, first, *a good listener.* Get family and friends to give you candid feedback and, of course, *listen.*

239. Take a Communication course to improve interpersonal skills. Continuing education programs at most colleges offer them, and good workshops abound.

240. Learn the importance of the verbal, vocal and visual aspects of Communication, noting the enormous importance of the *visual* dimension. Unless you are in a cultural setting where it's considered impolite, maintain *good eye contact* when conversing.

241. Remember people's names. *Use their names* when talking with them. Set up a file of business cards or other means to help you keep track of where you met, common interests, etc. Before going to a business meeting or social gathering, review the names and try to envision the faces of the people who are likely to be there.

242. Keep your communications positive. Translate anger into concern. Translate concern into genuine caring for other people and their viewpoints. Remember: *People don't care how much you know until they know how much you care.*

243. Don't be a whiner. The quickest way to lose the ability to interact effectively is to be a constant complainer and critic.

244. Work on body language. Do you use facial expressions, gestures, postures or movements that may interfere with your efforts to relate well with others? Do you have annoying habits such as clicking a ballpoint pen, putting your fingers across your lips when others are talking, keeping your arms folded during a conversation, shifting from one foot to the other, etc.?

245. Be a *good listener.* Make the people with whom you are trying to communicate feel *important.* Whenever applicable, let the *other person* speak first, and work toward establishing rapport by genuinely being interested and asking good questions.

246. Learn to be a *good negotiator.* Take a course or turn to books and tapes to develop your skills. Learn the *principles* of good negotiations, especially how to work toward *win-win outcomes.*

247. Honor the language. How you use it makes a *strong statement about you,* good or bad. *Speak* it well and *write* it well, and it will *serve* you well.

248. In the workplace, look, act and speak as a *professional.* Stay above "office politics" and direct your interactions toward building good Relationships. Focus on helping people, and the organization itself, achieve their goals.

249. **Book:** *Getting What You Want: How to Reach Agreement and Resolve Conflict Every Time,* Kare Anderson, Dutton.

250. **Book:** *The Art of Talking So That People Will Listen,* Paul W. Swets, Fireside/Simon & Schuster.

251. **Book:** *Nasty People: How to Stop Being Hurt By Them Without Becoming One of Them,* Jay Carter, Contemporary.

252. **Audio, Video or Live Seminar:** *Interpersonal Communication Skills™,* With Debra Sutch, CareerTrack.

Relationships

____ **Clear Road**   ____ **Steep Hill**   ____ **Roadblock**

253. Make a list of people with whom you have the most *positive* Relationships and a list of those with whom your Relationships tend to be negative. Determine *why* people are on each list and how they got there. How can you make Relationships on your positive list even stronger? How can you shift people from the negative list to the positive list?

254. Always try to contribute *more* to a relationship than you expect to receive from it. Identify Relationships in which that isn't the case. Work hard at making changes.

255. Recognizing that *people like people who are like themselves,* try to find ways you can strengthen Relationships with others by actively seeking out areas of common interest.

256. When trying to resolve conflicts, challenge the issues or situations, *don't attack the people.* Try to resolve such situations with rapport or at least mutual respect.

257. Find joy in the achievements of others. Build rapport by making people feel they are successful in your eyes.

258. Put your highest priority on Relationships *within your family.* Loving, trusting, caring family Relationships provide a good basis for strong and mutually rewarding Relationships outside the family.

259. Know when to seek professional help when family Relationships are at risk. There are many good counselors, clergymen and programs available. When *professional* Relationships are at an impasse, consider the good offices of a third party skilled in the art of mediation.

260. To strengthen your career pursuits, establish *mentoring* Relationships in which one or more trusted people take a direct and active interest in your success. And *be a mentor.* Support *others* in the same way you are seeking support.

261. Reallocate your pronouns. You will strengthen Relationships through both your spoken and written communications if you

severely ration the word "I" and use liberal helpings of "you" and "we."

262. **Book:** *Personality Plus,* Florence Littauer, Revell.

263. **Book:** *A Guide to a Happier Family,* The Schwebel Family, Jeremy P. Tarcher Inc.

264. **Book:** *Bus 9 to Paradise,* Leo Buscaglia, Slack.

265. **Book:** *Just Friends, Lilian B. Rubin,* Harper & Row.

266. **Audiocassette:** *Relationship Strategies,* Tony Alessandra, Nightingale-Conant.

267. **Film:** *Brian's Song,* RCA/Columbia.

• *Self-Confidence* •

____ **Clear Road**　____ **Steep Hill**　____ **Roadblock**

268. Make a list of *your successes.* Think of positive feelings that came with them. Harness those positive feelings to achieve future results.

269. Seek feedback. Take satisfaction in the positive and treat the negative as an opportunity to learn and, when appropriate, to change for the better.

270. Update your resume or prepare a new one, even if you're well-satisfied with your current job. Getting your qualities on paper can help reinforce what you "bring to the party" as well as your Self-Esteem.

271. Build upon your Relationships — at home, in the workplace, through professional and civic associations, and anywhere else where your positive qualities can be practiced and good feedback can be obtained.

272. Think of the two or three most self-confident people you know of. Were they always that way? What are their "secrets" in *developing* Self-Confidence?

273. Stop worrying about things you can't control. Concentrate your mental energies on making a positive difference *in the things you can control.*

274. When facing a challenging situation, imagine it being handled by the most capable and confident person you can think of. Cloak yourself in the same imagery. Envision yourself in that person's shoes — handling the situation, enjoying success.

275. *Prepare!* If it's important enough to be concerned about, and it involves communications skills, it's important enough to do a run-through. Raise your Self-Confidence level by practicing a presentation before a video camera. Record yourself making key points. Have friends or associates critique your performance. Role play before a key negotiation, discussion or debate.

276. Don't bottle up your worries. Talk them out with friends. Remember that *you will not fail!* You'll succeed or have a learning experience or gain from both. Besides: If *you're* not confident in you, why should anyone else be?

277. **Book:** *The Ultimate Secrets of Total Self-Confidence,* Dr. Robert Anthony, Berkley.

278. **Book:** *Stand Up, Speak Out, Talk Back,* Robert E. Alberti, Ph.D, and Michael L. Emmons, Ph.D, Pocket Books.

279. **Book:** *The Confidence Quotient,* Meryle Gellman, World Almanac.

280. **Audiocassette:** *The Science of Self-Confidence,* Brian Tracy, Nightingale-Conant.

Recognition

_____ **Clear Road**   _____ **Steep Hill**   _____ **Roadblock**

281. Be assertive, not aggressive. *Assertive people* earn positive Recognition that will lead to success. Aggressive people bring out anger in themselves and other people, weakening or destroying Relationships and creating *roadblocks* to Success.

282. Write down the two or three most important areas in which you could be more assertive in gaining *deserved* Recognition. Identify barriers and develop strategies to overcome them.

283. Put your efforts to be recognized for your strengths and achievements in the context of your principles and *the best interests of everyone* involved. Winning Recognition no matter what can exact a cost higher than you may want to pay.

284. Arrive at meetings early to meet people and strengthen Relationships. Introduce yourself to the hosts and offer to help with any last-minute challenges. Use your Communication skills to build rapport and be recognized as a team player.

285. Speak in public. Volunteer to give speeches or presentations for your employer or on behalf of non-profit organizations. Teach. Offer to help train others in your organization. *Communicating to groups* is one of the best ways to earn Recognition.

286. Pattern your manner of dress, understanding of the organization and general work habits after people in leadership roles whose Recognition of you will help you achieve your goals.

287. Develop a personal marketing strategy. Get specific about exactly what must be done by when and through whom in order to achieve deserved Recognition. Work with your mentor or with other people you trust to develop the strategy and carry it out.

288. Never cast aside or deflect Recognition that is deserved. Be gracious in accepting praise and be generous in sharing with others who deserve it.

289. Remember that Recognition also involves *your* ability to recognize Opportunity, which is the gateway to Achievement. If you are climbing a ladder to success, make sure it's leaning against *the right building!*

290. **Book:** *You Are the Message,* Roger Ailes, Doubleday.

291. **Book:** *Developing Positive Assertiveness,* Sam R. Lloyd, Crisp.

292. **Audio or Video Seminar:** *Assertive Communication Skills for Professionals™,* With Carol Price, CareerTrack.

The Achievement Imperative

____ **Clear Road**   ____ **Steep Hill**   ____ **Roadblock**

293. The biggest achievers are the people who can be *agents of* change as well as *adaptive to* change. Look back at your pursuits over the past year or so. To what extent were you an agent of change? Were you, at times, *resistant* to change? What were the results? Based on how you see things in the year or two ahead, write down ways you can do better as an agent of change and as a person adaptive to change.

294. **Book:** *Psycho-Cybernetics,* Maxwell Maltz, M.D., Pocket.

295. **Book:** *Beginnings: 24 Who Achieved Success Tell How They Got Started,* Thomas C. Hunter, Crowell.

296. **Book:** *Mary Kay — You Can Have It All,* Mary Kay Ash, Prima.

Opportunity

____ **Clear Road**   ____ **Steep Hill**   ____ **Roadblock**

297. Purge from your thinking process any notion of *the good old days.* If you think there were greater opportunities in times past, you will find it harder to recognize the opportunities before you *now.* These *are* the "good old days," *if you are determined to make them so.*

298. Measure opportunities against the motivational attributes, especially your Plan. Ask yourself whether each Opportunity would help you fulfill your Plan or deviate from it. If the latter, decide whether to pass up the Opportunity or change your Plan.

299. Check opportunities against your values — especially in matters with potential impacts on family and other aspects of your life. If your basic values will be compromised, don't do it.

300. Beware of anything that sounds too good to be true. Assemble facts. Sleep on it. Weigh it carefully. Then decide.

301. Cherish luck but don't depend on it. While some people

may seem to be luckier than you are, most often it's a lot of *hard work* that preceded the luck.

302. Capitalize on setbacks and adversity. There are opportunities hidden within *everything* that goes wrong. Search the lessons learned carefully, and you will find them.

303. Never give up the pursuit of an Opportunity too soon. There are countless cases of people throwing opportunities away, stopping just short of Success. Before ending a pursuit, be certain that *every* avenue has been totally checked and discounted.

304. Get good advice. Find good sounding boards, especially among people who can view an Opportunity from perspectives different than yours.

305. Make sure an Opportunity *feels right* before pursuing it. Have faith, but don't plunge ahead on *blind* faith.

306. Conquer fear. There are few rewards without risk and few opportunities without risk-*taking.* Fear is the biggest barrier you can place across your pathway to Success. Fear produces worry, self-doubt, indecision and procrastination. Fear-generated worry produces stress and, in turn, illnesses both physical and mental.

307. **Book:** *Think and Grow Rich,* Napoleon Hill, Fawcett.

308. **Book:** *You Can't Steal First With Your Foot on Second,* Burke Hedges, INTI Publishing.

309. **Book:** *101 Best Businesses to Start,* Sharon Kahn and The Philip Lief Group, Doubleday.

310. **Audiocassette Seminar:** *Getting Rich in America,* Brian Tracy, Nightingale-Conant.

Expertise

____ **Clear Road**   ____ **Steep Hill**   ____ **Roadblock**

311. Identify your main areas of Expertise. Considering the people you work with, what of importance can you do better than anyone else? In what areas are you considered the *expert?*

312. Identify several areas where your Knowledge and experience points *toward* becoming an expert. Set priorities and goals to concentrate on in the areas most worth pursuing.

313. Find out who the leading experts are in the fields in which you want to develop your own Expertise. How did they become experts? What could you do to emulate them?

314. Teach. There's no better way to build an outstanding body of Knowledge and Expertise. You not only learn to teach but *learn more as you teach.*

315. Publish. Whether it's an article in your company's publication or a whole series of books, the research and discipline of

writing will help build your Expertise. It also will provide an excellent means of gaining Recognition and Influence on the job and beyond.

316. Assess the market value of your Expertise in relation to the arena in which it is being applied. Are you earning a satisfactory return on the investment in acquiring it? If not, weigh carefully your alternatives.

317. Keep your resume up-to-date as an inventory of your Expertise and achievements. Use the MECCA Matrix as a guide to the strengths you have to offer.

318. Review your Plan and your Focus. With mastery of specific areas comes the need to make a decision. Should you optimize what you have or build Expertise in new areas?

319. **Book:** *Skills for Success: The Experts Show the Way,* Soundview.

320. **Book:** *The Executive Resume Book,* Loretta D. Foxman, Wiley.

321. **Book:** *Being the Best,* Denis Waitley, Pocket Books.

Influence

___ **Clear Road**   ___ **Steep Hill**   ___ **Roadblock**

322. Consider carefully whether you prefer to assert Influence mainly as a subject-matter expert or as a leader. Both avenues offer power, but the risks and the rewards are much different. Not all influential people make good leaders, and not everyone *needs* to become a leader in order to be a successful person of Influence.

323. If you seek leadership, re-examine your areas of Expertise. The transition from subject-matter expert to leader brings a need to shift Focus, especially in how you relate to people. The bigger the leadership role, the bigger the need for Expertise in Communication.

324. If you *want* to lead, *get good training.* While most of your capabilities may have been acquired in the School of Hard Knocks, you can still gain much through a first-rate leadership development program.

325. In whatever capacity you seek to Influence, concentrate on style. Go through an assessment center or other program to identify your personality type and related strengths and weaknesses. Experiment. Get professional and peer feedback. Make adjustments.

326. Build Influence by heeding organizational culture. Every work environment and even every household has certain ways of doing things and communicating. Find ways to work within the culture, strengthening and nurturing it for positive change.

327. Become a leader or influential resource for your *professional association.* Power and Influence in a professional association often translates into power and Influence in your profession.

328. Accept responsibility for *everything* over which you have control. Your Influence will be diluted or enhanced in proportion to the amount of responsibility you are *willing* to accept.

329. Show appreciation — for the work of others and for the Opportunity to serve, especially in times of need. The more you appreciate the work of — and Relationships with — other people, the more they will appreciate you.

330. Help *other people* succeed. It's the primary responsibility of every leader and person of Influence. Being a champion of your boss's career, for example, can give you a tremendous amount of Influence without being perceived as a threat.

331. **Book:** *Lincoln on Leadership,* Donald T. Phillips, Warner Books.

332. **Book:** *Everyone's a Coach,* Don Shula and Ken Blanchard, Zondervan.

333. **Book:** *Leadership Secrets of Atila the Hun,* Wess Roberts. Ph.D, Warner Books.

334. **Book:** *Bringing Out the Best in People,* Alan Loy McGinnis, Augsburg.

335. **Audiocassette Seminar:** *The New Manager and the New Organization,* Tom Peters, CareerTrack.

Character

____ Clear Road   ____ Steep Hill   ____ Roadblock

336. How you *handle* Influence is a much bigger test of your Character than how you handle the lack of it. Write down at least three *basic principles* you will follow when asserting Influence over others.

337. Another true test of your Character is *adversity*. How do you handle situations that go awry? With power? With grace? With integrity? Make a list of some important things that have gone wrong in your life. Review how you handled them. Are you pleased with your actions? Dissatisfied? What would you do differently?

338. The more power you gain, the harder it is to get good feedback. If you're becoming an *emperor,* find trusted advisers and become an *empowerer.* Be sure they're empowered to be candid and honest before you "try on any new clothes." Then, no matter *how negative* the message, vow to *thank* each messenger gracefully, not "*shoot*" each messenger angrily.

339. Ask (or re-ask) yourself this question: "Who or what *really* is my higher power?" If the answer is "me" or "the Board of Directors," re-examine the elements of Motivation and get help. The people of greatest Character are also the people of deepest spiritual commitment.

340. Are you a *humble person* or are you *extremely proud* of your "humility"? Strength in Character comes with dwelling *less* on yourself. Remember that Character is the *Communication* of Achievement, that self-centered people tend to lack charisma and that charisma is the conveyor of Influence.

341. Do a "values audit." Where do you *draw the line* with your integrity? At what point do you refuse to compromise your principles, no matter *what* the consequences.

342. Develop a personal crisis strategy. What are the toughest tests of integrity you might face? How should you handle them?

343. Shun the *trappings* of power. The more power you gain and the *less* you try to distinguish yourself *from* others, the *more distinguished* you are likely to become *among* others.

344. Develop Expertise in the *ethics* of your chosen field. Search out the literature, attend seminars, take the courses. Write articles, lead discussions and help in other ways to strengthen your own ethical foundation as well as that of your profession.

345. Write your own code of ethics, standards of integrity or personal credo. Use it as your guide in making decisions and handling difficult situations.

346. Treat people right, heed their opinions, help them grow and cherish positive Relationships with them.

347. **Book:** *The Power of Ethical Management,* Kenneth Blanchard and Norman Vincent Peale, Morrow.

348. **Book:** *Principle-Centered Leadership,* Steven R. Covey, Summit.

349. **Book:** *Compassionate Capitalism,* Rich DeVos, Plume/Penguin.

350. **Book:** *Hand Me Another Brick,* Charles R. Swindoll, Bantam Books.

351. **Film:** *The Sound of Music,* 20th Century Fox.

• *Self-Fulfillment* •

____ **Clear Road**   ____ **Steep Hill**   ____ **Roadblock**

352. Self-Fulfillment is the Achievement of Achievement and is the *prerequisite* of *true* Success. Consider, then, this distinction

between Self-Fulfillment and Success: A self-fulfilled person is one who *feels the joy* of living a successful life. A successful person who is *not* self-fulfilled has Success mainly in the eyes of other people. How does that distinction apply to *you?* Look again at the five "cities" along the roadway. If "Mecca" is where you would like to take up residence for the continuation of your journey through life, is it possible for you to feel successful without the joys of Self-Fulfillment?

353. Be wary of purely numerical measurements when assessing your achievements. Give credit to yourself for outcomes that add to Self-Fulfillment because they build upon Character, Influence and other important Attributes. Count your blessings, not just your money.

354. Review the Emerson exercise on page 165. Each of the 10 components is a seed that could help you *grow* in Self-Fulfillment. Which seeds would help you the most and how should you grow them?

355. Increase your Self-Fulfillment by sharing the *secrets* of your Success with others.

356. The further you go in life, the more you should seek and find joy in the *little things* of life — the precious moments, the day-to-day victories and even the Opportunity to learn from the setbacks. If you are joyful about the little things, the big things will give an even *greater* abundance of Self-Fulfillment.

357. Constantly strive for excellence in all that you do, maintaining a realistic and healthy mix of Good Relationships, Satisfying Work and Material Wealth.

358. Define and pursue happiness in ways that will strengthen your personal Plan. Above all, make time for joyful living. Without joy, there can be no ongoing sense of Self-Fulfillment, no living in "Mecca."

359. **Book:** *You and Your Network: Getting the Most Out of Life,* Fred Smith, Executive Books.

360. **Book:** *Effective Thinking for Uncommon Success,* Gerald Kushel, Amacom.

361. **Book:** *Life's Not Fair But God Is Good,* Robert E. Schuller, Thomas Nelson/Nashville.

362. **Book:** *When All You've Ever Wanted Isn't Enough,* Rabbi Harold Kushner, Times Books.

363. **Audiocassette Seminar:** *The Awakened Life,* Wayne Dyer, Nightingale-Conant.

364. **Film:** *It's a Wonderful Life,* Republic Video.

365. **Film:** *The Prize,* Inspiration Video.

You Have Access to All the Power You Need

Success in life, no matter how you define it, is a direct result of how much Personal Power you are willing develop and how you choose to use it.

If "Mecca" is where you want to be, you will develop and deploy "power" much more in terms of magnifying your own good qualities for the sake of helping others rather than exerting authority over others for the sake of personal gain.

You have access to all the power you need to be where you want to be and become whomever you choose to become. You have unlimited access to the power that comes from above and, increasingly, access to the power of far more self-development resources than you could possibly absorb in 10 lifetimes.

Greater access to the former requires a stronger spiritual dimension to your life. Greater access to the latter requires a stronger grasp on exciting new technologies.

> I think this is a wonderful time to be alive. There have never been so many opportunities to do things that were impossible before. It's also the best time to start new companies, advance sciences such as medicine that improve quality of life, and stay in touch with friends and relatives.
>
> Bill Gates
> *The Road Ahead*

Greater access to power offers greater potential for success in all three slices of life explored earlier — Material Wealth, Work and Other Activities, and Relationships. It also offers a greater potential for failure.

The difference between success and failure will have far more to do with personal values and choices than merely plugging into newer and better systems.

Chapter 12

Keep Growing & Going

- What You've Experienced So Far
- Some Thoughts About Values & Personal Choices
- A Favorite Story
- Never Give In!

You live in a land of plenty, filled with opportunities. But there are times, no doubt, when you feel surrounded by people unappreciative of the plenty, unwilling to take full advantage of the opportunities and downright oblivious to their own potential power.

Now and then, you may be *outraged* by examples of needless, self-imposed misery such as this:

> Sometimes I wonder why we haven't all committed mass suicide because we have so little to look forward to.

Chicago Tribune columnist Mike Royko teased his readers with seven possible sources of that quote, including a factory worker who lost everything in a flood, a woman in a public housing project whose youngest child was killed in a gang shootout and an illegal immigrant facing deportation to his Third World homeland.

The *actual* source? A young woman in a Jacuzzi complaining to friends about how *awful* things are in America.

What You've Experienced So Far

Part 1 of this book offered you a context for planning a better life. It summarized lessons from history, many of them still widely unlearned. And it emphasized opportunities in times of great change. Above all, Part 1 was about Positive Values — *doing the right things.*

Part 2 offered you a process for planning a better life. It

challenged you to come up with your own best answers to the Five Crucial Questions for Life's Journey. Above all, Part 2 was about Positive Attitudes — *doing things right.*

The process in Part 2 is *Values-neutral.* For example, the Five Imperatives for a Successful Life could help anyone succeed at *anything* — taking lives as a paid assassin, saving souls as a minister of the Gospel, making huge profits as a corporate raider, or finding a cure for cancer as a dedicated scientist.

Likewise, the 25 Personal Attributes could help a corrupt politician feed better at the public trough. Or, they could help you or anyone become a better employee, entrepreneur, spouse, parent, child of God, etc.

The First Crucial Question, after all, gives a *choice* of destinations. Most likely, that choice is between "Mecca," where Values are deep roots for a joyous life, and Fat City, where Values often are viewed as circumstantial bridges or barriers to conventional happiness.

Some Thoughts About Values & Personal Choices

There is a *single* Value that underlies all others:

I will accept full responsibility for my own actions.

Any time you or anyone compromises *that* Value, it becomes easy to compromise *all other* Values.

We are affected by six decades in which this Value has been undermined *systematically* by government welfare programs, welfare-rights groups, suit-happy trial lawyers, radical educators, and a largely liberal news media. And, too often, it also has been unintentionally undermined by parents, teachers and others who have come to accept relief from responsibility as the norm.

Not MY Fault

My boss is always bugging me just because I make a few mistakes and show up late for work. *Not MY Fault!*
So all the stress from work is making me smoke and drink more and now I don't feel so hot. *Not MY Fault!*
And my spouse doesn't understand me and gets mad just because I'm tired and gripe a little. *Not MY Fault!*
So I stopped at a bar after work one night and met this great person who *really* understands me. *Not MY Fault!*
And we had a lot of laughs and a few drinks and decided to make a night of it. *Not MY Fault!*
And now the only things *Positive* in my life are the results of the lab tests. *But that's Not MY Fault, either!*

Relief from responsibility has a willing companion. It's the gap between what you want and the resources you believe *you should have* in order to *get* what you want.

In Part 2, you learned the Three Vital Questions: What do I *Want* out of life? What is the best *Way* to get it? What *Work* does it involve and am I willing and able to do it?

All three of these questions have a lot to do with Values and the temptation to compromise them.

How many people have caused themselves, or others, pain because they compromised Values in what they *Want* — someone else's spouse or property, for example?

Or perhaps what they wanted was consistent with *positive* Values, such as buying a nice home, but the *Way* they tried to buy it was wrong — torching an unprofitable rental property to get the money, for example.

Or maybe the *Want* and the *Way* were all right, but Values were compromised in the *Work* — doing the minimum necessary and expecting a bigger paycheck. Or slipping poor quality materials into a project. Or padding the number of hours charged to a client.

Insufficient resources to have or to do things is the most common cause for compromising Values.

> I took it because I needed it.
> I took it because I wanted it and couldn't afford it.
> I took it because even though I *could* afford it, I wanted to use my money for something *else* I wanted.

The insufficient-resources excuse compounds itself:

> I took it because everybody else is taking stuff.

Two questions: (1) Do you believe most people would improve their Values if they were simply *given* sufficient resources? Or (2) do you believe that if most people *improved* their Values they are more likely to *have* sufficient resources?

If you answered *yes* to the first question and *no* to the second, welcome to the 1960s and the social welfare boom of the Great Society. If you answered *yes* to the second and *no* to the first, welcome to the reality of the 1990s and the Millennium to come.

But, you may ask, even if people improve their Values, would resources be *available* to fill people's needs and wants? What about *decent* people who have positive Values and still end up destitute?

Values are reflected in the *choices* people make, and the choices people make can have a tremendous impact on resources that become available to them.

Choices can be good or bad or questionable which, quite often, is a matter of opinion.

You may be quick to agree that studying hard in school would be a good choice, and choosing to quit school in the 11th grade would be a bad choice. But what about a seven-foot-tall teenager choosing to neglect his studies and "waste" thousands of hours trying to become a good basketball player?

Is choosing to believe that God favors the poor and, therefore, it is perfectly acceptable to stay impoverished, a good, bad or questionable choice? When the town's only major industry closes, is staying and collecting welfare rather than leaving to find a job elsewhere a good, bad or questionable choice?

Where resources are concerned, let's explore choices that may be a bit easier to categorize as "bad" or, at least, "questionable."

If you're a sports fan, you probably read the "box scores" in your daily newspaper to keep track of team standings and other statistics. Here's a brief "box score" on America. "Box" is spelled differently, however, for this *BOQC* stands for *Bad Or Questionable Choices*. It's a bit unscientific and the dollar amounts may harbor some duplications, but it should drive home the point:

The BOQC Score

Values-Based Choices	Annual Impact on U.S. Economy
Alcohol abuse	$ 70,000,000,000
Legal gambling in casinos, at racetracks, etc.	500,000,000,000
Government-run lotteries	34,000,000,000
Illegal drugs & associated crime	500,000,000,000
Overeating & related health problems	80,000,000,000
Sexually transmitted diseases (not including AIDS)	50,000,000,000
Smoking & other use of tobacco	75,000,000,000
Workplace theft & sabotage	200,000,000,000

That's well over *One and a Half* **Trillion** *Dollars Annually* worth of Bad or Questionable Choices — an *enormous* chunk of the U.S. economy!

Perhaps the tally would soar past *two* trillion dollars if it included the economic impact of accidents caused by irresponsible behavior; divorces that could have been avoided if people simply respected each other; bankruptcies that resulted from greed; tax fraud; government waste; adding to a huge international balance-of-trade deficit by purchasing imports when domestic products are just as good, and big-ticket items not even listed, such as *illegal* gambling and all the crime *not* related to illegal gambling, drugs and workplace theft.

The point is that you and everyone can offset or overcome almost entirely whatever *economic bad things* seem to befall people by strengthening Personal Values and making better life choices!

What are *your* most important Values? They are implicit in your reactions and responses to the three parts of this book:

- *Part 1:* **Your Context**

Through what political and philosophical "filters" did you accept or reject the overview of history, the 10 trends and the call for renewal of the American spirit?

- *Part 2:* **Your Conquest**

What Personal Values are reflected in *how* you answered the Five Crucial Questions? How did you score on the Victor/Victim exercise? What do you aspire to and what do you feel entitled to? How about your personal assessment on the Five MECCA Imperatives and their associated Personal Attributes?

- *Part 3:* **Your Curriculum**

Of the 365 ways to strengthen your Personal Power, which ones were most compatible with your Personal Values? Which of the books, tapes and other resources will you turn to and for what purpose?

Of all the information and activities presented here, your Personal Values will be most evident in how you answered the Second Crucial Question: *Whom Do You Choose to Be for the Journey?* This question helped you define yourself in terms of what you consider most important in your life.

How much importance you put on Material Wealth (Having), Work and Other Activities (Doing) and Relationships (Being), says a lot about your Values.

Here is the author's reflection on Personal Values and Choices, identified and prioritized during the development of the *Meccanize!*® process.

Using the simple beauty of the Have-Do-Be concept, all three slices of life were considered *important,* but the *order* of importance begins with Being, which holds the key to successful Doing and abundant Having. The five most important Personal Choices and three dominant Personal Values are identified and prioritized for each slice of life.

Perhaps it will help you identify the most important values and choices in *your* life:

Above all, I am a Human-*Being*.
As such, I choose to:
1. Have, Heed and Honor a Higher Power
2. Respect and Do Right by Others
3. Cherish Life
4. Set and Achieve Worthy Goals
5. Keep Growing and Going

My Most-Important Values for Relationships Are:
Reverence • Loyalty • Humility

But I also need to be a Human-*Doing*.
As such, I choose to:
1. Love What I Do
2. Work with Heart *and* Head
3. Deliver What I Promise — And More!
4. Be Valuable to Others
5. Maintain a Good Perspective on Life

My Most-Important Values for Work and Other Activities Are:
Integrity • Diligence • Courage

And, rich or poor, I am a Human-*Having*
As such, I choose to:
1. Meet or Exceed My Obligations
2. Manage Resources Carefully
3. Put Integrity Above Gain
4. Live *Beneath* My Means
5. Share With Others

My Most-Important Values for Material Wealth Are:
Generosity • Frugality • Gratitude

As tumultuous and challenging as the 1990s may seem, you will succeed beyond your wildest dreams if you have:

• Strong and positive Personal Values that are an inspiration to yourself and others,

• A well-thought-out Personal Plan that charts a good course for your life, and

• A full measure of Personal Power that will enable you to carry out your Personal Plan.

The Five MECCA Imperatives and the 25 Personal Attributes related to them, encompass your Personal Power. You must harness all five Imperatives and be free of Roadblocks among the Attributes if you are to achieve *total* success and reach "Mecca."

A quick review of the Imperatives:

M otivation gets you started and keeps you going.

E ducation adds substance and worth to your efforts.

C oncentration adds direction and gets you focused.

C ommunication adds outreach and acceptance.

A chievement brings success and invigorates **M** otivation.

Life really is a journey. And there's no better time to be making that journey than right now. May your journey be filled with the joy and happiness, self-actualization and "spiritual" fulfillment to be found in "Mecca."

A Favorite Story

The stage for this book was set by the story of four couples gathered for a New Year's Eve party to celebrate the advent of the 1990s. The hope and optimism for continued prosperity were shattered as all four of the principal breadwinners lost their jobs within the first 14 months of the new decade.

The executive among the four was fired two months after earning the biggest performance bonus in his career and one month after learning he was to receive his professional association's highest international honor.

As described earlier, the ritual outplacement he went through — and has been experienced by hundreds of thousands of people in recent years — can be described as a CROP: Corporate Rite of Passage. More than six years later, and happier than ever as part of America's burgeoning entrepreneur movement, he recalls a favorite story:

> There once was a man who worked very hard. Deep down inside, he longed to break away from his toil and travel to distant parts of the world. But he was never willing to risk his savings to pursue what he saw as purely personal pleasure.
>
> One day, he saw a newspaper ad with these words in big, bold type: "Europe. 40 Days, 40 Dollars." There was no phone number, only the address of a travel agency. Surely, he thought, this was too good to be true. It must be some kind of gimmick.

Nonetheless, he was so intrigued by the idea of seeing Europe for so little money that he stopped by the travel agency having convinced himself that, if the deal were real, he would take the trip.

He showed the ad to the agent. "Is this true?" he asked. "Can I really see Europe for just $40?" he asked. "Absolutely!" she replied. "Just give me $40, sign this form and you're on your way." The man enthusiastically produced $40 in cash and signed the form; whereupon, the agent reached under the counter, pulled out a big wooden mallet and — Bonk! — knocked him unconscious.

When he came to, he found himself sitting on a bench in the hull of a large wooden ship. He was chained to an oar, as were a hundred or so other people. They were seated in pairs, two to an oar, behind one another for the entire length of the ship.

No sooner had the man gained awareness of his surroundings than a sweaty, bare-chested, bald-headed giant wearing black leather shorts and steel arm bracelets began cracking a long whip and shouting; "ROW! ROW! ROW!"

A great groan went up as everyone began pulling on the oars. "ROW! ROW!" the giant-of-a-man shouted, cracking his whip again and again. The big wooden ship moved out to sea.

Forty days later came an order to stop rowing and word spread that the ship had entered a European port. Their chains removed at last, everyone struggled to their feet and prepared to file out of their place of toil.

Still a bit dazed and confused by the whole experience, the man turned to his companion on the oar and asked: "I've never been on one of these cruises before. Should I tip the whipper?"

Have you been subjected to a Corporate Rite of Passage — or another form of *CROP* in which someone bumps you off the road to success? If so, and if you've kept moving onward and upward toward "Mecca" no matter *what* the circumstances, write your own ending to the story. Maybe it would go something like this:

"After being chained to a corporate oar for 30 years, should I thank the CROP-er for cutting me loose? Well, no — I'll just thank God instead."

Never Give In!

The fundamental distinction between winners and losers in life is a simple one, oft-repeated: Winners never quit. They do *whatever it takes* to succeed in every aspect of life. They know what they *Want.* They find the best *Way* to get it. And they *Work* at it, and at it, and *at it* — until they *achieve their goals.*

Similarly, quitters never win. They may *Want* something more out of life. They may even find the best *Way* to get it. But they allow themselves to be defeated by the *Work* involved, latching onto whatever excuse puts the best face on the decision to quit.

Who pays the higher price — a winner or a quitter?

> You have always heard that people pay a price for success. And it's true: hard work and sacrifice are necessary. But I believe the price is low in comparison to the price you pay for failure.
>
> Mary Kay Ash
> *You Can Have It All*

So, don't quit. Never give in. Dream big. *Know* what you *Want,* find the best *Way* to get it, and become *passionate* about doing the *Work.*

> The only place success comes before work is in the dictionary.
>
> Donald Kendall

Commit to memory and recite often Sir Winston Churchill's last, shortest and, perhaps, most profound public speech. To the students of his boyhood school, Harrow, just before the end of his life, here, in its entirety, is what Churchill left as a legacy for generations of winners to follow:

> Never give in! Never give in! Never! Never! Never!
> Never — in anything great or small, large or petty — never give in except to convictions of honor and good sense.

But Sir Winston's immortal words too-often are quoted only

in part, focusing totally on "never give in!" The part usually left out —"convictions of honor and good sense"— is just as important, for it encourages people to avoid mindless pursuits of *doing things right* that trample upon the moral imperatives of *doing the right things.*

The most successful people in the years to come will be those committed to doing both.

> The next century — Century 21 — will belong first and foremost to a new mental breed of humans driven by a strong, sensitive, spiritual individualism.
>
> Dr. Robert H. Schuller
> *If It's Going to Be, It's Up to Me*

May God's blessing be upon you and yours as you continue that most-exciting journey called *life!*

Index

The MECCA Factor

The Ultimate Way to Manage Your Career and Life Plan!

ISBN 0-9649284-2-6

Handy companion to *The MECCA Factor* has easy-to-use looseleaf pages to record personal and shared Missions and Visions for the Future, keep track of Key Objectives, Goals, and Do-It!s, and even note your location on the "road map." Fits mid-size Franklin, Day-timer and other popular 7 and 3-ring planners. 52 two-sided sheets, 2 wallet cards for Mission, etc., star and locator dots for the map, and complete instructions.

$13.50 in U.S., $16.50 in Canada. Ask for it in your favorite book store, or add $3.00 for postage and handling and send a check / money order to Capstar Corporation, P.O. Box 18411, Tampa, FL 33679-8411.

Growth-Oriented Programs That Energize and Delight!

Let Tom Ruddell enrich your organization with a keynote address, seminar or other program focused on the issues, principles, and planning techniques covered in this book.

The 5 Imperatives for Success in Anything!

This lively 30 to 90-minute keynote presentation, tailored to your audience, uses plenty of participation, humor and hard-hitting realities of the times to provide a fresh perspective on what it will take to enjoy success in all dimensions of life.

Meccanize!®: How to Get the Most Out of Your Life

Seminar of 2 to 6 hours goes in-depth, offering a wealth of tips and techniques, and putting participants among an elite few who have a well-thought-out, effective career and life plan. Workbook, personal planner and other materials available.

Look Above Your Bottom Line!

Management-oriented programs of 30 minutes to full day focus on turning your organization's people into highly motivated, goal-oriented team players.

P.O. Box 18411, Tampa, FL 33679-8411
(813) 837-2672 • FAX (813) 831-7688